PRAISE FOR *THE LAST HART BEATING*

"Nattie is a one-of-a-kind, living, walking legend who has chosen to share her story of the fight inside and outside of the wrestling ring. A unique story that is rich in history and truly captures it all, from self-love, self-discovery, family, heartbreak, lessons, relationships, losing and gaining people, forgiveness, empathy, and unconditional love!

You will laugh as you can hear Nattie's voice and sense of humor pop off of the page; you will cry through the hard times, clap and cheer through the good; but most importantly you will feel, heal, and learn through the lessons, insight, and stories that show what is truly important in life by defining your own happiness and success. This is more than just a wrestling story. This book isn't just wanted. It's needed."

—Bianca Belair, WWE Superstar

"As soon as I started reading this book, I wished it was an audio version so I could hear it in Nattie's voice. I've known and loved Nattie for over twelve years. Not only for her mentorship or how much she's always looked out for the girls, but because she is one of the greatest storytellers of all time! When Nattie is in story mode, she does not skip a beat, an emotion, or a detail. And EVERYONE in the locker room listens. And laughs. A lot! As a longtime wrestling nerd, I think this book has everything and then some. But as a forever Nattie nerd, I promise this book will make you love her even more."

—Bayley, WWE Superstar

"Reading this book felt like having wine with Nattie on the couch—if that wine came with tears, belly laughs, and a crash course in resilience. I thought I knew everything about her (she's one of my best friends!), but I found myself laughing, crying, and texting her mid-chapter like, 'Wait, what?!' She's raw, real, hilarious, and truly one of the most badass women I know."

—Leah Van Dale, former WWE Superstar and influencer

"I could not put this book down. Nattie has such a beautiful gift of telling stories. I laughed, cried, and yelled while reading this book. It's a true story of courage, strength, perseverance, and true love"

—Nia Jax, WWE Superstar

"Nattie Neidhart was not just a part of the women's revolution, she was the architect of its design. Nattie's longevity and unrivaled grit has produced a career unlike any other in sports entertainment. Her tender account of her family, tragedy, and triumph provokes both perspective on a woman succeeding against all odds and inspiration on finding your own self-worth within."

—Beth Phoenix, WWE Hall of Famer

"Most second- and third-generation kids are arrogant, egotistical, and delusional. But readers of this funny, poignant, and revealing book will now see what everyone in the wrestling business has known all along: Nattie is none of those things.

I can count on one hand those who are universally respected by their peers in this business, but Nattie will receive a three-minute standing ovation for that reason when she's inevitably inducted into the WWE Hall of Fame. You read about it here first.

I'm so excited for everyone to finally learn how Nattie took on the incredible task of furthering the Hart legacy, and not only did she succeed in proving herself, she created a whole new generation of fans along the way. What a read. What a story. What a book."

—Cody Rhodes, WWE Superstar

"People are going to be obsessed with this book! There are so many moments that it had me crying out loud laughing. It's so funny! This book is such an honest read. It's SO good."

—Liv Morgan, WWE Superstar

THE
LAST HART
BEATING

THE LAST HART BEATING

From the Dungeon to WWE

NATTIE NEIDHART

with Paul O'Brien

BenBella Books, Inc.
Dallas, TX

The events, locations and conversations in this book, while true, are recreated from the author's memory. However, the essence of the story, and the feelings and emotions evoked, are intended to be accurate representations. In certain instances, names, persons, organizations, and places have been changed to protect an individual's privacy.

The Last Hart Beating copyright © 2025 by Natalie Neidhart Inc.

All rights reserved. Except in the case of brief quotations embodied in critical articles or reviews, no part of this book may be used or reproduced, stored, transmitted, or used in any manner whatsoever, including for training artificial intelligence (AI) technologies or for automated text and data mining, without prior written permission from the publisher.

BenBella Books, Inc.
8080 N. Central Expressway
Suite 1700
Dallas, TX 75206
benbellabooks.com
Send feedback to feedback@benbellabooks.com

BenBella is a federally registered trademark.

Printed in the United States of America
10 9 8 7 6 5 4 3 2 1

Library of Congress Control Number: 2025022368
ISBN 9781637747872 (hardcover)
ISBN 9781637748220 (signed hardcover edition)
ISBN 9781637747889 (electronic)

Editing by Leah Wilson
Copyediting by James Fraleigh
Proofreading by Sarah Vostok and Rebecca Maines
Text design and composition by Aaron Edmiston
Cover design by Sarah Avinger
Cover photo by Chuck Jackson
Case collage images TM & © WWE and courtesy of the Hart Family Archives
Makeup and hair by Mickey Fitzpatrick
Photo insert: Photos on pages 1, 2, and 3 (top) courtesy of The Hart Family Archives. Photos on pages 13, 14 (bottom left), 17, 18, and 19 (top left) TM & © WWE. All rights reserved. Photos on pages 14 (top) and 22 (bottom right) courtesy of Steve Argintaru/@stevetsn. Photo on page 14 (bottom right) courtesy of Emanuel Melo Photography. Photo on page 19 (bottom) courtesy of Mike Mardones aka Layzie The Savage. Photo on page 20 (bottom) courtesy of TJ Wilson. Photos on page 23 courtesy of Chuck Jackson. All other photos are courtesy of the author and family archives.
Printed by Lake Book Manufacturing

Special discounts for bulk sales are available.
Please contact bulkorders@benbellabooks.com.

For my dad

CONTENTS

Preface by Bret "Hitman" Hart | xiii
Foreword by Dwayne "The Rock" Johnson | xvi

Prologue | xviii

PART ONE

Hall of Fame | 3
The Harts and Their House | 9
The Anvil | 15
The Good '80s | 20
The Bad '90s | 30
Back to Canada | 40
That Little Shit | 46

PART TWO

Practice, Practice! | 55
Matrats | 63
Here I Come! | 69

A Tale of Two Tours | 76
The Harts and the McMahons | 83
Trying to Break In | 89
Deep South | 94
Florida Championship Wrestling | 101
Losing Myself | 108
Finding Myself | 114

PART THREE

Debut | 121
Divas Title | 128
"You Gotta Find Your Voice" | 133
Voice Found | 139
Divas Champion | 147
Control Versus Chaos | 152
Dropping the Title | 158
Divas of Doom | 163
Vince's Big Idea | 170
All Vince's Sides | 176
Total Divas | 182
My Wedding | 188

PART FOUR

TakeOver | 197
Hashtag | 205
The Dark Match | 211
Hangman Fracture | 219

The Revolution | 226
Ignored and Featured | 231
Sorry | 236
The Ashes | 241
Champion | 248

Epilogue | 255

Acknowledgments | 258

PREFACE

It's probably safe for me to say that Nattie is my favorite of my nieces and nephews. I always felt we had a unique and special bond, and that, as her uncle, I had a duty to look out for her.

When I first heard that Nattie was training to become a wrestler, I thought it was innocent enough. She was being trained by Tokyo Joe, an excellent teacher and one who taught the most vital intricacies of wrestling—specifically and most importantly, how to protect your opponent and yourself. But when she came and told me she was interested in entering the ring professionally, it was during a dark time for me. My brother Owen had only recently fallen to his death in a tragic and poorly thought-out stunt in 1999. His death all but dashed any love I had for being a pro wrestler.

Nattie was always a very sweet, funny, and smart girl, so when she first approached me asking for any advice or support, I was blunt with my words. Knowing how much potential she'd always had, I was quick to tell her that she had far better options than to wade into the ugly, hurtful world of professional wrestling, especially as a woman. I told her that it was a tough life, that girls like her are "swallowed by lowlifes and predators . . . and spit out. You have so much going for you. Don't waste it trying to make it as a wrestler. It's not for you, Nattie."

I looked deep into her eyes and could see my words weren't what she was hoping for. She accepted what I told her, but carried on pursuing her dream.

Initially, I was certain I'd given her the right advice, but over the next few days, I began to second-guess myself. Who was I to shoot down her hopes and dreams? Did I not live *my* dreams, when so many saw pro wrestling as a black hole? I realized that it was unfair for me to be so negative when clearly she had that same fire in her eyes that I once had.

About a week later, I went down to the Dungeon and found Nattie. I told her that everything that I said was the truth, but then again, it wasn't fair to pour water on her dream. Despite all the heartache, there were many positives: the chance to make a lot of money, see the world, stay fit and strong, and most importantly, defy expectations and live your dreams. "If you really want to do this, I promise to always help you in any way I can. It's not right for me to be unsupportive and negative."

I could see that big sweet smile on her face and I was glad I came around in my thinking. Why not? In truth, I loved my life as a professional wrestler, despite the tragedy, the deceptions, the false hope, the slimeballs, and the constant pain of tumbling and bumping around in hard rings, onto floors, and into walls, chairs, railings, tables, hockey boards, and so on.

Nattie was a dark pony among her cousins Harry and Ted and even her future husband, TJ. Despite having the least-best chance to make it, she outworked, outlasted, and outsmarted all those who doubted her. She's been at the front of the herd for twenty-five straight years, leading the way. She's always followed her heart and lived her dreams,

Preface

and her proudest claim is that she's never injured one opponent in her long, illustrious career. She's one of WWE's all-time greats, and she can boast as proudly as I ever did that she is the best there is, the best there was, and the best there ever will be.

—Bret Hart

FOREWORD

Nattie Neidhart is not only a trailblazer—she's a trailblazer in one of the toughest industries in the world to survive in, let alone thrive in: professional wrestling.

While our paths through this business have been different, they're rooted in something we both understand deeply—family, legacy, and the relentless grind that comes with growing up in the world of pro wrestling.

Our family histories go way back. My grandmother, Lia Maivia, was one of the first female promoters in the game. Nattie's grandfather, Stu Hart, built Stampede Wrestling into a powerhouse in the territories. My dad, Rocky Johnson, wrestled for Stu's promotion. And Nattie's uncles and father—Bret, Owen, Davey Boy, and Jim "The Anvil" Neidhart—wrestled for my grandmother's. There was always mutual respect between our families and a shared commitment to building something bigger than ourselves.

Like me, Nattie was born into this wild, unpredictable, beautiful business. And when you're born into wrestling, you quickly learn: It's not something you *win* in, it's something you *survive* in. And if you're lucky—and you work your ass off—it's something you *thrive* in.

Nattie has done exactly that. She's carved out a hell of a career—on her own terms. Multi-time WWE Women's Champion.

Six-time Guinness World Record holder. And now, the longest-tenured female athlete in WWE history—eighteen years and counting.

But what I admire most about Nattie isn't just the records or titles. It's how she's carried herself along the way. With heart. With grit. With grace. And always with kindness and a smile—even when things got tough.

In my book, that's the mark of a real champion.

As a father to three daughters—including Simone, who's now proudly continuing our family's wrestling legacy—I have deep respect for women who kick down doors and lead with strength and authenticity. Nattie carries the spirit of the women who came before her—including my grandmother—and she's helping shape what the future of this industry looks like.

Nattie Neidhart is a trailblazer.

Thank you, Nattie, for everything you've given to this business we love.

—Dwayne Johnson

P.S. Cheers to the Anvil and the Soulman smiling away in that squared circle in the sky!

PROLOGUE

I come from a dynasty of professional wrestlers going back to the 1940s. My grandfather, my dad, my uncles, my cousins, and my husband were all wrestlers. My grandparents had twelve children, and their eight sons became wrestlers, and their four daughters married wrestlers. From those marriages came more wrestlers, including me, the first and only woman from my family to wrestle—and I feel the weight of that legacy on my shoulders every day. Part of that weight is always trying to make sure my family's achievements in this fast-changing business are never forgotten.

When you grow up in a large family like mine, you either make yourself bigger to stand out—or smaller, to fit in. In the middle of the rapid river that is the Hart family, I grew up feeling like smaller was safer, but over time I learned that bigger was who I really was.

If you ask anyone who knows *of* the Hart family, they'll probably tell you we've been up and down, together and estranged. We've been put through the wringer and hoisted on a pedestal—neither of which we probably deserved.

But as someone *in* the Hart family, I can tell you so much more.

Even though I've given many interviews over my career, I've mostly kept to myself, and so much of my story has been private.

But now I want to share, and write, and maybe purge a little too.

I've been body slammed and dropkicked a lot, but this is my story, and this is how I remember it.

Most of all, I want to be open, just in case there's someone else out there who doesn't feel right being made to feel small, when there's something big pulling at their heart.

PART ONE

HALL OF FAME

On March 25, 2019, I was in Central Park with my mom and two sisters as we tried to hold back our tears. My dad, the three-hundred-pound force of nature Jim "The Anvil" Neidhart, was now just three pounds of ash in our hands.

I don't know what made us do it—maybe the serendipity of being in his favorite city, on the day he was getting inducted into the WWE Hall of Fame, and finding a giant oak tree straight out of his funeral eulogy—but we opened his urn and scattered his ashes right there in the park.

It was closure.

It was beautiful.

It was fitting for so many reasons.

And, as we were just about to find out, *it was also illegal.*

"Stop!" came a rattled voice from behind us.

We were filming a reality show at the time, *Total Divas*, and through my tears I could make out the head producer of the show, Russell Jay, who came running up to us frantically, waving his arms and shouting, "Stop! We can't film this! It's against the state law to spread ashes in a public place in New York City!"

"Nattie, did we just use Daddy to commit a crime!?" my now-panicked mom asked from behind her tissue.

"We need to get the hell out of here," I told her as I ushered her to the park exit.

My dad wasn't unfamiliar with being arrested, but my mom was a whole other story.

"We can't just leave him there if it's a crime," she said.

"What do you want me to do, vacuum him up?!"

Okay, I'll admit, I was stressed out. We were only in New York that day for the Hall of Fame induction ceremony, where my dad and his tag-team partner—my legendary uncle, Bret "Hitman" Hart—would be inducted as the Hart Foundation, and I started to envision headlines reading "WWE Wrestler Arrested for Felony in NYC."

When I looked around, my sisters and the production crew were already in the wind, so I dragged my mom out of there toward our safe house across the bridge (the Barclays Center) where I knew Bret was waiting.

Nine months before, when my dad passed away, I'd worked up the courage to go see World Wrestling Entertainment's Wizard of Oz, Vince McMahon, to ask him to finally put my dad in the Hall of Fame. Vince's office was usually packed with people, with even more waiting outside to get a minute of his time, but that day, there was no one waiting; I had a clear road.

The then-owner of WWE had been amazing since my dad died, so I thought it was worth the ask.

"Natalie," he said, "I thought your dad was in already."

Vince was pissed off at whoever had overlooked my dad (Vince!) and immediately offered to include him in the upcoming 2019 class. But I knew teaming with Bret was the most special time in his life, so I requested he go in as part of the Hart Foundation. Like in the movie *Planes, Trains, and Automobiles*, my dad was John Candy to Bret's Steve Martin.

Back at the Barclays Center, where everyone was setting up for that night's live broadcast, my mom wanted to go find my sisters while I went and found Bret, who was in the empty seats going over his speech.

He looked very pensive. I knew this night meant a lot to him, and I could see that written all over his face as I approached.

"You want to hear it?" he asked, inviting me to join him.

I knew this was going to be special. Inside and outside the ring, Bret is a master storyteller—one of the greatest in the world, I think—and as we settled into the empty upper deck and he read his speech to me, I was reminded of that fact once again. Every sentence flowed beautifully—until he suddenly stopped.

"Nattie, why are you looking at your phone so much?" he asked.

I flashed him the stopwatch on my screen. Without pauses or clapping or any sort of engagement from the crowd, it was already forty-three minutes long.

"Okay, well, how long did they give us?" he asked.

"Fifteen."

"Minutes?!" I could see Bret getting instantly overwhelmed as he scoured through the twenty pages he had yet to read. "How am I supposed to cut Jim's life down to *fifteen minutes*?"

I felt caught between Bret's beautiful writing and Vince's militaristic timing. We were going live, and he hated when anyone ran over.

"Well, is there anything in there we can tighten?" I offered, trying to find a middle ground. "Maybe we take out the story with King Kong Bundy?"

But as anyone in wrestling could tell you, when it came to Bret and Vince—whose storied past peaked with Vince getting knocked out and Bret leaving the company he considered his home—finding a middle ground was tough.

"If he didn't want me to, you know, read my speech the way I wanted to write it, then he shouldn't have fucking invited me in the first place!"

Bret had a point, and I could see he wasn't going to budge. So I was pretty nervous later that night as Bret and I hit the ring that acted as a stage in the now-packed arena.

On the way through the ropes, I said a little prayer to my dad above and asked him to please make sure we got through this: *Daddy, I'm sorry about the park earlier, but please find us the time for Bret's speech. Or please try to keep Vince calm backstage if we go an hour... Get us through this...*

Bret was dressed in a crisp suit and I was in a custom-made pantsuit and a twenty-inch ponytail, which pictures of Jennifer Lopez at the time had convinced me was cool. It was not cool. *And* it kept yanking my head back every time I accidentally sat on it and then tried to move. By the time I made it to the ring that night, I felt like I had a twenty-inch dead ferret hanging by a thread from the back of my head.

But all I wanted was some kind of miracle to happen that would give Bret the time to honor my dad the way he wanted. It felt like this was our last chance as a family to really say goodbye. And I didn't want to say goodbye at all.

I kept my part of the speech short, unlike my deeply regrettable hair, so I could give the floor to Bret, who began his speech... word for word like I'd heard earlier. *Okay, he's going for it!* The audience was there for him, too, just they'd been his whole career, except this time they were hanging on his words instead of his athleticism. With Bret it was storytelling all the same. No one is a better storyteller than Bret.

I was just starting to wonder when Vince would shut us down when I heard a commotion behind us. I didn't want to turn around because it would look like I wasn't paying attention to Bret's words. Then I saw someone enter the ring from the corner of my eye, and thought, *Oh, shit, here it is, we're getting pulled offstage. Vince must think we're going too long already.*

Until I suddenly realized that, no, this wasn't somebody from WWE, this was somebody from the crowd who'd stormed the ring—and he was tackling Bret to the canvas.

Bret has endured a lot after his wrestling career, including a very serious stroke that took a huge toll on him, and it's made us all very protective of him. Instinct kicked in and I grabbed on to my uncle as he was being taken down. In an effort not to land on him as we fell, I sent myself flying over him instead, like I was taking a bump.

A split second later, Travis Browne, Ronda Rousey's MMA-heavyweight husband, appeared in the ring (the fastest heavyweight fighter I've ever seen!), along with a flurry of wrestlers piling in from all sides a second behind him.

If there was one guy the whole locker room would run through walls to defend, it was my principled, honest, outspoken, and singularly talented uncle. The attacker was quickly pinned down, and some of the rescuers started giving him a wrestler's welcome that involved introducing their fists to his face.

And in the chaos, with Bret secured and his attacker seeing stars, my next thought was, *I hope this fucking ponytail is still on my head.* I'd taken a solid tumble in the middle of everything, and I was horrified to think the camera would zoom in on me on live TV and everyone was going to realize that I didn't have any real hair left. Fortunately, it stayed put.

And through the stampede of black pants legs and shiny shoes all around us, Bret and I shared a smile from the canvas. We realized in that moment that nothing could have summed up the craziness, mayhem, and comedy that my dad loved about this business more. Not only did the attack that night not stop the Harts, but it granted us all the time we needed to give my dad the send-off of a lifetime. Who could say no to Bret going long after all that?

We never did find out why the man attacked Bret. But after he was hauled out, bruised and battered, Bret got to deliver his speech in full while everybody laughed, clapped, and hung on his every word about my dad.

Video of the event trended worldwide for two days afterward. As I said to my mom as we left the arena that night, "I felt like Daddy wanted to make sure that we stole the show in the most Jim Neidhart fashion ever."

And as we both quietly remembered my dad on the ride back to the hotel, I was reminded all over again what "the most Jim Neidhart fashion" had meant in our lives—good and bad.

That's the thing about spending your life with someone who's always unapologetic about who they are—sometimes you're in awe, and sometimes you're left aching to hear them say "Sorry."

We told the world a lot about my dad, but I was still struggling with how to carry his memory and not get crushed by it.

But that was the journey of any Hart.

You step into the ring to honor those who came before you, but you fight to figure out your own place in that historic family lineage.

A lineage born from a chance meeting in the very city we were in many decades before.

THE HARTS AND THEIR HOUSE

Even though the Hart family name is synonymous with Canada, our legacy began with a couple of chance meetings in the heart of New York.

In 1946 my grandfather, Stu Hart, found himself in Manhattan as a tourist after World War II. As fate would have it, he decided to grab a bite at boxing legend Jack Dempsey's restaurant, where he was approached by none other than the legendary wrestling promoter Toots Mondt. Now, not only did Toots have the best name in wrestling, but as a wrestler, trainer, and future co-founder of Capitol Wrestling Corporation (which later evolved into World Wrestling Entertainment), he also had a great eye for talent.

"You gotta be a wrestler with a neck like that," Toots said to Stu after seeing him waiting in line. Those words changed the course of my family's history forever, because Toots was right—Grampy *was* a wrestler. As an amateur, he qualified for the Canadian Olympic team, only to have his heart broken when the Olympics were canceled due to the war. And as a professional, Stu "broke in" up in Edmonton, having been trained by Jack Taylor, and had worked three jobs to buy the Edmonton wrestling territory with his good friend Al Oeming.

Once Toots heard that Jack Taylor, who had been *his* trainer, had also trained Stu, my grandfather quickly found himself working regularly at the iconic Madison Square Garden. Toots knew Jack only trained the best, and it didn't hurt that Stu had the "look" that New York loved to promote.

My grandfather was billed as a "tall, dark, and handsome" young man who "had a build that would put movie stars to shame." But that wasn't all he was, and all the old-timers who loved to test the greenhorns by legitimately hurting them in the ring learned fast not to mess with Stu.

He might have been young and handsome, but he was also tough as nails.

My grandfather's work in the ring soon led him to working the rest of North America against the likes of star names like Buddy Rogers and Lou Thesz. But it was back in New York where his life would change again—this time at the beach, where he met a beautiful woman named Helen Smith and helped her remove tar from her heel with a Popsicle stick.

It was a case of "opposites attract" that day, when Stu went to Coney Island with his fellow wrestlers, and Helen with her girlfriends. Younger Helen had been raised as a well-educated, well-to-do New Yorker with well-connected parents, while Younger Stu had lived in a tent in Tofield, Alberta, in 40-below weather. When the Great Depression hit, Helen's family lost everything in New York, while Stu was made a ward of the Salvation Army after his teacher found out he was living outside with just some dogs for heat and a slingshot for hunting. While Younger Helen found her calling in her academic gifts and was top of her class on Long Island, Younger Stu discovered his own vocation at the YMCA, where he learned amateur wrestling from older wrestlers. Those wrestlers were extremely hard on him, but they taught Stu everything they knew, and finding refuge at the YMCA—in wrestling—saved my grandfather's life.

But even though Helen Smith and Stu Hart grew up in different countries and in different worlds, fate dragged them together in 1947 on that beach in New York. They soon fell in love and married, and with a family to now support, Grampy's always-ambitious plans became even bigger, as he dreamed of moving from "only" being a wrestler into becoming a promoter himself.

At the time, North America was divided into regional wrestling territories, and my grandfather—with Toots's backing and connections—ventured further into the world of wrestling promotion, setting up shop in Great Falls, Montana, while running shows in Edmonton, Salt Lake City, and Spokane.

Stu ran the wrestling end of things, while Helen was hugely instrumental in the operation and marketing of it all. She handled the business end involving payroll and taxes behind the scenes and wrote out the programs by hand. She was also the one who found the famous "Pomp and Circumstance" music for Gorgeous George and Big Time Wrestling when she rented it for a dollar at the Calgary Public Library.

Stu quickly spent the money they made from a few good years of promoting to buy the Calgary territory for $50,000. This still left some money for him and Helen to buy an old orphanage-turned-mansion on twenty-eight acres for $28,000 from a retired judge in Alberta. Stu didn't mind that the place needed a lot of attention; he loved salvaging things that others deemed "unfixable and broken," like the old broken-down Cadillacs he'd collect. And he wanted a house big enough to fill with a lot of kids, pets . . . and people looking to break into the wrestling business.

People like Lia Maivia, the matriarch of the Maivia family, whose territory would often exchange talent with Stu's after she took over her husband's Polynesian Pacific Pro territory following his death in 1982. People like Fritz Von Erich, the patriarch of the famous Von Erich family, who lived at the Hart House while my grandfather trained him and broke him into the wrestling business.

And people like Jim Neidhart, a former NFL football player and national shot put champion, who was also looking for his way into the crazy world of professional wrestling.

My dad had heard about my grandfather from "Judo" Gene LeBell, the iconic judo pioneer, wrestler, and stuntman (who once choked out an all-too-cocky Steven Seagal on the set of one of his movies). LeBell and Stu had been introduced by a strength-training coach who thought my dad's physique was perfect for wrestling. Gene's mother, Aileen Eaton, was a future Hall of Fame boxing and wrestling promoter in Los Angeles who worked with Sugar Ray Robinson, Muhammad Ali, Lou Thez, and Gorgeous George. So when my dad and Gene met about him getting into the business, Gene told him the best place in the world for a former football player like my dad to train as a wrestler wasn't in California, but in Calgary, with former Canadian Football League alumnus Stu Hart.

So my dad made a call.

And just like that, in 1978, the former Oakland Raiders and Dallas Cowboys tryout left California for Calgary on a Greyhound bus, with fifty bucks in his pocket—because that's all my grandfather told him he'd need.

As big as the Hart House was, at the time my dad arrived, it was full. Even the small coach house out back was taken, by a young artist (who has since gone on to become world renowned) named Katie Ohe, so my dad stayed above my uncle BJ's gym about twenty minutes away instead.

BJ's was *the* gym that all the wrestlers used, and it wasn't long before my dad made friends with everyone while learning all the ins and outs of the business. My dad was actually the last person my grandfather personally trained, after training Jake "The Snake" Roberts, Bret

"Hitman" Hart, Owen Hart, Gorilla Monsoon, Brian Pillman, Junkyard Dog, Superstar Billy Graham, Davey Boy Smith, Dynamite Kid, and so many, many hundreds more. And because Stu saw so much in my dad, he kept him financially afloat while he trained him too. My grandfather treated my dad like he was one of his own children and gave him every tool he could to help him succeed.

But as easy as it was for my dad to get Stu to invest time in him, he struggled to get one of Stu's daughters—my mom, Ellie Hart—to even look in his direction. My mom wasn't interested at *all*.

There were a couple of reasons for this. One, my mom was told she wasn't allowed to date any of the wrestlers. And two, my uncle Bruce had convinced my dad to dye his hair with bleach to look like Ric Flair, and it turns out peroxide hates red hair. So my dad was walking around for months with a red beard and puke green hair.

Fortunately, as happened with most people, my dad's personality began to grow on her, and she agreed to one date, sure that he'd be a refined gentleman.

"Do you mind if I smoke a doobie?" he asked the waitress as they were being seated for their date.

Okay, maybe not.

"Oh, I don't mind at all," the waitress deadpanned back. "But he might."

She nodded over at the next table, where a police officer was watching. My mom laughed at my dad as he whistled his innocence at the ceiling.

My mom knew then that she'd never seen or met anyone like Jim Neidhart before. He was a big, funny, charming, charismatic, outrageous Californian who drank Chivas Regal on the rocks, and she was a beautiful, petite, quiet, artsy Calgarian who'd never even *seen* anyone drink anything except beer.

Big-city guy and small-town girl.

Opposites attract, and wrestling was once again the matchmaker. Now all my dad had to do was find out if Stu knew.

He got his answer one day in the basement gym the wrestlers called "the Dungeon," when my grandfather stretched him to the point of agony. Stu was always tough, but this training session in that small, damp room with its low ceilings and flat wrestling mats, he made my dad hurl from sheer pain and exertion. My dad—one of the strongest men in America at the time—crawled off the mat, eyes bloodshot from the holds . . . and told Stu he loved my mom.

He said that even though he might not be welcome, he was going to keep coming back to show my grandfather what he was made of—both as a wrestler, and as a man who wanted to date Stu's daughter.

Until, finally, my grandfather gave his blessing.

Three months after their first date, my parents were married. And soon after that, they moved into the small coach house Katie had since moved on from and began a family of their own.

THE ANVIL

I am the middle child, with one sister who's older than me by a year and one who's younger than me by a year. I was a big baby—almost ten pounds—and I'd probably attribute that to my dad being built like a tank and maybe on a little juice at the time. Actually, my sisters and I were all really big babies, so maybe it wasn't just the juice. Either way, my poor mom had to have C-sections with all of us because of how big we were and how small she was.

By the time I came along, my dad's career was starting to pick up, and my grandfather wanted to pour some promotional gasoline on his new, strong-as-an-ox wrestler by entering him into the Calgary Stampede anvil-toss competition.

The Calgary Stampede was—and still is—a massive annual rodeo and festival event, described by its originator in 1912 as "the greatest outdoor show on earth." It welcomes more than a million people from all over the world to celebrate Western heritage and culture across hundreds of different events over ten days and nights. With that many people gathered, my grandfather figured it would be a great place for my dad to show the world just what he could do. The promotional gasoline was Stu publicly offering $500 to anyone who could out-throw the Californian blow-in, Jim "The Rhino" Neidhart.

And it worked.

The eyes of the Stampede were on my dad as he stepped up to show the gathered masses just what he could do. With everyone out to win the money *and* out-throw the outsider, there was immense pressure on him to do well. But, as it turned out, my dad did as exactly what my grandfather knew he would, and he won the competition outright with a toss of 11 feet, 2 inches—a festival record that still stands today.

After this incredible feat, my dad became Jim "The Anvil" Neidhart—and his new name and tales of strength helped sell him to other wrestling promoters around the world. Europe called, then Japan, and all of a sudden my dad was on the road, and away from the Hart House—and his family—more and more.

Like a lot of working wrestlers in the 1980s, he'd often be away for more than three hundred days a year, getting enough work to stay on the road and be on regional TV—but not making enough money to take any time off.

That's the thing about being a working professional wrestler. It's very much a "make hay while the sun shines" kinda business. You've got to keep going when the bookings are there, because wrestlers are always one move away from being done—something I found out intimately later in life.

So, unless you're the name on the top of the card—which my dad wasn't—being "successful" meant you had to stay on the road, and sometimes bring your family with you.

Which is what he did.

In September 1983, when I was barely two, we all moved from the Hart House in Calgary to Baton Rouge, Louisiana, where my dad went to work for "Cowboy" Bill Watts in Mid-South Wrestling. It was a short and challenging stay, as my little sister, Kristin, got pneumonia when we got there, and it almost killed her. (That was when she got her nickname, "Muffy," after the kids' show we used to watch when she was recovering.) Then, before we could even settle into our new life, our new home, my dad was almost immediately traded to Tennessee, because Watts and Memphis promoter Jerry Jarrett had a talent trade in place to freshen up their rosters.

Back then, there was no real national penetration when it came to wrestling. A fan in Memphis had no idea what was happening in New York, and a California fan didn't know there was a whole new territory operating in Texas. This meant that wrestlers could do their "act" in several different territories without getting stale. But it also meant that even more road needed to be traveled, to keep the bookings going.

So after just a few months in Mid-South, and a few months in Memphis, my dad moved territories again, in August 1984, when Eddie Graham in Florida asked him to come in and work there.

Most wrestlers loved working the Florida territory because of the weather, but also because getting from one town to another required far fewer miles than in, say, Texas. This meant less time in the car, and less cost for the wrestlers to get around. Florida was also a high-paying promotion where the wrestlers knew if they worked hard and made the towns, their money at the end would be better than in most other territories at that time. Lastly, Florida was run by Eddie Graham, who was known as a fair and talented booker, and for building long-term storylines that meant wrestlers could stay there longer and put down some roots.

My dad loved working for Eddie Graham too. On one occasion, he asked Eddie if he could borrow some money to buy us Christmas presents, as sort of an advance. And when my dad went to pay him back, Eddie told him to keep the money instead. It always meant a lot to my dad. Shortly after, Eddie Graham ended up taking his own life. The wrestling business had taken a toll on him.

I remember, at our school in Florida, because my dad was on TV, we were known as the rich, famous wrestling family—but everything in our world was boom or bust. Sometimes we were riding to school in a nice car because my dad had a good month or two; if the money was good, so was the car. And if the money wasn't good, then it was back to a shady used-car lot. When I was three, my dad bought an old Volkswagen Beetle convertible to get us around. I know that doesn't sound too bad, except it was permanently a convertible because it had no roof. Or seatbelts. Or back seat. But the floor back there was carpeted like a house for some reason, so we would all just sit there on the floor as we cruised around in our roofless, shag pile death machine. It also had no muffler, so when the engine was running it was so loud you couldn't hear yourself talk.

I can still remember my mom praying to God that it didn't rain.

But no matter what was going on financially in our family's life, my mom and dad always made sure that, during the summers, we could go back and visit my grandparents at the Hart House, where Stu always had a big wrestling ring set up on his lawn. That's where my cousins started a promotion called the Kids Wrestling Association. We would set up lawn chairs, and family and friends would come outside on the Hart House lawn to watch.

Every Sunday, when was I growing up, my grandfather would have these elaborate Sunday dinners where fifty to seventy-five people would come and eat every single week. It meant Stu had astronomical grocery bills and sometimes very little money to pay for them, but he would still go shopping at Safeway every Saturday with my aunt Georgia (BJ's wife and my mother's sister), who was a gourmet chef. My grandfather loved making his famous spaghetti, prime rib and mashed potatoes, and beef stew, and my grandmother would make Jell-O with fruit and the best iced tea you've ever had.

No matter how old Stu got, he never forgot what it was like to be hungry, so food was a huge deal to him. He was one of the most compassionate and generous people I've ever known, and he never cared if anyone crashed one of his cars or even stole from him, but if somebody made themselves a plate of food and didn't finish it, they immediately went on Stu Hart's proverbial shit list.

I was *never* on that shit list. I used to lick those plates clean because I wanted to stay as long as I could. The Hart House felt like home, and as a young girl, all I knew was that everything had gotten harder when we'd moved away.

That was about to change, though, because it was at one of those family dinners that my grandfather announced that he'd sold his territory to Vince McMahon in New York, and that, as part of the deal, several of his wrestlers would be getting WWE (then World Wrestling Federation, WWF) contracts, too—including my uncles Bret, Davey, and Tom, and my dad.

Grampy could see the writing on the wall for small, regional territories like his, and he wanted to make sure that his wrestling family could not only make enough to keep their families fed, but also, for the first time in their lives, make much more than he ever did.

This was the Harts' first-ever national break, and everything was about to change.

THE GOOD '80S

My dad's ginger billy-goat goatee bent in the wind as he weaved his Ninja motorcycle through the Florida traffic. He was on "Hart Time," which meant he was late as fuck, but he was also on cocaine, which meant he was going to be perfectly on time. This was 1988; professional wrestling was on fire, and The Anvil was headed to my school on his one day off a month.

As I sat in class and waited for the other parents to tell us about their jobs, I could only wonder what my dad was going to say when he got there. I was six, and he was a big star on TV now, the kind that people would line up outside arenas across the country to meet. In my few short years on earth, my dad had wrestled in the regional territories in Calgary, Mid-South, Tennessee, and Florida—but it was only when he signed with WWE in 1985 that all our lives started to change.

Back then, Hulk Hogan was one of the most famous people in the world, and WWE was a big part of pop culture, with shows on USA, NBC, and MTV. It was the era of Jake "The Snake" Roberts, The Honky Tonk Man, Andre the Giant, "Macho Man" Randy Savage, Ultimate Warrior, and so many, many more.

My dad and my uncle Bret were now big stars in the tag-team division as the Hart Foundation, which brought them national and international fans. McMahon's takeover of the smaller territories—and the marketing blitz that followed—turned the biggest, scariest guys in the business into plush toys, action figures, and Pez dispensers.

And that's how most of the people in my school knew Daddy not as my dad, but as "The Anvil," an unhinged powerhouse who pulled on his pointy beard and laughed maniacally down the lens of the camera. As he barged into my classroom, he did little to change that perception.

He was six foot one and three hundred pounds, wrapped in Spandex pants, wearing Air Jordans, a leather fanny pack, baby pink flat-top hat, wraparound Ray-Ban sunglasses, a $20,000 Rolex, and an AC/DC T-shirt dripping in sweat from the Florida heat. I still remember him waving at me from the lineup of the other, suit-wearing parents in all his eccentric, loveable, antiestablishment glory. Ladies and gentlemen, Jim Neidhart.

And then it was his turn to speak.

"School doesn't matter, kids," was his opening line to the class. "Well, it does," he said, immediately correcting himself as he pulled at his beard, "but only the sports part." My dad saw the teacher's attempted intervention like a referee trying to interfere in his match: he just worked around her and continued to play to his audience. "Now, take me," he continued. "I never attended a single college class, but I have a degree in political science. How? Because my coaches in track and field paid people to go to class for me."

My teacher tried again to object, like an opposing lawyer losing grip of her case. But my dad was on a roll.

"People were paid to go to school for me," he said to his now captivated audience. "Because I got a scholarship to UCLA from . . . that's right—sports!"

And at that point my teacher gave up trying to intervene. The kids were fully engrossed, and my dad was in the zone, working the room, getting laughs, milking applause, while telling his story.

Once he was done, he was mobbed by the other kids, who gravitated to him, his TV persona, and his "honesty" in giving them "the truth."

And that was my dad.

Or that was my dad in the eighties.

Or that was my dad in the eighties when things were good.

Either way, I've been scarred ever since. See, there were a few Jim Neidharts, and for better or worse, over the course of my life I'd meet all of them.

But this day, when he was finished delivering his message, he hugged me, left my school, and was gone again for another month. That's the way it was in WWE back then. There was no health insurance, no guaranteed contracts, no safety net—and definitely no time off. If you weren't on the road, you weren't working, and if you weren't working, you weren't earning money. So everyone in that company, from the main event all the way down to the ring crew, moved from town to town, show to show, every day of the week and twice on Sundays.

If you were injured, you took a pill of some sort, laced up your boots, and continued anyway. If you were tired, you took something to get you up, and if you were full of adrenaline after a show, you used alcohol to take the edge off on the long, long drives from town to town.

Every wrestler on the card was a little banged up or a lot banged up, rolling into different towns every night—but at this point, they were working their way through a wrestling boom, and the pain, loneliness, and endless travel were a lot easier to swallow when everyone could wipe their tears with hundred-dollar bills. The other truth is, they were having a lot of fun—maybe the time of their lives. They were as famous as rock stars, if not more so.

We'd had some good payoffs in the territory system before, but nothing like this. The WWE gold rush meant we could live in the biggest house on the street, which to my young eyes looked like a spaceship. It was painted black and white and had massive windows, a huge yard, and large trees all around it for privacy. It was big enough that my sisters and I could all have our own rooms, but we all still slept in the same bedroom anyway. My dad might have had a little money, but we hadn't grown into it yet. My sisters and I were super close and loved being together all the time, sleeping in the same bed and staying up late talking to each other until we fell asleep.

But the life we lived in that house flipped between a normal childhood and . . . let's call it a "different" childhood, depending on where my dad was at the time. At the start of the boom, he'd come off the road, and we would pick him up from the airport and go straight to 7-Eleven, where he would let us get anything we wanted. To this day, I love 7-Eleven convenience stores. They remind me of my dad coming home. That was our thing with him. He'd want us to have whatever we could carry, then take it back home. My mom always made us eat healthy. That's how she grew up. A wholesome peanut butter and jelly sandwich for lunch with milk and an apple—nothing fancy or fun ever. My dad, being the "big kid," let us break all the rules.

Once we got home, we'd go through all my dad's luggage, which always smelled like Icy Hot pain relief spray, and marvel at little things like a sewing kit from a hotel room in New York or an eye mask from Delta first class—all these trinkets and clues of a much bigger world that my dad was living in.

My mom would make his favorite meal, BBQ chicken with her special rice, and my dad would make margaritas that were 99 percent tequila, a splash of lime juice, with egg whites to "add protein and a bit of froth," and then slip us our own when my mom wasn't looking. On those nights, we would stay up until two in the morning swimming with my dad in our pool and listening to his favorite song, The Doors' "Riders on the Storm." Then my mom would call in to school the next day and tell them that we weren't feeling well. Maybe my mom liked to break a few rules sometimes too.

With my dad on the road so much, we didn't see him a whole lot, so we made sure to maximize those minutes with him. I loved all those minutes, more than I can put into words.

I knew he felt the same about us too. As the boom continued, my dad would really try hard to make our time together memorable, like when he turned our whole yard into a racetrack after buying us a badass go-kart, only to come home the next time with a bass fishing boat because go-karts were boring now. He was like a big kid, and my mom was The Parent. The disciplinarian. The one in charge. She was the person raising us and my dad was her fourth child, sometimes the problem child, coming in, wreaking havoc, and then leaving again.

Our house wasn't the only one hit by the gold-rush times. If you were on the WWE roster and out on the road, you were probably making more money than you ever had in your whole life. And because we were in Florida, where a lot of other wrestlers lived, our house was always full of my dad's "work colleagues," which was far more like a brotherhood than a bunch of coworkers.

Wrestlers like the permanently tanned Brutus "The Barber" Beefcake would come over and "smoke the good stuff" while wearing the smallest Speedos you've ever seen—I'm talking so small it looked like he had a thong on back-to-front. That wouldn't have been so bad if he wasn't constantly bending over like a giant flamingo. Grabbing beer off the bottom shelf, diving into the pool, getting out of the hot tub—every action that bent Brutus at the hips strained his stringlike swimwear to its limit, and sometimes past it. As a kid, it was hard not to look! I was surprised to find out, about a year into him coming over, that he had a torso. Whenever Brutus was around, it meant we sometimes went to class with a little hint of "the good stuff" on our clothes. We really liked to keep our poor teachers at school guessing. I should add, we all loved Brutus. He was a very loyal friend to my dad.

The Iron Sheik would stay with us regularly too, riding my dad's quad racer like a child before exploring the swampland at the back of our house in the middle of the night looking for snakes and Florida wildlife while shouting, "I'm not afraid!"

I'm not sure what motivated the fearless Sheiky to walk into the swampland, but I'm guessing it was the cocaine he and my dad were indulging in together.

Daddy was also really close friends with the slimy tax man known as Irwin R. Schyster to the fans, but Mike Rotundo to us. In real life, Mike is a great guy and the one who suggested my dad move to Florida in the first place. Mike said, "Hey, I'm down here, it's beautiful down here, the airport's really good and the beaches are really nice. You should move here." And so we did.

I remember when Mike's first son was born, he came to our house and he was so proud of his little boy. He pulled up in the driveway and we all ran out so that Mike and his wife, Stephanie, could show us their brand-new baby. I think we were the first people to see little Wyndham—who WWE fans would know later as Bray Wyatt.

"Macho Man" Randy Savage and his wife, Miss Elizabeth, came to our house too. Elizabeth was so pretty, so sweet and so shy, just like I'd seen on TV, and she was even more beautiful in person. I remember the contrast of looking out the window and seeing a drunk Randy crash my dad's motorbike into a stop sign on our street, while inside my mom and Elizabeth were chatting over coffee like nothing was happening.

As we were growing up, my sisters and I were always taken by how beautiful and glamorous all the wives were. So much so, we would pretend I was Michelle Rude, Rick Rude's wife, and my little sister Muffy was Linda Hogan, Hulk Hogan's wife, while my older sister Jenni was our aunt Diana, the British Bulldog's wife. We'd prance around in my mom's clothes while our "husbands" were out of town and go "shopping" in our kitchen, talking about our husbands and their lives as wrestlers.

The tough, wonderfully mustachioed "Ravishing" Rick Rude lived just down the street, and I remember one Easter he celebrated with us by dressing up as Big Bird and bringing over several real bunnies my mom soon found out were meant as a gift. Rick and my dad were best friends, and bad gifts seemed to be their thing together. Like one time, while drinking Champagne on the road and talking about how much they missed their wives, they decided it would be a great idea to blow tens of thousands of dollars on new wardrobes for them. While my mom was at home, knee deep in rabbit shit, my dad walked in the front door delighted with himself because he'd gotten her a line of women's dress suits from Lillie Rubin—the kind that were big with politicians' wives in those days. Google Nancy Reagan or Hillary Clinton in the '80s and they're guaranteed to be wearing Lillie Rubin suits.

If buying your stay-at-home artist wife political pantsuits wasn't bad enough, they were all the same horrible maroon color.

My dad was so happy.

My mom was so furious.

"What am I supposed to do with those?" she asked.

"Wear them?"

"Am I fucking running for office, Jim?!"

My mom drove two hours to the shop, buzzing like an angry wasp, and took everything back. She didn't want my dad wasting precious dollars on stuff she was never going to wear. She preferred worn-in Gap blue jeans and a plain white T-shirt.

When that didn't work so well, my dad bought her this crazy expensive Rolex watch. Again, she got mad. "Jim!" she told him. "I don't need this watch, and I don't want this watch. I appreciate it, but we're going to return it."

It might have been a boom time in my dad's world, but my mom grew up with the changing nature of the wrestling business. Her family had been very poor at times, especially when my grandfather's wrestling promotion was struggling. In a way, she knew how wrestling worked financially better than my dad did, so she was always trying to get him to be sensible with his money. But he would spend it just as fast as he would get it. While my mom just wanted to make sure we took care of the house and paid the bills, my dad always had very grandiose plans that included the most expensive luggage, coolest shoes, finest cashmere sweaters, and the best Champagne. Möet Chandon, to be exact.

In the meantime, the good times continued to roll, with my dad and Bret winning the WWE Tag Team Title in 1987.

It seemed like nothing could stop the party . . . except, by then, we could all see my dad was struggling. He was getting more banged up on the road, his money was going quicker and quicker, and his moods were swinging wilder and wilder. And as the decade rolled on, his friends around the house turned from the usual faces to people who were also struggling.

Hawk, the giant, scary-looking mouthpiece of the famous Legion of Doom tag team, began to stay over at our house a lot, partying with my dad into the wee hours of the morning. The woman who would "replace" Miss Elizabeth on-screen, the villainous "Sensational" Sherry, would come over too. I was in awe of her because on TV she was a bit deranged, but in person she was so nice and so sweet. One time she gave me a little ring as a birthday present. But I knew, even as a kid, that she and Hawk were people who struggled with demons. I knew because they reminded me of my dad in ways that, back then, I couldn't put my finger on.

Now that I'm older, I can see my dad suffered from anxiety and depression. He liked to drink a lot, but I never saw him get sloppy drunk—he could really hold alcohol well. One of his regular drinking partners was Andre the Giant, who could out-drink anyone. They enjoyed a lot of beers together after the shows. That's how my dad got one of his first big breaks, because Andre had as much power as Vince in WWE back then. He wanted my dad and Bret featured more, so they were.

But as the years wore on, the charm of those raucous, star-studded parties wore off, and my dad's returns home turned from celebration to confrontation.

One morning, when my sisters and I were going through his luggage like we always had, we pulled out his WWE tag-team championship belt. My sisters and I wore the title, ran around the house with it, played with it, and showed it off to the neighbors. We had it in our room. We brought it outside. Our dad was a world champion wrestler on TV!

My sisters' excitement wore off over the course of the day, but I became more and more fascinated with the title. The weight of it, the design, the leather strap. I held it over my head, and looked at myself in the mirror. Maybe I didn't want to be a wrestler's *wife* after all.

I remember how that title belt made my whole family feel so happy and close, like we had achieved something amazing. And that feeling lasted until the next day, when, on the ride back to the airport, my dad freaked out when he realized his title wasn't in his bag.

He had a meltdown, yelling, "I'm going to get fucking fired!" over and over again the top of his lungs, until my mom swerved the car, drove back home like a bat out of hell, and found the big, shiny belt where my sisters and I had left it near the pool.

That morning I saw something different in him—an anger none of us kids had ever seen before.

After that, each time my dad had to go to the airport, it became more and more stressful. Because he was working so much, he never had time to recover, so he was leaning harder and harder on drugs, alcohol, and anything else he could get his hands on just to get through the day.

We could see he was running on fumes from too many late nights and too many early-morning flights. The atmosphere in the house became more tense as his moods got worse, and all my mom could do to keep my dad in line was match his energy in a "fight fire with fire" kind of approach. This tiny woman would turn herself into Joe Pesci from *Goodfellas*: when he began to bark, she'd bark louder and longer to quiet him down. My mom was doing the best she could, but it was becoming more and more challenging to snap my dad back to reality as the decade wore on. We were walking on eggshells every day, holding on to hope that this would pass.

When I was about eight, I began to notice how much happier we all were when my dad was out of the house, because it was such havoc when he was home with his friends, and then it was such a production to get him back on the road again. It felt like once he was at the airport, we all began to breathe again. My dad's craziness and instability sometimes really scared me. I feel like I grew up too fast because my sisters, my mom, and I were more like his parents than his family. That's why I don't want to have a kid of my own, because that feeling of responsibility was etched into me as fear and not joy.

As much fun as my dad could be—and trust me, he could be *the* life of the party—he was very much like a pendulum. He could be outrageously outgoing, so fun, bright, and charismatic. And then there was another side to him—when he'd been on the road for three hundred days, and he was hurting, and tired, and hungover—where he'd veer between brooding and explosive without rhyme or reason. As an adult, I can see that my dad really struggled with his mental health, and he self-medicated. A lot.

As we headed toward the end of the '80s, it also felt like the end of the party. The bottle of Champagne to celebrate the good times with his brotherhood turned into him locking himself in a room for days with a couple of other wrestlers who were struggling too. It all began to affect his work, and WWE began to trust and book him less. I was okay with that. I thought if the money lessened, the chaos might do the same.

I was wrong.

THE BAD '90S

One morning in 1992, I woke up to get ready for school. It was a typical beautiful Tampa morning outside, and a nice quiet morning inside, because my dad was on the road.

Or at least that's where he was supposed to be.

It was that morning, when I was nine, that I remember our life changing forever. And it began when I noticed our car, a gray-and-white Dodge Ram Charger, wasn't in the driveway.

I knew our mom would never just drive off and leave us all in the house on our own, so immediately I felt something wasn't right. I made my way to the kitchen, and I could see in my mom's face that she was upset.

"I have to figure out how to get you guys to school," she said.

"Why, where's the car?" I asked.

"They took it during the night."

"Who took it?"

"I'll . . . I'm . . . Just give me a second here."

Our car had been repossessed.

Our house was nowhere near the "fun" of the '80s anymore, and even though I was still very young, I knew that things had been going off the rails between my parents. I'd felt the tension and heard the explosive fighting become more and more frequent. My dad's erratic behavior and partying were causing so much stress in our house that the rest of us were spending more and more time worrying about him, and what would happen next.

Like one Super Bowl Sunday at a small, local restaurant called Yachts of Fun, when my dad got into a fight with somebody at the bar. I wasn't watching the game, I was watching my dad—we all were, because we were just so on edge, waiting for something to happen. And just as we feared, as I was coming back from the bathroom, some big loudmouth, blowhard guy tried to shove my dad.

And then it was on.

And even though I was just a kid, I was so scared of my dad getting arrested or in trouble that I ran between these two giant guys to break up their bar fight. I'll never forget it. Even at a very young age I felt a responsibility to try to control the situation before my dad got in trouble. If I just tried hard enough, I thought, I could control the craziness for him.

It wasn't just my dad's drinking and fighting that were pissing my mom off. It was also his flippant approach to making dates for WWE and managing his money. My mom knew the peaks and valleys of professional wrestling better than most. When her father's wrestling territory was doing well—which wasn't often—her father, Stu, would buy "fancy things." When a big name like chain-smoking, barrel-chested Harley Race would come through Stampede Wrestling, tickets would boom, and Stu would buy chandeliers, oriental carpets, leather couches, Cadillacs, alligator-skin cowboy boots, and anything else extravagant that he could afford. Stu, who once lived with dogs just to stay warm, loved and appreciated opulence more than anyone. Grampy never spent his money in bars, or other shady places, but my grandmother Helen still used to get furious with him. Helen, who had been born into money but lost it all, always said it was worse to have it and lose it than to not have it at all. My mom grew up knowing it was best to hope for the boom but save for the bust. The hard times were always right around the corner.

But my dad never planned for tomorrow.

And now in the early '90s, wrestling in general was less popular, and all the money metrics started to plummet. Attendance was down, PayPerView numbers were down, merchandising was down. Hulk Hogan wasn't as much of a draw, and WWE was struggling to build new stars. All the revenue streams that paid the wrestlers' salaries were evaporating, which meant jobs in the wrestling business were getting more and more precious as companies began to downsize their rosters just to stay alive.

And at a time when others were trying to be on their best behavior to make sure they wouldn't be the ones who got cut, my dad was unraveling, and his relationship with Vince McMahon was becoming strained.

A few years prior, a flight attendant had accused my dad of assault because she denied him drinks on a US Airways flight from Tampa to Pittsburgh. In the end, he was acquitted of all the charges, and his attorney brought a successful malicious prosecution suit that paid out $400,000 to my dad. But it was Vince who put up the initial money to defend my dad, in a case that also brought McMahon and his now notorious lawyer, Jerry McDevitt, into each other's orbit. Vince was so impressed with how Jerry handled my dad's case that Vince hired McDevitt to be his personal lawyer—a relationship that would last decades and span across many high-profile, high-stakes cases for WWE's head honcho.

However, my dad blew all his award money in a couple of months in a whirlwind of spending . . . and never paid Vince back. At one point he was driving around with $225,000 in a small bag in the back of his Ninja motorcycle he had just purchased. Not only did he spend it all, but he crashed the motorcycle, too, at the front of our neighborhood.

I think he had intended to pay Vince back, but the money was all gone, and I don't think things were the same between them from then on. But Vince loved my grandfather and respected Bret, so he kept my dad on the roster because of how loyal he was to our family. I also think Vince, very much like Stu, saw the raw potential of my dad as an incredible athlete and as a very charismatic person. I do believe, in my heart of hearts, that Vince had a soft spot for my dad, because Jim at his best was a truly exceptional talent and someone who could make him money. Vince stood by him when so many would have walked away. Especially during the US Airways ordeal.

But then my dad began to miss shows—a cardinal sin in the wrestling business, especially as guaranteed deals weren't a thing yet. My dad was slipping.

It all came to a head one morning after my dad slept in and missed his flight, which prompted Linda McMahon, Vince's wife, to call our house looking to speak to him. WWE was a much smaller, family-owned business back then, which made everything more personal in nature. But my dad wouldn't, or couldn't, get out of bed to take her call, even though my mom frantically begged him to please get up, please take Linda's phone call, and please make the flight.

The following day, Vince's right-hand man, the legendary Pat Patterson, called and fired my dad. I'll never forget that day.

And that's why our car was no longer in the driveway.

We couldn't afford to pay for it.

Or our house.

Or anything, really.

Once you stopped getting booked in wrestling, there was no lead time, no adjustment period, no payment to see you on your way.

The money just stopped.

And we had no "rainy day" fund.

Everything was gone.

My mom was devastated, as the thing she'd seen coming—the thing she'd always feared the most—had happened.

My dad quickly spiraled further, selling anything he had of value to get by. All his wrestling gear and wrestling boots. His Rolex watch. His Oakland Raiders jersey, his Dallas Cowboys helmet. Family heirlooms.

My mom called Rick Rude, Curt Henning, Hawk, Hulk, The Bushwackers, Randy Savage, Brutus, Davey, Bret, Owen, Stu, and anyone else in the wrestling business she could think of to try to get my dad some work. My mom was fighting for my dad and for us kids and doing everything she could to keep us afloat. She was the Little Red Hen, all 5'2" of her, trying to save a sinking ship. But even though my dad had some small runs in World Championship Wrestling (WCW) and on the independent wrestling circuit, getting back into WWE was a Vince McMahon call. So my mom tried to contact Vince through Jim "JR" Ross's office. JR was running talent relations at the time. After leaving several phone messages looking to speak to Vince with no response, my mom wrote him a letter instead. That finally prompted a reply:

Dear Ellie,

Based upon your recent telephone conversation with JR's assistant, I can only assume that you're hurt and upset. I'd like to apologize to you if you in any way felt I disrespected you by not responding directly to you.

JR is in charge of talent relations and therefore, under normal circumstances, would handle inquiries of employment, nonetheless, considering our family situation, I could have been more sensitive to you in responding directly.

As you know, Jim has had many opportunities here in the past, and for one reason or another it just didn't work out. Considering Jim's track record, I'm not willing to give Jim yet another chance.

This is a business decision which has nothing whatsoever to do with my appreciation and affection for you and other Hart family members.

This business and I will always be personally indebted to your father, to you and to other Hart family members who have contributed so mightily to the success of our organization and "the business."

Warmest regards,
Your friend,
Vince

I remember this reply really broke her heart. Not because she thought Vince was wrong, but because it felt like her last chance to get my dad work and save our family.

My dad fell into a black hole of depression and substance abuse, while my mom had to go to food banks and food auctions just to feed us. She would come back with tuna fish and crackers in a snack pack with little packets of mayo and relish all in one container. The food was stale. We would go for weeks and weeks without going to a grocery store because we couldn't afford to. A grocery store was a luxury to us because we simply didn't have the money.

My mom and my sisters and I were so terrified all the time because my dad was falling apart and we had no idea what was going to happen to us. Everything felt so uncertain. Every day I felt like we were holding our breath, ready for the rug to be ripped out from under us.

Now, as an adult looking back, I know a few things that my younger self didn't about what was wrong with my dad. After my dad died at sixty-three years old, WWE wrestler turned neuroscientist Chris Nowinski called me after hearing the news online and asked if I was willing to donate my dad's brain to the Boston Brain Bank for research.

It was just hours after my dad had died, and I just wanted him to be left alone, but I figured this might be a way to help advance science and give us answers about what had really gone on with my dad. Doctors had told us before he died that he most likely had Alzheimer's or something very similar, but we struggled to get concrete answers.

It took the Brain Bank fourteen months of extensive study of my dad's brain before they had the results: stage 3 chronic traumatic encephalopathy, or CTE, a disorder stemming from the death of nerve cells in the brain from repeated head injury.

The woman who did the research—Dr. Ann McKee, one of the country's leading neurologists—said my dad's CTE was extensive and very consistent with football, though she couldn't say for sure it was entirely football without knowing what head trauma he might have experienced during his wrestling career and other parts of his life. My dad started playing football when he was eleven years old. He had played nose guard and defensive tackle, where he used his head a lot, and they didn't have proper concussion protocols in the NFL back then or even proper helmets. The doctor said that when they looked at my dad's brain, they could see the brain injury had been manifesting for a long time, over the course of many decades, and guessed correctly that our family had started to see the signs of my dad's CTE when he was in his early thirties. Essentially, my dad was living for most of his adult life with a traumatic brain injury that stemmed from his teenage years. The doctor's timeline was so consistent with when my dad really started to spiral out of control that everything made a lot more sense.

Now that I understand what happened with my dad's brain, I also understand that by this point, CTE had basically robbed him of his ability to think rationally.

When Ann McKee called to give my mom, sisters, and me her findings, she also said my dad had hippocampal sclerosis—a loss of neurons in the hippocampus, the part of the brain that regulates motivation, emotion, learning, and memory. Ann said that my dad had been dealing with a shrunken hippocampus for a long time, at least three decades but most likely more.

So, in simpler terms, my dad didn't even have a chance when it came to "managing" himself and changing his behaviors. The area in his brain that might have controlled that was damaged. It was something our family had always suspected, but now we had science to back it up.

Back in 1992 nobody knew the effects of CTE, and how repeated concussions could cause memory problems, confusion, impaired judgment, depression, anxiety, impulsivity, aggression, mood swings, substance abuse issues, and so much more. The era my dad came up in was the "walk it off" era. Men in general and athletes in particular were taught not to talk about their "weaknesses" or mental health but to push through by any means necessary. My dad would tell us stories of how he repeatedly had his bell rung playing football but would be rewarded by his coaches for pushing through it and getting back out on the field. They praised him for working through concussion after concussion, saying things like, "If everyone had the heart and toughness that Jim Neidhart has, we would win every single game hands down." Knowing what I know now, I do believe that those early years getting his head hit repeatedly and going back out on the field hurt my dad a lot and came back to haunt him later in his life, and early in mine.

I watched him bury himself in a hole until he couldn't find a way out anymore. And it broke my heart to watch it. It still hurts even to write about it. I loved my dad so much, but I didn't have age or the wisdom or enough information to understand just how lost he was and why. To the naked eye, he was "just" a drug addict. "Just" an alcoholic. "Just" a fuckup. Now I understand, and I really look at my dad so differently. I feel bad he struggled so much. I also feel strongly that my dad was using the drugs and alcohol to try to self-regulate how confused he felt inside. I can't imagine what he went through, silently struggling with this brain injury for so long.

We didn't know how to help him, and back then, we were in survival mode, focused on keeping him going while we struggled to keep ourselves afloat. It made my mom and my sisters and me really strong, but it also left deep scars—ones that would take years for us to heal. Some we still haven't healed from.

Still, he was my dad, and I would have done anything to look after him, to protect him, to keep him safe from himself. I would try to protect him my entire life, even when he was in the wrong. But especially when he was right.

But as he slid further downward, the only thing that kept us from the streets was my grandfather Stu secretly sending my mom money. My mom absolutely hated asking my grandfather for help. And Stu wasn't a rich man by any means, as he wasn't promoting wrestling much at that time. But even a small amount of money was a lifeline that allowed us to eat.

Things got so bad that one month, my mom, who was working as a hostess in a restaurant but still struggling to pay the bills, out of sheer desperation had to ask my twelve-year-old sister, Jenni, for the $1 an hour she made babysitting the neighbor's kid all summer long just to keep our power on. All the while, at school, everyone thought we were rich because my dad had been a famous wrestler on TV (emphasis on *had*). They had no clue we were living off scraps, scared to death of what the next day would bring as we tried to keep my dad from going completely off the rails.

Everyone hoped that, with time, my dad would get better, but over the next couple of years he just got worse. He also showed no signs of *wanting* to get better. Even when he got a chance to return to WWE in 1994, in a storyline with my uncles Bret and Owen, he couldn't keep it together and was gone within the year.

Finally, in 1996 my mom began to talk about us packing up the few things we had left in Florida and heading back to the Hart House. I'd be lying if I said I wasn't happy about the idea, as I was excited at the chance to see my cousins again, and see them wrestle once more in the ring Stu built and had set up for them in his front yard.

Since things had gotten bad with my dad, we'd missed a few summers in Calgary because we couldn't afford to go, and I longed for the wildness and freedom that came with being there. I was even more thrilled when I'd heard the Kids Wrestling Association was now thriving and my cousins were putting on even more elaborate matches, practicing new, high-flying moves on each other until the sun went down.

Unfortunately, it was in that little brotherhood of kids that something truly tragic was about to happen and make my mom's decision to move for her.

BACK TO CANADA

The Kids Wrestling Association (KWA) promotion was started at the Hart House by my cousins Teddy, Matt, and Harry; and Matt's friend from school, TJ Wilson.

The Hart House was like going to Disneyland if you loved wrestling. In addition to the family itself being loaded with huge names, the Sunday dinners attracted just about every other top draw in the business at one time or another. And it was in this environment that the KWA was born, as the Hart kids practiced, perfected, and innovated wrestling moves to showcase for the after-dinner entertainment.

As I got a little older, I, too, wanted to get in the ring, but my grandfather was always protective of the women in the family getting involved in a very much male-dominated, cutthroat, and sometimes dangerous business. Grampy wasn't wrong—the ring was dangerous, and the wrestling business can still be brutally tough, on so many different levels. And I was also afraid of trying and failing. Still, seeing my cousins in there really did pour gas on that little spark that I could feel growing inside me since I'd first held up my dad's title belt.

All the boys were serious about getting into the business when they were old enough, and the Hart House was filled with role models they could emulate. WWE Superstars who were on TV one day were walking the halls the next. It wasn't like that for me. I didn't have anyone in my family I could follow. And back then, there weren't many paths for women in wrestling. The few that were there were getting their clothes torn off in "catfights" or just waving to the crowd in a bikini.

Neither of these appealed to me. I wanted to do what my cousins were doing. But getting into the wrestling business was a very distant dream for a girl like me. So instead I got involved in the KWA by being, at various points, a bell ringer, a manager, and the person introducing the boys to the ring.

I loved being a part of it, even if my role was small. Our family was close in general, but there was a real sense of brotherhood connecting those in the family who wrestled. Every summer, I watched them with a mixture of joy and longing as they spent hours outside in the ring on my grandfather's lawn, working on new moves, putting matches together, and planning their eventual takeover of the wrestling business. Harry, Ted, TJ, and Matt were young, eager, talented kids who always wanted to absorb everything there was to know about the wrestling business, and for minds like that, the Hart House was the greatest education in the world.

My uncle Owen actually took it upon himself to teach the boys, before Sunday dinners, how to do backflips off the top rope. He always knew how to have fun and was very mischievous, being the baby of the family. My grandfather would watch out the kitchen window, where he could see everything going on in the ring, and worry a little about Owen teaching the kids highflying—Stu always liked to keep his feet on the ground. "Goddamnit! Someone's going to break their neck out there!" Grampy would say from the sink.

When times were tough in Florida, I couldn't wait to get back to the Hart House again—to hear the hollow sound of the ring, see my cousins, taste my grandparents' cooking, and feel free as bird wandering around the property.

However, when I, my two sisters, and my mom arrived at the Hart House in 1996, it wasn't for the summer, it was for good.

My mom never stopped loving my dad, and she never stopped praying for a miracle. But when we moved back to Canada, my dad stayed behind, because he couldn't look my grandfather in the eye. Even when our house got foreclosed on, Dad stayed on friends' couches and floors instead of joining us at the Hart House.

I remember leaving our bags on the old red carpet of our new room—my mom's old bedroom when she was a kid, where she, my two sisters, and I were all going to be staying—as we began our new chapter. There was a king-size bed where we'd all sleep together, one old dresser that used to belong to my mom in the '70s, an original fireplace from 1905, a small closet to hang coats in, and a picture window that overlooked the whole city. It was a far cry from the spaceship house in Florida, but it was cozy and I loved the calmness it brought. I felt really safe there. Even if the whole house did smell of cat pee. That was part of its charm.

Through the window, I could see the KWA wrestling ring that pissed off Stu's rich neighbors to no end. When my grandparents first bought the house, the hill it occupied was far away from everyone, but over time, very expensive houses were built around it. Many of the new arrivals were prominent doctors and lawyers and upper-class families, and most of them considered the wrestling ring an eyesore. I guess if you didn't love wrestling or understand the Harts, you wouldn't get why someone would have a twenty-by-twenty-foot professional wrestling ring on their lawn surrounded by dozens of broken-down Cadillacs and more than twenty stray cats.

My mom and sisters gathered behind me, and we all looked quietly at the ring, where it sat unusually empty. The usual suspects—my cousins Harry, Ted, and Matt, along with their friend TJ—weren't wrestling out there as the Kids Wrestling Association like they always had been.

Because the last time they were all in that ring together—just a couple of weeks before we moved back—Matt, who was just thirteen at the time, had to stop wrestling because he took a bump in the ring that gave him a pain in his groin. There wasn't anything else that seemed out of the ordinary at the time, but later that night Matt told his father he didn't feel good and had a sore throat. Within minutes, Matt said his eyes "felt foggy." He kept repeating, in a near delirious state, "I need my glasses." Matt had never worn glasses in his life.

His dad, BJ, who was a veteran firefighter, took him to the hospital. Unfortunately, it turned out Matt had Group A streptococcus bacteria—the common bacteria in strep throat, which in very rare cases can cause far more serious infections.

Unfortunately, this was an extremely rare and very deadly case.

Within hours of admittance, Matt fell prey to streptococcal toxic shock, which weakened his internal organs and dangerously lowered his blood pressure. And despite swift and early treatment, the bacteria spread quickly, evading all attempts to treat it. Over the course of just days, Matt faced the worst of all scenarios: necrotizing fasciitis, commonly known as flesh-eating disease, began to run rampant through his young body. After a whirlwind of excruciating meetings between his parents and medical professionals, it was established that the only chance Matt had was to remove several of his infected limbs, in a last-ditch effort to stop the spread and try to save his life.

Only a few people were allowed to see Matt. When TJ and Harry went in to visit him, they had to wear hazmat suits, and they said Matt was unrecognizable, that his skin was black and the texture like "a burnt tree."

In the end, after twelve days in the hospital, there was nothing else anyone could do. Matt was completely sedated when he died—the first strep fatality that Dr. Taj Jadavji, the head of pediatric infectious diseases at Alberta Children's Hospital, had seen in eleven years of practice.

And just like that, Georgia and BJ's son was gone. Ted, Annie, and Angie's brother. My cousin. TJ and Harry's best friend. Stu and Helen's grandson. Gone. To say we were all devastated is an understatement. Matt was a one-of-a-kind person, and his loss was immeasurable. A huge gaping wound in the fabric of the Hart family.

I knew what a great person Matt had been, having spent every summer with him as kids. He was a talented young wrestler and maybe an even better poet. For someone so young, Matt was so well rounded as a person, and everybody said he reminded them of a young Stu. He was so compassionate. He loved animals. He was a good kid who got up early, never caused any problems for his parents, and loved his brother and sisters and his cats. Matt was so agreeable and so happy and so full of life.

Then he was gone.

And it was a nightmare for his family.

Matt's mom, Georgia, was my mom's closest sister and best friend, and Mom wanted to be there for her. Georgia was born right after her, which made them the first two girls in the Hart family. This bond had kept them extremely close their whole lives.

So with everything we were going through in Florida, and everything that our family was going through in Calgary, my mom decided enough was enough, and packed up a small U-Haul with the few belongings we had left.

I wasn't sad to leave Florida, as it held a lot of anxiety for me because of how our lives turned out there. But I was sad about leaving my dad. All I knew is that he didn't come with us to Canada. It was just adult stuff, I figured at the time, but I missed him the second we left. We all did. But there was relief mixed in with my sadness. I felt surrounded by safety in the Hart House, while I'd been surrounded by dread in mine.

When we arrived in Calgary, we found out that Owen, who was now also a WWE Superstar, had paid for Matt's entire funeral because he didn't want Matt's parents to have any additional stress. After the funeral, Owen and his wife, Martha, also paid for Matt's parents to take a trip to Hawaii to get their minds off things, while my uncle Ross, a high school teacher, watched their kids.

I could feel right away that everyone was pulling together. Even with the trauma of what had just happened, there was a sense that the family was strengthening even more at the Hart House. And although there wasn't much space left, we were welcomed back with open arms by everyone, especially my grandfather Stu.

Still, I didn't want us being a burden on a family already stretched to its limit, so I knew we had to find our feet. I was a young teen now, but after living so hand-to-mouth for years, I knew I never wanted to feel like the rug could be pulled out from under me again. I wanted to stand on my own two feet and take control of my own destiny.

I wanted to be someone my family would never have to worry about.

I guess that's what happens to the kid of a parent who can't be depended upon—they want to become super independent just to make that feeling of helplessness go away. My whole life, I wanted that feeling to go away.

So, hoping to be a good girl, and no bother to my family, I decided to look beyond the ring on the front lawn of the Hart House, and down to the twinkling Calgary lights instead. I thought if I wanted to stand on my own, the way to do that was down there somewhere.

I needed to resist what I wanted to be, and be who they needed instead.

THAT LITTLE SHIT

A lot changed in my family in the months after Matt passed away. Even though my mom had earned a degree at art college, she knew being an artist wasn't going to feed her family. Having been a stay-at-home mom for so long, with little work experience, her options were very limited—but she kept applying to ads until she finally landed a job as a hot dog vendor at Costco. The job paid her $7.50 an hour, and it helped keep us afloat. My mom was never afraid of hard work, no matter what it was. She would just roll up her sleeves and handle it.

My sister Jenni, now fifteen, soon followed my mom's lead and got a job packing bags at the local IGA grocery store. At thirteen, my other sister, Muffy, was too young to work yet, and at fourteen, I was, too—but I hated the feeling of being poor.

Back in Florida, we were always worried about bills coming in and how we were going to pay them. That anxiety about losing it all has never left me. So, after watching my mom and sister get work, I figured the best way for me to control that terrible feeling was to get a job too. I wanted to be like Jenni and have my own money and the sense of independence and security that came with it.

So I asked everyone who came and went from the Hart House to let me know if they heard of anywhere that was hiring. It only took a couple of days before my uncle Davey Boy Smith, "The British

Bulldog," said he had a lead for me. Davey went to a breakfast place called Humpty's religiously when he was off the road, to get a Southwestern Panscrambler and black coffee to start his day. Davey knew the owners there, and dropped into conversation that his niece was looking for work. He lied, telling them I was sixteen, but said I was a hard worker and ready to do whatever they needed done around the place. Turns out the owners were huge wrestling fans and loved Davey, so, as a favor, they decided to offer me a trial run where I'd make $4.50 an hour.

And I can't tell you how much I instantly loved that job. Truly.

I cleaned the tables, scrubbed the urinals and bathrooms, mopped the floors, and emptied the ashtrays. I also did the dishwashing and helped the waitresses bring out food when it was busy. It was such a great feeling to take power over one of my biggest fears as a child by earning my own money. And when I saw how my efforts were helping my family, it flipped a switch in me that has stayed "on" to this day.

For the first time I could remember, I felt helpful instead of helpless. Every ashtray or toilet bowl was another chance to feel the rush of independence. I didn't need a spaceship house or a racetrack in my backyard. I just needed to feel that my family could sleep well at night knowing nobody was going to take everything we had.

What we had was very little. But it was ours.

So even though I was going to school, I still managed to work a full eight-hour shift five days a week, which meant that every two weeks I would get a paycheck for $360!

I was rich.

R-I-C-H.

The more work I took on, the less anxiety I felt, and I quickly rose through the ranks from cleaner to busser, to hostess, and finally, to waitress. It was still me, my mom, and two sisters living in one room at the Hart House, so I kept my head down and worked as hard as I could.

The only breaks I took were when I gravitated toward that ring in my grandfather's yard.

As I moved into my late teens, I still loved being around my cousins—but not so much their friend, my future husband, TJ Wilson. When I first met him, I thought he was a little shit, and that opinion hadn't changed in the three years since.

I knew TJ because he was Matt's best friend from school, but even after Matt passed away, he continued to come to the Hart House. My problem wasn't with TJ, the person, so much as the cocky attitude he seemed to be developing. TJ had been hanging out more with Matt's older brother, Ted—not because they were particularly suited personality-wise, but because TJ didn't really have anywhere else he wanted to be. Ted was very smart but mischievous and, at times, restless, and he and TJ became inseparable.

I will say, TJ was a respectful, kindhearted person right from the start. I knew this because he'd been around our family since he was a kid, and by that point he was like part of the furniture at the Hart House. All the adults loved TJ because he was a quiet, polite kid who stayed out of trouble and was obsessed with learning the wrestling business. My aunt Georgia and uncle BJ took TJ into their lives as if he was one of their own children.

And TJ loved our family back. Everyone could see the kick he got out of walking into the Hart House and seeing Bret and Owen and the British Bulldog going about their day. He couldn't believe the Harts had a wrestling ring on their lawn, and a "Dungeon" where all the top names in the business came to train. For a boy who idolized the wrestling business, this was a dream come true.

However, after Matt died, TJ kinda took on Ted's personality a little, and it got on my nerves, because now all of a sudden he was always trying to be a tough guy, and I knew that wasn't him.

What I couldn't see back then was that TJ was lost.

He came from a broken home where he never met his dad, and he and his mom lived in women's shelters growing up because they had no money. He first came to the Hart House very malnourished because they didn't have money for food. So Matt and Ted's mom, Georgia, took TJ under her wing and pretty much let him live with their family. Years later, after TJ was the first in his family to graduate from high school, his mom wrote Georgia a letter saying that TJ meeting the Hart family saved his life.

Looking back, I guess Ted was lost too. Both he and TJ were young and hurt and angry about their brother and friend dying. So they found solace in each other.

Even if they didn't have much else in common, they had Matt.

And wrestling.

Everybody in my family had wrestling as their North Star.

Or should I say, every male member of my family had it.

On TV, a retooled Hart Foundation appeared on *Monday Night Raw*, with my dad even making a comeback, joining Bret, Owen, Davey, and a close friend of the family, the unpredictable and hugely talented Brian Pillman. They were a heel anti-American faction who feuded with the biggest names in wrestling like "Stone Cold" Steve Austin, The Undertaker, and Shawn Michaels.

It was at this time that Vince told Bret he couldn't make his contract payments, and that Bret should go to WCW where he'd get much more money. Bret hadn't wanted to leave, but he had no choice if Vince couldn't pay him. Unfortunately, Bret and Vince couldn't agree on a plan where Bret would drop the WWE Title on the way out of the company. This led to Vince "screwing" Bret by having Shawn Michaels beat Bret in Canada, even though it wasn't the planned finish of the match.

This moment and match went down in wrestling history as the "Montreal Screwjob"—and had huge ripple effects in my family. Bret left WWE, and my dad and Davey followed him to WCW. Only Owen stayed.

Now that my dad was back in the business, he had a whole new purpose and happiness about him. Mom and Dad became closer again. And when I saw him on TV, I understood where I'd gotten the bug to do the same someday.

I knew I was the only Hart woman who felt drawn to wrestle, and that dream felt scary to even say out loud. It was something that I had buried and hidden well. Or, at least I thought I had.

"You should get in there, you know," TJ said to me one day on the lawn, nodding to the empty ring.

"No, it's not for me," I lied.

I didn't want him to see that I was terrified of not being good enough. One thing about growing up around the legends of any business is, you can't help but wonder where you might fit in. I didn't want to be the one who was so terrible that I dragged the whole family legacy down. I kept picturing me making this dramatic statement that I was going to be the first woman in our family to do this, and then being terrible at it.

"Well, I think you'd be great," he said, like he was reading my mind. His voice had that gentleness that I remembered from him before Matt died.

I don't know why I wanted to open up to him. I also don't know why I didn't. Our interaction that day was three sentences. But his words stuck in my head when I was trying to sleep.

The way I looked at it was, I had security working in the restaurant business. I knew my shifts, knew my pay, knew my future—as much as a teenager could predict something like that. Going into the unknown of the wrestling business meant inviting back that uncertainty that had twisted me up as a kid and was still my worst fear as a teenager. Wrestling was something I felt in my heart of hearts I was meant for, but I had seen so much turmoil and hurt and trauma in that world that I was scared to even think about it.

That's why I never went looking for any opportunities in the business: because I was afraid of getting a "yes," not a "no."

But much like everyone else in my family, the wrestling business had other plans for me. As in, I didn't seek it out, it sought me. Well, the KWA did, to be exact.

And it was that little shit TJ Wilson who would take that journey with me.

PART TWO

PRACTICE, PRACTICE!

In 1999, my uncles Bruce and Ross ran a regional promotion under my grandfather's old Stampede Wrestling banner that featured guys they trained in the Dungeon. They figured that even though Vince made a deal with Grampy to buy the territory and intellectual rights, WWE had never used the Stampede Wrestling name, so they resurrected it, eventually landing a local TV slot in Alberta.

It was during this time a TV producer called Graham Owen came aboard to shoot that show, and in his introduction to Ross and Bruce's version of Stampede was also introduced to Teddy and TJ, who blew him away with their matches.

Graham said he saw something in them that he could package and sell to a much bigger market if they were interested. He pitched them his idea for a new wrestling promotion where smaller, faster, much younger talent would compete in high-speed, nonstop, explosive matches. A younger wrestling show for younger wrestling fans.

All they needed to do, Graham said, was shoot a pilot for him to shop around—so that's what they arranged to do. Graham booked a studio space in Calgary for December 2000, where the new promotion "Matrats" would shoot the pilot they would pitch to all the North American networks.

My cousin Ted, who at twenty was the oldest of the group, was taking the calls on the project through his dad, so that made him sort of the leader. Ted had a vision for the pilot and the confidence to execute it, so the early meetings about the shoot usually started and ended with his input.

When I first heard the KWA were now being called Matrats and were going to be shooting a pilot in a fancy studio, I was genuinely so happy for them, but honestly I was also a little jealous. It felt like their train was leaving the Calgary station for the big time—and I wasn't on it.

I mean, I had no right to be on it. Up till that point, I hadn't found the courage to do even a single wrestling move. The only person I'd even talked to about wrestling was TJ, and that was only to deny I was interested.

I don't know why I didn't tell him the truth. He had an upbringing that was chaotic like mine, which I guess drew us together as sometime-friends in the quiet moments when nobody was looking. We had this thing where we should share the most vulnerable things about ourselves with each other, and then just spend months nodding at each other from afar while all the other boys were around, until we'd find ourselves alone somewhere and talk again.

He was the one I'd confided in the year before when I was told my dad, now out of the wrestling business again, was finally coming to Calgary to rejoin us as a family. He was also the one I'd turned to that same year when my uncle Owen fell to his death from the rafters of the Kemper Arena to the ring below on a WWE PPV.

Even before we lost Owen, my whole world was already spinning backward. My mom thought of my dad moving back in with us, in a small home my grandfather got us near the Hart House, as a fresh start, but my dad was struggling to find purpose when he couldn't find work in the business, and was disappearing more and more into drugs and alcohol. He was erratic, silent one day and explosive the next, and I was soon back to being on edge, waiting for something bad to happen, always planning in my head for the "worst case scenario" so I would somehow be ready.

And then Owen died, and over that summer, I dropped suddenly from a normal size to 110 pounds—a 50-pound weight loss. I fit into kids' clothes, my hair turned brittle, my skin was really dry, and I was calculating every piece of food I put into my mouth down to the calorie. I only ate a few different types of food, because I needed to know exactly how many calories everything contained. If I had a small orange, I'd round it up to 100 calories just to be safe. I never wanted to go over the daily limit I allowed myself in my head. It became a numbers game. At the time, I thought it was just the perfectionist in me coming out, but it was really me grasping for control because I felt I had none in the rest of my life.

And it was TJ who was the only one I told I had developed an eating disorder.

He was the one who listened, advised, never judged, and never told a soul. I felt I could tell him anything.

Except that I wanted to wrestle.

How could my dream be to enter the business that had caused my family so much pain?

But as Ted and the guys discussed the lighting and the smoke machines, and what they'd wear and the moves they'd do for their pilot, I couldn't help but desperately want what so many in my family already had—and that they were now about to have.

As I stood slightly back from their circle in the Dungeon, wondering how I could possibly find my way in, it was TJ who brought me closer when I was standing apart.

"You should do it, Nattie," he said.

Everyone's head slowly turned toward me.

"Do what?" I asked, like a panicked student caught not listening by their teacher.

"They're looking for a ring announcer for the pilot," Ted said.

"And?"

I waited for them to tell me who they had in mind, but their stares and silence gave me their answer.

"Me?!" I said, shocked that I was even an option.

TJ smiled. "And you should do a cool move too. Surprise everyone. Show them what you can do."

Now I was totally anxious. Heart thumping somewhere between terror and exhilaration. "What do you mean, *what can I do*? I can't do shit, TJ!" I suddenly jumped from being sad I wasn't involved to being terrified that I was. "I've never even . . . what move?"

"Dragonrana," Ted answered like he'd just gotten inspiration from the gods.

Now, for anyone who doesn't know, a Dragonrana is one of the more high-risk, high-flying moves in professional wrestling. You jump off the top rope, do a somersault midair, land in a sitting position on your opponent's shoulders, and lock your legs around their neck, before quickly doing a backflip, taking them with you so it creates the visual that their head "spikes" the mat.

It's definitely not a move an untrained newbie should be trying for their first-ever outing. I should've been starting with a lock up or a headlock! But before I could decline, TJ jumped in again and offered to help me himself. I should say that he *very eagerly* offered to help me. So much so that it kinda took me aback a little. Up to this point I'd known him only as a very reserved person. I hadn't seen him get too excited about *anything* before. But he was so adamant that we could do this that I think I saw his cool-guy mask slip a little.

I was terrified, but there was something about TJ's faith in me that elevated my confidence a little. It just felt to me that, with TJ involved, I could pull this risky move off—so I took the boys up on their offer. We were going to do this pilot together!

I guess I didn't have to tell TJ my deep secret, because he just knew.

And there was something about his smile in the middle of everyone's excitement, celebrating what was about to happen, that made me wonder for a second if he might *like me* like me.

Then I thought that would be ridiculous.

So, I entered the wrestling business for the first time because TJ literally held my hand. When my uncles Bruce and Ross found out, they were also supportive of their niece being the first female wrestler in the family, and let me train with them in the Dungeon with the boys.

But I still kept it a secret from the rest of my family, even as I started practicing with the rest of the Matrats. I knew I was only going to do a couple of moves at most, but I wanted to train the same as everyone else. I wanted to learn how to wrestle and take all the bumps the others were taking, so I could feel like less of a fraud and imposter.

But that imposter syndrome gave way to new confidence when one day my uncle Davey walked in to take a look. When I saw him standing there, I wanted to stop what I was doing and leave. I felt kind of silly learning wrestling moves in front of a big WWE Superstar who had seen and done it all.

"Holy shit," he said, loud enough for everyone to hear. "She's doing stuff that I've never even done!"

I've never forgotten his words and how they made me feel ten feet tall. They gave me a confidence I'd never had before from anything. *Anything.* I wasn't sure how everyone was going to react to me being the first girl in the family to wrestle, but Davey made me feel great about myself and the progress I was quickly making.

Over the weeks my trepidation turned into obsession, and all I wanted to do was wrestle, wrestle, wrestle. I wanted to add to the Hart name and not take from it. My dad hadn't seen me wrestle yet at this point because I wanted to be sure I could make him as proud of me as Davey was before I invited him in.

And as the pilot date came closer and closer, I really began to feel like I was a part of something special. Like I belonged. Like I was supposed to do this.

Like I was a natural.

Wrestling is a crazy-hard sport to learn, but I was the happiest I'd ever been while learning it. Every Dungeon practice felt exciting and left me on a high.

And right there beside me was TJ.

Patient and calm. Cool, but not cold. Always ready to come over and practice more, show me more, teach me more. Looking back, I think he always felt that he had chemistry with me, but I didn't always feel chemistry with him. As a matter of fact, I thought we had negative chemistry, because I thought he liked my sister Jenni. I'm sure he did at one point. Everybody liked Jenni, so I just presumed TJ was the same. I presumed a lot about TJ that I shouldn't have.

I sometimes hear guys say they never know if a girl is interested in them, and they miss all the signs. Well, I guess I was the "guy" in this situation, because I didn't think anything of it when TJ offered to take bumps for me and get black eyes for me, and catch me on cross bodies and front flips and stay countless hours with me after practice to get beaten up. I mean, he got *so many* black eyes from me; I must've dug my heels into his eyeballs probably thirty times learning to do the front-flip Dragonrana. I crashed into him so many times with that move, and he would get right back up and tell me, "I'm fine, I'm fine, I'm fine."

Now I realize TJ wanted to wrestle with me and help me and work with me as a way for him to connect and bond with me. But I was so in my head about doing a move on a wrestling show that I missed all his new signs and signals.

I could kind of feel that he wanted to spend a lot of time with me. I remember telling my sister Jenni that TJ was getting on my nerves because "he wants to do everything with me, he wants to drive me around, wants to tag along with us, he keeps asking when I'm going to be at the gym, and it's like, he's just being so annoying, and it's just like, it's enough, you know?"

I mean, I enjoyed wrestling with him very much. I just wasn't used to a guy being around so much. I'd grown up with two sisters and a mom who'd had to act like both parents. My dad was away nearly three hundred days a year sometimes. So TJ just being there for me felt like it was too much. I had never seen it before. Didn't understand it.

But once TJ was booked on a two-week wrestling tour in Saskatchewan with my uncles in the middle of our training for the pilot, something began to change in me.

Before he left, he told me not to worry, and to wrestle with the other guys to keep my training going. But I hadn't been planning to stop. I was a natural after all, and I was sure I could wrestle anybody.

At least, I was sure for the first thirty seconds of TJ-less practice that I could wrestle anyone. Because that's all the time it took for me to realize that working with other guys instead of TJ was like going from a Ferrari to a broken-down Dodge Neon. (I had a Dodge Neon that I nearly totaled when I was seventeen and it never ran right after that!)

Now it was *me* getting the black eyes and being dropped recklessly. Oof.

No, wait, I thought, *I'm a natural.* Maybe everyone was just having a bad day. So, I tried again. But the next day was even worse. I felt like my superpowers were gone. I couldn't fly like I was flying before. I couldn't land like I was landing. And then it hit me: holy shit, *TJ* was the reason I was doing so well this whole time.

TJ was making me look good!

TJ was the MAGIC.

He was the one that was helping me find confidence.

All of a sudden the signs he'd been sending me over the years, all the help he'd given me, all the kindness he'd showed me, all the patience he'd had with me hit me. And suddenly I felt like an idiot.

An idiot who really missed him.

The rest of those two weeks he was away felt like forever, and when he got back I told him before his bag even hit the ground that I missed him. And he said he'd missed me too. And then he got me ice for my black eye.

With our big break waiting and our big pilot show coming, it felt like we were back to the races—back to the Dungeon, back to practicing, back to growing.

Back to having a really big dream to chase.

Everything was back to being the way it was.

Well, except one thing.

The way I now felt about TJ.

MATRATS

Our rented-out studio space was dressed to feel like the hottest nightclub in Calgary. Our casting call for audience members asked if they could "dance like they were in a rave," so everyone would know this wasn't your grandparents rasslin' show.

As the opening bell drew closer, I was waiting backstage to get my camera-ready hair done, trying not to throw up from nerves. TJ and Ted were leading the charge, explaining to everyone the plan for the night, stopping only to check out their freshly spray-tanned abs in every mirror like they were afraid someone might have stolen them.

I guess they were making sure they were camera-ready too.

But once they were talking to each other, for some reason they insisted on using this "language" they and their friends literally had made up in school, which I couldn't understand. So, while they were talking gibberish amongst themselves, I took a quick second to talk to someone quietly under my breath who I hoped *would* understand my gibberish.

God, please protect me, and please protect everyone else in the ring. Please let me get out of there without any injuries, and please let me hit my cue, and not look like a fucking idiot. Sorry. An embarrassment. I've found something I love with all my heart, so please help me be good at it. And if you can make my Dragonrana look amazing on

TV, I'd be very grateful. And lastly, can you maybe remind my dad to watch. I would really appreciate it. Amen.

To this day, I say a prayer before every match to focus my mind, but in December 2000, I was doing it because I was terrified. Terrified I'd mess up on my first time out there, but also terrified that I was going to get hurt, or hurt someone else.

My uncle Bret had to retire that year after an errant in-ring kick gave him a severe concussion, and Owen's tragic death the year before was still seared into my mind. I grew up knowing our family business was dangerous, but seeing the effects—Owen's grieving wife, Martha, and his two young children, Oje and Athena—shook me to my core. I'll never forget the strength they showed, but Owen's passing changed them in ways I can only imagine, and they wore it on their faces every day after that.

For family member after family member, I'd seen what could go wrong in this business, and even though it terrified me, wrestling still felt like something I had to do. The wrestling business was our family business. It was in my bones.

As I waited for the show to start, TJ and I shared a silent smile through the sea of people milling around. He knew the path we had walked to get me to this point.

Until I started to train, I had no idea how to "fix" my eating disorder. Then I took my first bump in wrestling practice. I quickly found out that if I wanted to wrestle, I had to put on some weight to lessen the blows a little, as I had no meat on me to absorb any of the shock. So I suddenly began to look after myself again, because I needed to wrestle more than I needed control.

Wrestling had saved me by giving me purpose and direction.

Just like it had with TJ.

"You ready to get started?" the hair stylist asked. I think she could see I was so nervous I was stuck to my seat, so she moved all her stuff over to me. It kind of blew my mind that I was working at a restaurant bussing tables, and then all of a sudden, I had a clothing allowance, a hairstylist, and a makeup artist for TV.

I was physically and metaphorically a long way from my grandfather's backyard, but it felt natural. Which brought me a little peace—until the lights, the music, the excitement from the rabid crowd poured backstage.

It was showtime.

This was the pilot that was going to make us stars.

And it was time to find out if I was going to add to my family's name—or tarnish it.

The studio was packed, darkened for the grungy look the production team was going for, and I could feel the wave of energy all around the ring. There's something magical that happens when you gather like-minded people in the right atmosphere and encourage them to go absolutely ballistic.

And then it was on me to start the show.

"Weighing in at a rock-solid 159 pounds," I yelled into the mic, thinking that's how it was done. "Hailing from Calgary, Alberta, Canada, he is Pistol Pete Wilson!"

And we were off. Cameras were rolling, the matches were cooking, and the crowd was howling. Wrestler after wrestler, bout after bout, I pushed down my nerves about my one move, coming in the main event, and focused on what was going on in the ring.

This show set the stage for a style of wrestling that was to dominate professional wrestling for decades to come. Jack Evans, Jake Evans, Marky Starr, Keishi Matsunaga, TJ Wilson, Teddy Hart, Pete Wilson, Harry Smith, and Renee Dupree might have been unknown back then, but they were already innovating a faster, more complex, high-flying, all-gas-no-brakes style of professional wrestling that influenced the style of a lot of promotions that followed. On commentary we had the voice of Extreme Championship Wrestling, Joey Styles, along with future WWE veteran Mauro Ranallo and current All Elite Wrestling manager Don Callis.

The excitement grew and grew as wrestler after wrestler killed it. They may have been all under twenty-one, but a lot of these guys had been waiting a long time for their break, and they were sure going to make the most of having cameras at ringside.

But for me, their excellence just made my upcoming contribution more nerve-wracking. I could see just how intricate the matches were getting, and how rabid the fans' reactions were, and I couldn't help but wonder what I was doing there. These guys were pulling off moves most wrestling fans had never even seen yet, and there I was, clinging to the hope that I didn't mess up my one big move, my one big moment, and expose myself as a Hart who didn't belong.

I consoled myself with the fact that "all" I had to do was hit my cue, climb the top rope, and hit the Dragonrana on TJ. *You've got this, Nattie.* We had gone over it a thousand times, and if there was one thing that was seared into my brain, it was that cue.

It seemed like hours as I waited and announced at ringside, until eventually the six-man main event was set up in the ring—and then, boom, there it was.

MY CUE!

FUCK!

SHOWTIME!

I slid into the ring, only for TJ to subtly hold me back as he continued his match. But I got this, TJ! It was my cue!

"Yoh tu eahlay," he whispered.

"What?" I whispered back, trying to get past him to find my mark.

"Yoh tu eahlay," he replied again.

"TJ! I'm going to miss my cue!"

I was so mad at him for choosing *this exact moment* to try speaking

Ted's gibberish—until I looked closer and saw that TJ's garbled words were because of a giant fat lip that got split open from an earlier head-butt. His mouth was both filled with blood and covered in medical tape.

"Yoh tu eahlay!" he said again.

"You're . . . too . . . early," I mouthed along, translating his garbled words to myself.

Oh, I'm too early? I'm too early!

I'M TOO EARLY!!

I whipped around to get out of the ring as fast as I could, but TJ guided me again without breaking stride.

"Nattah!" he whisper-shouted.

Turns out that I *was* early for my cue, but I'd spent so long trying to understand TJ that it was now my cue to stay.

Jesus.

Now I was shaking with adrenaline and nerves and weighed down with self-doubt in front of an audience whose energy was peaking.

TJ nodded to the turnbuckle. This was it. This was my moment.

I climbed the top rope like I'd practiced, and time stood still as I launched blindly into the wrestling version of the *Dirty Dancing* lift, where I would land crotch first on TJ's neck.

As I flew through the air, I was sure would either make my wrestling career or break my neck before it even started. I could see the wide eyeballs in the crowd, feel their clenched buttocks in fear of what was about to happen, but as I saw TJ waiting in perfect position to catch me, I knew everything was going to be okay.

Then I felt him under me.

I felt myself rotating.

And I felt myself go sprawling across the mat.

I lay there, eyes closed, trying to figure out whether I'd hit the move or not, until I got the guts to peek—and saw the glorious sight of TJ sprawled out on the mat in front of me, selling the move to the audience like I'd killed him!

And with that time hit its normal rhythm again.

My Dragonrana was in the bag, and I didn't hurt anyone else, or myself!

My internal volume went from mute to full as the audience unclenched and lost their collective minds—a sound and sight I continue to crave to this day.

I did it.

We did it.

And we celebrated that night just like all rock star wrestlers celebrate: by finding a walk-in clinic for TJ to get sewn up as his lip bled for six hours nonstop.

This was our first time in a hospital together for an injury to TJ, and unfortunately it wouldn't be our last. But here we were at the start of something beautiful.

We were young and happy, and we were going to be professional wrestlers on TV.

HERE I COME!

Unfortunately, it wasn't meant to be.

We were so ready to sell that pilot and be megastars, just like everyone we'd grown up idolizing. And for most of 2001, it really did look like it was going to happen. The pilot ended up piquing the interest of Eric Bischoff, the former executive vice president of WWE's main competitor, World Championship Wrestling.

Under Eric's leadership, WCW had transformed from a smaller, more Southern-leaning organization into a cool national juggernaut that overtook WWE as TV's most watched wrestling show for almost two years. However, over the course of Eric's tumultuous reign (which included his firing, and re-hiring, and re-firing), not only did WWE reclaim its spot on top, but it eventually bought WCW—a company that was making $200 million in 1998—for just $2.5 million just three years later in 2001.

You see, that was a big part of the problem. Eric was ecstatic about Matrats in February 2001, because he was in the midst of pulling together financing to buy WCW himself. It was his plan was to debut the Matrats talent in the new WCW to give it a much younger edge.

"We are going to kick Vince McMahon's ass," he told TJ and Ted after he'd seen the Matrats promotion live.

It was clear that Eric and his producing partner, *The Wonder Years* star Jason Hervey, saw huge potential for a wrestling show that targeted a teenage viewing audience, but once WWE purchased WCW, Eric became less and less enthusiastic about Matrats.

Until he wasn't interested at all.

Like happens a lot of times in the entertainment business, we went from being the hot new thing on the block to dead in the water.

And part of me wondered if the reason the pilot didn't sell was me.

My world was so upside down that I couldn't see the bigger picture, which was that wrestling—which really was now just WWE—had gone through years of the over-the-top attitude that was WWE's 1990s calling card, and advertisers were feeling skittish about being attached to the business. Any new wrestling project was going to be a hard sell, particularly one that was aimed at kids and teens.

We were told that the promotion was going to continue, and we did a few more shows, but in reality, without TV, it was dead as a company. We tried pitching other networks, and even streaming shows online, but in 2001, online-only content was just a little too ahead of its time.

And once reality set in that we weren't going to be wrestling stars on TV, TJ and I processed it like any good, mature teenagers would—by arguing.

I blamed the pilot dying on me missing my cue.

He threatened to quit, even though the promotion was already dead.

I worried they were going to fire me, even though the promotion was already dead.

He asked if I was going to practice that week.

I told him he was suffocating me.

So he stormed off.

So I stormed off.

Actually, I can't entirely blame it on us being teenagers because we still argue exactly like this. But the dream of making it big on TV like the rest of the Hart family was our whole world, and it was over. On top of that, TJ was being the most infuriating boy I'd ever met.

And the most wonderful.

So much so that a day or two later a letter arrived at the Hart House for me:

Nattie

I hope you are not mad at me. Trust me, the last thing I want to do is argue with you at all. I always feel really bad and upset after. I wasn't saying that you needed to tell me your schedule and everything you do. I would never walk out on our friendship, you mean too much to me. I was so proud of you. You announced really well, and you are the only girl that can do a dragonrana. Most of the time you make me feel really good and important. You are really important to me. When I wrestle with you, it makes me feel special. You learn so fast and are so grateful. I am never put out whatsoever when I wrestle you. I was really flattered when you were talking about some of my qualities and you're not like any girl I've ever met. I consider you my best friend.

My ideal day would be us having coffee and donuts. We would go tan, go work out, maybe go to Souvlaki Time. Come back to the house instead of having to wrestle at a show. I would rather practice (wrestling) with you. Then possibly go to McDonald's. I enjoy spending time with you. You're very easy to be around and get along with. I will talk to you later Nattie.

—*TJ*

When I read TJ's letter, a fog lifted, and I decided I didn't have to be so afraid of what I could feel happening between us. After all, the guy who could write such a sweet letter to me couldn't be something to be so wary of. I thought that maybe I should relax a little more and just see what happened. And do you know what happened? We ended up having our first kiss in the front seat of the broken-down, brakeless, pastel-yellow Cadillac that my grandfather gave me after my Dodge Neon got totaled.

But do you know what happened after *that*?

We moved in together.

Our relationship went from tortoise to hare.

I figured the best way to deal with my dad's volatile lifestyle and the feelings it brought back up was to remove myself from it, so I asked my grandfather if my sister Jenni, TJ, and I could live in the vacant old coach house at the back of the Hart House where my parents started out. Grampy was thrilled that we would look after it, and he loved TJ. So Jenni got one bedroom and TJ and I slept on the floor of the other on a blow-up plastic mattress.

And other than the mattress having a small hole in it, it was perfect.

TJ and I were close to the Hart House, close to the Dungeon, close to the ring on the lawn, and close to each other. After our MTV dream died, we had no idea what the future would hold, but we kept wrestling regionally in my uncles' revived Stampede promotion, and it felt like this exciting, exhilarating drug that we were both on together—and we didn't want it to end.

Like most of us in the Hart family, wrestling was the thing that had found me love.

Some couples garden together, some collect things together, but TJ and I wrestled together. When we had nothing else to our names to share, we shared wrestling.

And boy, did we have nothing. I was still working as a waitress, and TJ was shoveling barley 9 to 5—but once night hit, we'd both hurry to meet each other in the Dungeon and practice, practice, practice.

Disappointment at not being on TV didn't stop us or slow us down—it made us up our game and try even harder. We were having so much fun, and I felt like I was learning something new in the Dungeon every single day.

And that's when a longtime friend of the family, Tokyo Joe, began to see our potential.

Joe Daigo, who everyone referred to as "Tokyo Joe," was a revered Japanese trainer notorious for training legends like Jushin Liger, Kensuke Sasaki, Cobra, Hashimoto, Shinjiro Otani, Hiroyoshi Tenzan, Takano, and Hiroshi Hase in his home country. Being picked by him for private training was seen as an honor, something very few were chosen to do. Legends like Lou Thesz and Killer Kowalski would invite Joe to their schools when they felt they had real prospects for the business, and Joe would go and check them out.

Yukihiro Sakada was Joe's real name, and he had come to wrestle for my grandfather in the '60s as an up-and-coming talent, an accomplished sumo wrestler back home in Japan who also excelled in judo.

One night, after working one of my grandfather's shows, he was hit by an oncoming car during a torrential snowstorm while trying to move his own car out of a ditch. Joe was only thirty-one years old, but thanks to twenty-seven individual fractures, one of his legs had to be removed just below his thigh. His other leg was fractured in fifteen places but was able to be saved. He also damaged part of his arm.

When my grandfather heard that Joe could no longer wrestle, he wanted to take care of him, and gave him enough money to get set up wherever in the world he chose. Joe ended up staying in Calgary, as he had too much pride to go back home to Japan, and he loved my grandfather so much that he wanted to stay and find a way to repay Stu's kindness.

So Joe became a trainer and talent scout and liaison between New Japan and Stampede Wrestling, helping everyone from my dad to Undertaker to Fit Finlay, Bam Bam Bigelow, and Sid Vicious get bookings in Japan. He was *the guy* when it came to the Japanese style of hard-hitting, sports-leaning wrestling, and after seeing TJ and my cousin Harry wrestle, he felt they would flourish in that environment. Joe thought they were so talented that he came out of retirement to train them privately.

Soon, Joe invited me into his private training sessions too. I was the only woman there, and the only woman Joe would ever train personally, period.

Joe trained with us five days a week, Monday through Friday, for four to five hours a day. He really took me under his wing, and I learned a lot about shooting, precision, timing, and speed. I was working on so many new holds and moves that I hadn't worked on with TJ: German suplexes into bridges, how to do the perfect dropkick and lightning-fast headlock takeovers, and just generally taking in the hybrid style of wrestling that Tokyo Joe had mastered. I still remember the sheer amount of neck-strength training we did. I always told Joe he reminded me of a crocodile because he never blinked. He never missed anything. You could get nothing past Joe.

And while it was really intense training physically, Joe focused intensely not just on shaping us as wrestlers, but also as people. He was big on making sure the wrestlers he trained would know how to handle themselves like professionals. Respect was everything to Joe. While he was hardcore during training, after every practice we would take Joe to a restaurant he loved called Starlight Diner, and he would order eggs and toast and extra-hot coffee that would burn the roof of any mortal's mouth, then talk to us about our lives. And about his life. And about how to make it both within the wrestling business and outside the ring too.

Alongside training with Joe and wrestling for my uncles, I also got some work with a small promotion about three hours from the Hart

House, in Edmonton, with the Prairie Wrestling Alliance. The PWA let me work for them to get some experience, try out all the new things I was learning, and most importantly, fail. I couldn't grow the way I needed to without failing. Most of the shows we performed on were in front of fewer than fifty people. But it was the reps I needed to work toward my dreams. I'm grateful for the early days of my wrestling career, being surrounded by people who knew that becoming a wrestler isn't about perfection, it's about perseverance.

And perseverance was something I had plenty of. I wasn't going to give up no matter how hard it was. I wanted to show everyone in the business that I wasn't like my dad in terms of my professionalism. I wanted them to see that I would travel as far as needed, be on time, never no-show an event, never complain, and carry out whatever the booker of the show needed from me that night. I could be whatever they needed me to be.

Wrestling was now my life. Between training and wrestling, plus waitressing full time to pay the bills, I didn't have a free minute, and I loved it—because everything I did revolved around putting in the work to get better as a wrestler.

And people began to notice.

Opportunities started coming from various corners of the business. And while I felt scared and underprepared, it also felt natural, like something I was meant to do. I was about to do what countless members of my family had done before me.

I was about to go from crossing the Canadian Prairies to crossing the world.

A TALE OF TWO TOURS

There's that moment in all our lives where we first go into the world on our own and experience something so new that we can't help but think, *Wow, I'm a long way from home.* Sometimes it's the vastness of an iconic city, the beauty of a mountain sunset, or immersion in a new culture. Well, my first-ever *Wow, I'm a long way from home* moment was watching a guy in the UK clip his toenails and save those clippings in the drawer beside his bed. It wasn't a Paris sunset, but it was definitely something I had never seen before.

Let me rewind the tape a little here, because I get that this might need some context. In 2004, when I was twenty-one, I got my first overseas booking in the UK with a promoter named Brian Dixon. Brian worked a lot in UK holiday camps known as Butlins, and he'd sometimes bring over North American talent to do specific dates in the summer "busy season." And Tokyo Joe put me forward to be one of those people.

Joe's name carried such weight around the wrestling world that before I knew it, I was flying outside North America for the first time in my life—and I was doing it alone. That was a big deal for me, because I was used to being part of a litter of Harts and Neidharts, sandwiched between my mom and sisters or my grandparents and cousins. But my grandparents Stu and Helen were gone now, dying within just a couple of years of each other, and my sense of home was a little fuzzy without them there. And with the Hart House North Star not as bright anymore, I knew I needed to branch out more and see the world. Growing up in a family so big and close, I never had a quiet minute, or wanted one, so going thousands of miles away on my own was a huge adjustment for me, but it was one I knew I needed for growth.

The booking was to work with UK women, six to eight times a week, at the holiday camps. Not only was I going to be away from my family for the first time, I was also going to be away from my wrestling family—including TJ. All the people I had learned from and depended on to make me look good, the people who looked out for me, were staying behind.

I arrived in the UK nervous but excited at the opportunity to learn another style of wrestling. While the North American style tends to be flashy and story driven, and the Japanese style is competitive and hard hitting, the UK style is more like physical chess, where the focus is on holds, reversals, and outmaneuvering your opponent. So even though I was going to be thousands of miles from home, at least I would be in the hands of people who could teach me even more about . . . what's that? I was mostly going to "wrestle" women in schoolgirl outfits who'd never had a match before?

Okay, then. Let's fucking go.

I didn't know it then, but this tour gave me a great foundation in putting aside what you expect and making whatever the show needs to work, work. If they needed me to be the veteran who showed the other women the ropes, then so be it. That's what I tried to do, even though I was still learning and very green myself.

I was just happy to be working every day, making $40 a match. I was given my own room in a place called "The Digs" and I worked every day both teaching and learning at the same time. I loved it. The people were kind, the shows were fun, and with a little space to myself for the first time in my life, I began to learn what I wanted and didn't want my life to be.

It was in those auspicious Digs that a fellow wrestler clipped his toenails—while keeping perfect eye contact with me—and deposited the fallen clipping in his drawer for some reason when *the garbage can was right there*!

But it was on the short walk to my room after seeing it that I realized I wasn't only built for the ring—I was built for this life. I wanted to meet more people like the toenail guy. I wanted to be around the weirdness and kindness of people who lived most of their lives on the road, building relationships in the ring that lasted a lifetime. I wanted to be a full-time wrestler.

I wanted to follow in the Harts' footsteps and be the first woman from our family to make her way to WWE.

Still, I knew I had a ways to go, and I needed a lot more work, experience, and time on the road before daring to dream that dream.

And that's why I was thrilled when, the following summer, Tokyo Joe got me another three-month booking, this time in Japan for a promotion called the Next Entertainment Organization. NEO was a new promotion rising from the ashes of the famous All Japan's women's promotion called Gaea, which had just shut down the month prior.

Joe managed to get me booked over there as "the gaijin," which means "foreigner"—a role played by non-natives going back to the post–World War II era, where the Japanese hero would vanquish the invading gaijin who has come to their country looking for a fight.

While the UK tour the year before had been a great personal experience, Joe explained to me that this tour in Japan could be my big break into the business if I did well. There was a long, long history of North American wrestlers—everyone from Hulk Hogan to Ric Flair to my dad—going to Japan to "prove" themselves against Japanese talent. Time and time again, the gaijin who did well in the tough and unforgiving Japanese promotions boosted their prospects back home. If someone could handle and prosper in Japan's "strong style" of wrestling, then they had a real shot at getting booked back home too.

And that notorious strong style was the reason my dad didn't want me to go.

Not one little bit.

He'd been there, and seen how hard they wrestled. While he'd been a little wary of me going to the UK, he knew the style there was nothing compared to Japan's full-throttle matches. And they often wrestled the gaijin harder than they would their own, to make sure they earned it—something that made perfect sense to me, because, as Tokyo Joe would always tell us, "In Japan, respect is everything."

My dad told me stories he'd heard of other gaijin women and the injuries they'd received there, like the tough-as-nails Luna Vachon, who got her teeth knocked out. He was worried I was too green to understand yet what the wrestling business was *really* all about.

"You're always playing against the House in this business, Nattie. And look around! Nobody in our family has cashed out yet with their money and their health. If you want to be the first anything in this family, be the first to leave without being broke or broken. Be the first of us to beat the fucking House."

Like every one of his generation, who were on the road wrestling three hundred days a year, he now had daily pain that Icy Hot couldn't begin to soothe anymore. And he was worried I was going to end up like him, unable to get from one end of the day to the other without needing something to take away the pain, mentally and physically.

"These women are really rough, and I think you're in over your head," were his last words to me before I left for my flight.

But I was determined to prove him wrong. I was determined to prove myself in the family business. So I got on that plane. And I have no problem admitting that, while I'd been nervous about leaving for the UK the summer before, I was *terrified* of leaving for Japan.

It wasn't so much that I could get hurt. It was more that I could be exposed. I was about to enter a whole new level of competition, and if I failed now, it would be on a much bigger stage, in front of everyone who believed in me. And I was really afraid of not being good enough.

But I had to go. I had to find out if I had what it took to rightfully stand beside my family in the business they loved. I had to earn my place and not just rely on what my grandfather and father and uncles had done. So I arrived and settled into a little town outside of Shibuya in Tokyo called Motosumiyoshi, where I had a tiny little apartment that was really just a bed inside a very small kitchen. It was basic but perfect—except for the cockroaches (*gokiburi* in Japanese). I went to cook eggs one day and found one in my frying pan. It was the size of a mouse, I swear! I realized then that, despite having a deep voice my entire life, I could in fact scream if I needed to.

Every morning I would catch a train into Tokyo and go to practice with the intimidating Japanese girls. I immediately understood that I was the rookie here, as their dedication, skill level, and intensity were leagues above mine. Once again, I felt behind, not good enough, many paces behind everyone else.

And to make matters worse, when training was done, I'd just be alone. Nobody there spoke my language, and I didn't speak theirs.

It was hard not having TJ in England, but it was really hard not having him in Japan, and soon I was spending all my free time trying to reach out back home. In a time before cell phones were a thing, I spent what little money I'd earned to rent computer time in internet cafés to email TJ, and wait in there for hours just hoping he'd pop up on Messenger. Any money I had left over, I'd spend on pay phones and hope someone was home to pick up.

I found it hard.

Really, really hard.

I remember telling TJ that I wanted to come home because I was so lonely. "I don't wanna do this, I don't fit in and I'm really lost, and I just feel like I don't belong and I don't know how I'm gonna get through this. I've got months and months left of being out here and training with these girls who are so much better than me, and I'm just so lonely. Unless I'm training with the girls I'm all alone and I don't know if I can do this."

"Nattie, you can't come home," TJ said. "As much as I want you to come back home, you need to make it work because this is for you. This is your career and your dream, and you can't give up when it gets hard."

He wanted me to get strong and to be able to stand on my own two feet. He knew me being uncomfortable wasn't a bad thing, because lots of times growth only comes with being out of your comfort zone.

"You gotta keep going," he said. "Call me as much as you need, but you can't come home."

And he was right. I was used to hard work, and my training back home in the Dungeon had prepared me for times just like this. I decided I wasn't going to quit and I wasn't going to be carried. I knew I could hold my own and prove my worth even in a place where I knew nobody, and nobody knew me.

And once the other girls saw how hard I was trying, they slowly began to accept me and treat me like one of their own. Over the following days and weeks, we really began to connect during practice. I learned some basic words along the way, and some of the Japanese women put together enough words for us to connect a little more, but wrestling really became our universal language. And at night, when we'd do our shows, I felt like the girls really trusted me, wanted to help me, and wanted me to succeed. Wrestling brought us together.

My very first match there was with a woman named Sumie Sakai.

I tried to tell her how scared I was, and she told me in broken English not to worry, because "tonight we just dance." Her words immediately put me at ease. You're always in the hands of your "opponent" in the ring, but when you're as green as I was, you really are at the mercy of whoever is leading the match. And Sumie really, really took care of me out there. She even let me win.

I'll never forget her selflessness in letting a new girl beat her in front of her hometown. Sumie's way of looking at the wrestling business really made a lasting impression on me about how to conduct myself in an industry where fragile egos are common. I was still green, but I'd already made up my mind that if I became something in the wrestling business, I wanted to do for other new wrestlers what Sumie did for me that night.

As I gained experience over the course of that tour, wrestling in front of different crowds, in different settings, against women who were better than me, I was progressing rapidly, and I tried to absorb everything I could. I knew that if I could work any style against any opponent, I had a better shot of making it to the big time, to WWE. I figured that to have a good career there, I'd need a hybrid style, because at the time WWE was only hiring "athletic tens"—models—for their women's division, and I knew I wasn't that *at all*. Not even close. But I could become someone those "tens" could get in the ring with and have a good match.

Still, before I could even begin to think that big, I had my own little world to conquer first. As my Japan run was coming to an end, I began to lie in bed at night and play my dad's parting words to me over and over again.

No matter what happened, and what road I found myself on professionally, I was determined to be the first person in our family to "beat the House."

THE HARTS AND THE MCMAHONS

As soon as I got back from Japan, I began sending tapes of my matches to Dr. Tom Prichard, WWE's head scout and trainer, to see if WWE would be interested in hiring me. After months of silence on their end, Dr. Tom finally wrote me a letter saying, "We got your tape and we're reviewing it and, you know, just keep working hard but there's nothing for you at this time."

Okay, Dr. Tom had replied. They got my tape. I did my part. They knew I existed.

But twenty-three-year-old me was devastated. Being around the business my whole life, I knew that "nothing for you at this time" or "we're not hiring right now" really means "we're not hiring *you* right now." That's why professional wrestling, like any other form of entertainment, feels so personal when you're trying to navigate your way through it: you know that a major company like WWE doesn't stop hiring people, they just hire *other* people, and that rejection can really hurt. Just as I'd feared, they didn't want *me*.

I knew I needed to keep positive and keep hustling. But not only did I fear I might be the wrong kind of woman, at the wrong time in history—another, worse worry began to gnaw at me. Maybe I was from the wrong family too.

In 2005, World Wrestling Entertainment was the only major player in our industry, so if you wanted to make a real living wrestling, all roads eventually led to them. But at the time I was getting into the business, the Harts and the McMahons already had a long history, and a lot of the chapters of that history really weren't good at all.

At the start of Vince's time in wrestling, when he took over his father's New York promotion and began to buy up all the other regional promotions, one of the wrestling promoters he made a deal with was my grandfather—the deal that brought the Hart family wrestlers into the WWE in the first place. A huge part of Vince's strategy was to "raid" the top-drawing wrestlers in each territory, which would kneecap his competition by decimating their box office. But with Stu, Vince didn't have to do that because Grampy *wanted* his son and sons-in-law to go to a place where they'd have more earning potential and be able to wrestle on a national and international level. Stu knew WWE could offer Bret and my dad and my other uncles many more opportunities than he could, and if that meant selling Vince his TV time, and giving him access to his territory and talent, so be it. So in 1984, Vince and my grandfather made a deal for McMahon to buy Stampede Wrestling for $750,000, to be paid over ten years.

Even though my grandfather ended up never getting all of the money, he didn't say anything, because he didn't want to rock the boat for his sons, and sons-in-law, who were now making more money in WWE than they'd ever made in their lives.

Cut to 1997 and the most controversial match in WWE history: the "Montreal Screwjob." Bret was Vince's world champion, and originally, Vince had offered Bret a twenty-year contract. But then Vince told Bret he couldn't pay, and said that Bret should go to WCW, the competition at the time, instead. Bret reluctantly signed with WCW and told Vince he'd drop the title anywhere and to anyone, except in his home country of Canada to Shawn Michaels, who Bret felt had crossed the line of professionalism with him several times.

But anyone with even a passing knowledge of professional wrestling knows what happened next: after agreeing with Bret that he didn't have to lose to Shawn, Vince rang the bell during the match, stripping Hitman of the title live on PPV—even though Bret never tapped out.

That one decision resulted in a chain reaction that changed the business forever, but on the Hart–McMahon front, it resulted in Bret spitting in Vince's face on live TV, then knocking Vince out in the locker room afterward.

Bret felt like Vince had intentionally misled him and wanted to humiliate him—that he wanted to show Bret that he could do whatever he pleased, regardless of any past promises or how it would affect Bret.

Only a couple of years later, my uncle Owen fell from the rafters—also live on PPV—and died in a WWE ring when the harness that was used to lower him opened prematurely. This led to Owen's widow, Martha, suing WWE, and WWE in turn suing the company responsible for the defective harness.

So while your last name can be a good door opener in the wrestling business, I wasn't sure by the time I came around that my family name wasn't a door closer instead. There had been a lot of conflict between Vince and our family, and much of it still felt fresh. This worried me even more because making it in wrestling wasn't just my dream, it was TJ's, too, and we wanted to go on this journey together. I knew how insanely talented TJ was, and I didn't want any of what happened in the past hurting his chances, even if mine were slim to none.

Fortunately, I was ready for a challenge. I wanted to prove myself instead of getting favors because of my family, anyway. So I kept sending in tapes and trying my hardest to get booked on more shows. Working for very little if not for free. Driving hours and hours to wrestle in front of even ten people to get any experience I possibly could.

I even got to share the ring with my dad, tagging together on a small show in Ontario, Canada. It was one of our only times sharing a ring together, and I treasure the memory of it to this day. I had torn my ACL in Japan, but even though I was so limited that I couldn't train, when the opportunity came up I decided to gut through it to be in there with my dad no matter what.

And it was awesome.

He could see that I was as stubborn as he was, and that I wasn't going to back down when it came to being in the wrestling business. He knew I was my own woman, and I was going to do this with or without him, so he wanted to see me up close in the ring. He wanted to get a feel for what I could do and if I had a shot or not.

At the show he treated me like his daughter when it was just us, but like "one of the boys" in front of the other wrestlers. I watched his every move backstage, and how he handled himself. I watched him command the audience once we got in front of the crowd, and for the first time, his years of working nonstop all around the world were so evident to me, now that I could see what he was doing, wrestler to wrestler. I had never given my dad enough credit for how good he actually was as a professional wrestler. He was so good. And so agile for a bigger guy. I was so proud of him. And so proud to be his tag partner for the match. It really was a dream come true for me.

My dad was adamant that he and I do the same finishing move—the Hart Attack Clothesline—that he and Bret used to do when they were one of the biggest tag teams in the world. My dad would bear-hug our opponent and lift him in the air so I could run the ropes and flying-clothesline the guy my dad was holding in position for me.

"Take his head off, Nattie!" he shouted in character as I hit the ropes. I still smile about that line today. It was the first time I felt like he saw me as more than just his daughter. He saw me as a wrestler—one of his peers. It was awesome to be able to hold my own in there, and have my dad cheer me on up close and personal.

It was a revelation to see my dad go from the alternately depressed, withdrawn, and explosive person he'd become at home to the excited and focused star he became in that ring. Wrestling gave him purpose and meaning, and to watch him go from somebody so lost at home to somebody so at home in the ring really opened my eyes to him as a person.

He wasn't "just" my dad. He was a professional, a craftsman, a wrestler who had been to the very top of the mountain because of how good he was at what he had dedicated his adult life to.

And as much as I got to see a different side to him, my dad saw a different side to me too.

"You're good enough to be there, you know," he said to me in the car on our way home after the match.

"Where?"

"WWE."

And he left it at that. He was proud of me, which made me happy, but he was also confident in my abilities, which made me even happier.

He and Mom left Calgary shortly afterward, looking for another new start. With both my grandparents now gone, and the Hart House up for sale, the glue that held the whole family together was gone. My little sister lived down in Tampa, so my parents, who both loved the sunshine, decided to move back to Florida.

I stayed in Canada with TJ so I could prove my dad right about making it to WWE. I just needed an "in." And in 2006, when we heard that WWE was going to induct Bret into their Hall of Fame class that year, it felt like that "in" finally might have presented itself.

"Maybe this means fences are being mended?" TJ wondered.

Bret and Vince burying the hatchet was a good thing. Not just for us, but for Bret and the rest of the family too. It was like a weight had been lifted.

Still, even without the Hart–McMahon history in the way, TJ and I knew our chances were slim. WWE was considered "land of the giants" where everyone was six-foot-four and three hundred pounds, so TJ, at five-ten and two hundred pounds, was considered "too small." And I definitely wasn't the "athletic ten" they were looking for in the women's division.

I had proven myself in the UK, in Japan, and in the ring with my dad. But all of that was going to be child's play compared to the challenges that were waiting just around the corner.

TRYING TO BREAK IN

TJ and I didn't have to guess when it came to our odds of making it to WWE. Back in 2005, Carl De Marco, a friend of Bret's and president of WWE Canada at the time, had asked if we'd like him to feel out any interest in us. Carl didn't have any power when it came to hiring and firing, but he could have a quiet word with those who did. First, though, he was straight up with me and TJ, saying that us ending up in WWE was going to be a very tough sell.

We knew WWE seemed keen on my six-four, two-hundred-and-fifty-pound cousin Harry, son of Davey Boy. And at least *some* people in management weren't violently against TJ teaming with Harry there. But nobody from WWE wanted me there—something I saw firsthand when I attended Bret's Hall of Fame induction.

My ACL tear in Japan meant I couldn't train or work out properly, on top of having been a little chubby to begin with, so I arrived in Chicago for the ceremony about thirty pounds heavier than I am now. No makeup, no dazzle, just plain old Nattie, the lady wrestler, among the most in-shape, stunning women I'd ever seen. It was one thing to see these women on TV, but once I was beside them, around them, I couldn't help but compare myself to them.

I nearly broke my own ribs, I sucked in my stomach so hard.

And I realized then that my shot at getting into WWE wasn't

dependent on the thing I spent the most time on, which was wrestling. It was dependent on the thing I spent the least on, which was my appearance.

Every corner I turned, or room I walked into, I met a better version of myself. For the first time in my life, I wanted to be prettier, and smaller, and more glamorous. And because that wasn't going to happen in the next two minutes, I instead wanted to run for the fucking door. I'd spent years focused on how good I was compared to the guys but I'd forgotten about the girls.

That weekend, Harry got signed, and word was they were interested in Ted too. TJ was told to "stay busy," which meant there was a chance down the road. I got a flat "no."

TJ did what was asked of him, and took off for the summer to work the same Butlins tour I'd worked a couple of years before for promoter Brian Dixon in England.

And me?

One of WWE's upper management had told me straight up that I needed to change the way I looked. He said I needed to lose thirty pounds and tighten up my body—"a lot."

No promises, he said, but he'd take another look if I did.

I wasn't a fitness model, or a dancer or a cheerleader, and I had no idea how to even approach the visual illusion of being any of those things.

I couldn't do a best-body contest and win it.

I couldn't do a dance-off and win it.

I was a girl that wrestled.

But I wanted to get to WWE.

So as soon as I landed back home in Calgary after that Hall of Fame ceremony, I used my waitressing money to hire a fitness model with bodybuilding experience. Her name was Deb. She got me on a nutrition plan and a workout plan, and did weekly weigh-ins with me while I lost thirty pounds in just three months. I was determined to show WWE that in the era of dancers and bikini models, there was a place in their programming for a woman who was "just" a wrestler.

I sent WWE my updated tape and pictures, and the feedback was much better. Still no job offer, but at least they got straight back to me this time, and said they were impressed with the changes in my physique. And then, a few weeks later, while TJ was still in the UK, we both got the word we'd been waiting on for years: WWE was going to bring us to Georgia in the fall for a tryout.

Carl was honest. He told us that WWE wasn't really interested in us, but they wanted to make good with Bret, so they were bringing us in to say they at least took a look.

"You guys gotta blow this out of the water," Carl told us. "You have to go in there and out-wrestle and outdo everyone else to have any shot at all."

I knew that wouldn't be a problem for TJ. He'd already made a name for himself by outworking everyone in every town we wrestled in. Everything he'd done so far had prepared him for this: Tokyo Joe, Japan, wrestling with our family in the Dungeon and on the lawn at my grandfather's house.

TJ's tryout in Georgia was as smooth as could be. Even the thing he wasn't strongest at, cutting promos, he managed to overcome by delivering a passionate, captivating monologue when he needed to the most. I was so proud of him, and I could tell the WWE decision makers at the tryout were impressed too. We could all feel that he was in.

And then it was my turn.

I stepped through those ropes, and I was vibrating with nerves. But I focused, tightened my fiberglass knee brace to support my newly repaired ACL, and went to work.

I was up against a Canadian wrestler named Shantelle Taylor, and the second the bell rang I wanted every move I did to look snappy and quick. I put everything I had into every second, because I didn't want to be left behind in Calgary—to have all my training and hard work be for nothing. I wanted to make my family proud, and I wanted to prove that I was a safe and proficient wrestler who could work any style with anyone on any day and . . . *wait, is that blood?*

Oh, fuck, there's blood on the mat. I must have cut my opponent open, and it's bad. That's a lot of blood. That's a lot, a lot of blood.

The second I saw it pooling on the mat I panicked and went on autopilot. Tunnel vision, all the voices around me muffled, my heart pounding in my neck. This was my shot, I just wanted to do well, and I'd made my opponent bleed on my first tryout match.

No, wait.

It was even worse than that.

The blood wasn't hers.

It was mine.

Huh?

I instinctively reached up and dabbed my face—hot, wet blood. When I brought my hand back down, my fingers were covered in it. But I didn't care that my opponent busted me open. I just kept going. Locking up, transitioning into the next move. Blood wasn't going to stop me. Somewhere in my head I could hear the WWE trainers at ringside telling me to stop, that the match was over. They started yelling and waving for me to get out of the ring, seeing the ten stitches' worth of wound above my eye.

It was then I looked down and saw my fiberglass knee brace was open, and the sharp corner of it had my blood running down it.

Fuck! Did I just beat the shit out of myself?! Oh, that's even worse. I'm out here so freaked out and nervous that I literally cut my own face on my knee brace.

"NATTIE, STOP!"

The trainer's calls for me to stop finally registered, and I had to stand there like it was no big deal. To this day I have no idea how I managed to do it, but it meant the match I was basing my whole future on got stopped before I could even show them what I could do. And the cut was so deep and long that they wouldn't let me get back into the ring to try to finish what I'd started. I was no longer cleared for the tryout.

One of the referees drove me to the ER, and it was over.

TJ and I went back home, where I veered between sadness and self-hatred for weeks. I'd lost thirty pounds on this crazy diet and got into this crazy shape and finally got myself back from the ACL injury on my own, and then I blew it.

"Don't worry, they know that was an accident—don't let one bad day ruin everything," TJ said, trying his best to reassure me.

I hadn't expected to hear anything from WWE after that, but I was surprised TJ didn't either. I began to feel like an albatross around his neck. Like, was I so bad that I'd dragged TJ down with me?

After four weeks, we finally got a call from president of WWE Canada, Carl DiMarco.

"You're in," Carl said.

"Who's in?" TJ asked.

"You are," he replied.

"And Nattie?" TJ asked.

I knew the answer before I heard it.

TJ got a WWE developmental contract, and I did not.

DEEP SOUTH

I was beginning to feel like a stranger in a strange land after coming back from the tryout. Like I didn't belong. I couldn't help thinking that I was the only Hart to be terrible at wrestling and I should have kept my mouth shut and never gotten between those ropes in the first place.

At least things were going okay with my dad, who had moved to Tampa shortly after I got my tryout. We definitely got along better after he moved away, though I think that's partly because the distance meant it was easier for him to hide his growing addictive behaviors from me.

We also had something new in common. Even though he was trying to find any work he could in the wrestling business, he always hung on to the hope that he would find his way back to WWE in some way, even though that wasn't going to happen. It seemed like my dad and I were both waiting on a call from Connecticut that was never coming.

When I finally told him I didn't get in, he was more encouraging that I expected. He said it was only a matter of time before I got my shot, and that the wrestling business can change on a dime.

With only one real place to make money—WWE—wrestling was even more of a boom-and-bust business than ever. If you were out of favor with Vince's company, you didn't have many other options to build a career and feed your family. That's why I kept my waitressing job through everything. Even when I tore my ACL, I waited tables on crutches, because I didn't want to have to rely on anyone else to keep afloat.

TJ was still in Calgary with me, too, which helped.

Because he was a Canadian citizen, he had to wait a couple of months for his work visa to come through. So we both continued working our jobs during the day and training at night.

It was so hard showing my face at practice, because I felt like I'd let my family down. Like I'd failed everyone who helped train me, no matter how kind and encouraging they were about it. But my dad's words about how anything can happen in the wrestling business kept me there in body, even if I was struggling in spirit.

Then, on the morning of January 4, 2007, I got a call from WWE. Turns out there were huge changes happening in WWE's developmental system, and someone along the chain of command convinced someone with power to take a chance on me after all.

It wasn't a main-roster WWE contract, but it was a deal that got me into their new developmental pipeline, just like the one TJ had gotten. It might not have been a ticket to the top, but it was a chance to work my way up from the bottom. And I loved that.

It was a shock because I hadn't sent in any new tapes or made any fresh calls since the tryout. But from WWE's point of view, I was a cheap gamble who they could cut at any time if their suspicions about me not being the right fit for their women's division were proven correct.

Talent relations called shortly after with more details, saying I'd be starting in February, and my weekly pay would be $750. They were talking like this was a bad number, but I couldn't believe they were going to bring me in, much less pay me at all. Then, I got a second call twenty minutes later saying they changed their minds, and my money was cut to $500 a week.

It didn't matter. I just wanted a chance to be a wrestler in WWE.

After I called my dad—and after he finished running around my parents' house like I'd won the Super Bowl—he pointed out that the money changing like that meant I was caught in a power play somewhere along the WWE line. Clearly *someone* wanted to take a chance on me, while *someone else* just as clearly didn't. But I didn't care about the money one bit. I would have paid *them* what little money I had just for the opportunity to go live my dream, especially with TJ there too. And my dad was so proud of me.

I gave my notice to the restaurant where I was waitressing, and I couldn't wipe the smile off my face the whole last two weeks I was serving tables. I was finishing my work there strong and empowered. I knew I was about to start a new life. And when my two weeks were up at the end of January, I packed my bags. Despite getting my contract after TJ, I actually ended up moving down first, while TJ waited for his visa to materialize. At the time WWE had two developmental territories—Ohio Valley Wrestling and Deep South Wrestling—and I got assigned to Deep South, based in McDonough, Georgia.

I moved into a one-bedroom apartment that was about five hundred square feet and lived there alone for around two months until TJ could get his visa. I'd left everything behind with my sister Jenni in Calgary and moved with one suitcase and one carry-on bag, because I just figured that if I ever got to the main roster, I could go back and live in Canada and get all my stuff. And really, when I look back, the only things that mattered to me were family mementos and pictures and stuff like that. Everything else I had, like hand-me-down furniture and some old clothes, I didn't miss.

Without TJ, it wasn't perfect, but I was signed. I had my foot in the door.

I walked into Deep South on the first morning excited to be there, even if I was feeling a huge amount of pressure to deliver. I was also eager to feel at home again, even if it was in a tiny, no-air-conditioning facility, thousands of miles from anyone I knew.

But about an hour into our first morning, it hit me that although WWE's developmental system had recently gone through a huge overhaul, where the company itself was now staffing and financing its own pipeline, their hiring practices for the women's division were just the same. I was a *wrestler* in Deep South *Wrestling*, but I was in a room full of dancers and cheerleaders and models, and I felt like I was in their world, not mine.

All I wanted was a little crack, a little opening, a sign that I wasn't the wrong person in the wrong place, at the wrong time in history. Like anybody starting out in something new, I needed someone to believe in me.

And then I met the head coach assigned to our developmental, Dr. Tom Prichard.

Dr. Tom was the guy I'd been sending tapes to all along. He was a wrestler who loved wrestlers. He knew my family, knew the history of the business, knew just about everything there was to know about training wrestlers. He was even broken into the business by Paul Boesch, the promoter who introduced my grandparents on that New York beach back in the day.

And where others in WWE didn't give a shit if you could wrestle as long as you looked good, Tom was the opposite. I think Dr. Tom could sense I was scared. He told me on my first day to not worry or think about the mandate from WWE regarding my look or weight.

Of course, that was easier said than done when every week, we all had to weigh in to make sure we were still in the weight range the WWE sought.

For me, as the daughter of a man literally called "The Anvil," these were always panic-inducing times. I would try to starve myself for

Saturday and Sunday because the weigh-in was on Monday. There's nothing worse than having to publicly get on scales in front of a room full of the most petite women in the world, especially when your feedback is, "The company thinks you're a little heavy, and wants you to drop some more weight."

Especially when it was already taking everything I had in me to diet and train as hard as I was.

I kept a food journal where I logged everything I ate, and I worked out like crazy, but I was still too heavy. And the more I worried about my weight, the more weight I held on to. I already felt like a fat ugly duckling who was in the wrong place, so whatever I had to do was what I was going to do, even if it meant counting how many calories were in a strawberry and risking an eating disorder again.

The higher-ups wanted to see 135 pounds on the scale, but my dad was built like a giant rhinoceros and I inherited his beefy genetics in girl form! (Minus the goatee, thank God. At least I didn't have to worry about facial hair. Okay, a little mustache from time to time, but that's it!)

Dr. Tom could tell that I got really stressed out with it all, and after a few weeks of watching my pure dread, he came up to the scale with me, pen in hand to record the number, and whispered, "Hey, just give me a number. You don't even have to get on the scale. Just fucking give me a number you like, and we'll send that up to them."

I might not have been the tiny model WWE wanted, but I was the strong wrestler Dr. Tom wanted. He respected me because he knew I respected the business he'd given his life to. And just feeling that respect from him made me feel, for the first time in my WWE journey, like I might have a fighting chance at living my dream. At following in my family's footsteps.

And it all felt possible because of Dr. Tom.

Early on, I also figured that the easiest way for me to demonstrate my value, and be accepted more, was if I helped everyone. So I tried to be as much of a team player as I possibly could. My mindset was that if I could help all the models have really good matches, and if I could teach them and give them as much of myself as I could, then I would be somebody that would always be needed.

And I loved doing it. I loved being there for all the girls. Anytime a new girl came in and WWE wanted to see what she was capable of, they would put her with me. Anytime they were trying to get somebody else off the ground, they would put her with me. And soon the coaches started to see me as a leader. As much as I was scared shitless of not being good enough for WWE, a lot of these girls coming in, they were like, *Fuck, we need to learn how to do this*, and they kind of gravitated toward me.

I and the models and dancers and girls picked from a swimsuit calendar, we all had something in common: for one reason or another, we were all scared. Scared of the unknown. Scared of not being good enough. Scared of being exposed. Just scared. That's the human part I love about developmental. We were all in the same boat. Some worked harder than others and some wanted it and deserved it more. But no one wanted to get cut.

And as soon as I figured out how to be less selfish, and more selfless, it became easier for me to make friends, and I felt less alone.

Maybe I wasn't the odd one out after all.

Or that's what I thought until the day I heard a group of the girls who I had gone out of my way to help badmouthing me in the bathroom while I was in the stall.

"She has it easy because of her family."

"I thought it was her dad in the ring when I saw her."

I can still hear the way they were laughing at me, and about me, when they thought I couldn't hear.

For days after that, I felt sick coming into training. I knew exactly who it was that had been talking about me in that bathroom, but I also wondered if everyone else thought the same.

In the end, those who were mean to me or bullied me got fired for other reasons. I never opened my mouth because I knew I didn't have to. I knew they were going to fuck up somewhere else along the way and get shown the door. From listening to my family over the years, I'd learned that the people who aren't meant to be in this business get weeded out very fast.

And I wasn't going to let some mean girls stop me. I'd made it this far, and this was the wake-up call I needed to finally make some changes. If I was going to be one of the wrestlers who got to stick around, I needed a little sizzle to go with my steak. But as a recovering tomboy, I had no idea where to even start.

Fortunately, when it came to the glamorous side of the business, help was on the way. Actually, help was on the way times two.

FLORIDA CHAMPIONSHIP WRESTLING

About three months after I arrived in McDonough, WWE moved their developmental program from Deep South Wrestling in Georgia to Florida Championship Wrestling in Tampa. And not long after that, TJ's visa was finally arranged.

Once TJ got the paperwork he needed, wild horses couldn't keep him back home. He opened the mail, got the visa, filled our old silver Pontiac Sunfire with some clothes and personal items, and drove four days from Calgary to Tampa. And I was ecstatic to know that all I wanted or needed to rebuild and start over from scratch was finally on its way.

My parents and sister were already in Tampa, and after Bret's Hall of Fame ceremony, Ted and Harry were hired and sent to Tampa, too, though Ted didn't last long in WWE's very strict and rigid system. I wished it had worked out better for him, but he wasn't the kind to take direction easily, and that wasn't going to work in a machine like WWE.

So three kids from my grandfather's front-yard ring, Harry, TJ, and I, made it to WWE at the same time, and it was fun and exciting to be chasing our dream together.

Even though we'd all had some experience by this point, we knew we had to kind of start over and forget everything we'd learned about wrestling from my family and Tokyo Joe, and in England and Japan on the road—at least for the moment, until we could learn the WWE style.

Because WWE was, and is, a whole different style of wrestling.

It's a whole different vibe.

And it's a whole different energy when you're just starting out. You have to walk in there with an open mind, and even if you know something, you have to pretend you don't, because if you weren't there to be a student, then you weren't going to last there at all.

But TJ and I loved that. We loved the wrestling business so much that we couldn't wait to learn a whole new style. We wanted to soak up any and all knowledge and experience we could. If WWE had allowed aspiring Superstars to eat, drink, and sleep in the ring, that's what we would have done.

Our first night together in Florida was an emotional one for me. I was back in the place where I'd seen my dad's rise and fall as a kid, and now I was feeling like I'd made it—even though I was at the very bottom of a long and slippery ladder.

It was the spring of 2007, and FCW was run by Dr. Tom Prichard and Steve Keirn; Norman Smiley and Dusty Rhodes would soon come in to help too. And it was honestly one of the most fun times of my life.

I absolutely loved learning under Steve Keirn, and I loved working with Dr. Tom (who became a huge ally for me) and TJ and Harry too. Dusty came in at the tail end of my time in developmental, but I remember him being so kind and so sweet and so helpful. He once gave me a line for when I became a heel character, suggesting I was "Nattie by nature, naughty by choice." Dusty saw so much in the three of us because he really cared about people that cared about the business. He loved to cultivate and harness potential, very much like my grandpa Stu. Neither man ever wanted the brand-new luxury car off the showroom floor; they always wanted the car that was a little broken but could be salvaged and considered a "classic."

But as much as the developmental was run by wrestlers who loved training wrestlers, the company at large was not. So the chances of me getting out of FCW and on the main roster by being "just" a wrestler were very, very slim.

This was highlighted my first week in developmental in Florida, when Steve told me WWE wanted him to bring in these twins who, from what Steve understood, were models. He didn't really know what to do with them, but he asked if I would spend some time with them and show them the ropes. In explaining the twins' arrival, Steve rolled his eyes and kind of sighed like, *Welp, we'll see what we can do.*

Sure, I could help. I decided I would show these women everything I knew about the business. And if I could do that with two women at the same time who had no ties at all to this business, surely that would prove how valuable I was.

So in came the Garcia sisters, who fans would come to know as the Bella Twins. Brie and Nikki were, unsurprisingly, beautiful, but I also noticed a few other things about them. They were likable, funny, and had athletic backgrounds in soccer.

And they were sharp as a knife when it came to business.

They had a cool California vibe that seemed effortless, and they made friends with everybody in no time. Within a week they were the life of the party in FCW, which reminded me how important it was to not judge a book by its cover. I'll admit that when I first heard of them, and saw their pictures, I naively thought they were just models, that they didn't want this. But it turned out that they had a great work ethic. They were the first girls at practice every day, worked their asses off, and were the last ones to leave. They would do all this extra stuff, too, like hanging flyers and talking to the tiny number of fans who came to our shows. They were great for morale at FCW.

And then these wonderful girls had the audacity to also teach me how to do my taxes, and introduce me to people that could help me on the business side of things. They introduced me to a seamstress to get my gear made, and a good accountant to manage my hundreds of dollars. Any time I had an issue, the Bellas knew someone who could help.

They taught me about clothing and fashion, about my look, my energy, and my character. They made me feel better about myself, like I wasn't an ugly duckling. I knew I wasn't a model, but with the right styling and advice, I began to feel as beautiful as I could.

They taught me about storylines, and how to pitch ideas, and how to mingle and talk to people. They told me that it wasn't about politicking, but that you can't get ahead in the world without being able to communicate well. They were right. They knew everyone and everyone wanted to know them. One night they invited me out to a dinner gathering where I ended up putting Jimmy Fallon in a headlock after a few shots of vodka. Around the twins, I felt like I was learning to come out of my shell out of the ring, and I liked it.

They were a vast wealth of resources when it came to everything I didn't know anything about, and they taught me how to be a self-made businesswoman, which was what they were trying to be themselves. Far from what I thought they were, the twins really had their shit together, while owning this confidence that I wished I had.

And after them helping me so much outside the ring, it was my pleasure to help them inside. We were all moving each other closer to the big dance, and it never felt like competition because we all brought such different things to the table. And before we could even dream of getting to the main roster, we first had to help each other get noticed way out in FCW, which was a satellite system many, many worlds away from WWE's decision-making offices in Connecticut.

These days the WWE's developmental brand, *NXT*, has their own TV show and a direct line to the highest decision makers in the company.

But in FCW we had to rely on "reports" from visiting legends and the corporate higher-ups who visited every four to six months, which meant maybe we got our names mentioned somewhere, or someone who knew someone would pass Vince's assistant while she talked to someone else who could write it on the back of a piece of paper that Vince might someday glance at. It was that kind of feeling down there.

But one day, we got word that someone from Vince's inner circle was coming down to see how everyone was developing.

Now, the last time a guest had come to FCW, it was Tony Atlas—one-half of the first-ever Black WWE world champion tag team. His visit was exciting, but beforehand, I was too green to know two things. One, as nice as Tony was, he was retired and no longer employed by WWE at that stage, much less someone who had the power to get us a job there. And two, he had a serious foot fetish. So I was confused when he got into the ring and asked me to stomp on his face as hard as I could. I'd been trained to protect my "opponent," so while I didn't know the real reason he was asking, I did know that it was weird!

But this visit, from someone who we knew had actual power in the company, was much bigger. The second Vince's emissary walked through the door, Dr. Tom and the rest of the staff wanted to us to look extra productive. But they didn't have to tell us that. We knew this could be our ticket to the big time, so we were more than ready.

The Bella Twins, ever ready to put in whatever work was needed, wanted to make sure that the three of us got a glowing report. They wanted to make sure that we stood out among all the guys, and for all the names we knew were already shoo-ins to get called up to the main roster. So we thought it would be a great idea if we stayed busy by wrestling in one of the three rings set up in the FCW warehouse the whole time the visitor was there. When I say "busy," I mean we didn't stop practicing moves and putting on holds and running the ropes and taking bumps for each other for about three solid hours, just in case the special guest looked over and caught a glimpse of us working hard.

By the end of the day, we were exhausted, because we were beating the shit out of each other more and more every minute we weren't being noticed. I walked out of there feeling the most beat up I've ever felt in my entire life. And all because we were just so starved for anyone to take notice of us, hoping a WWE official would go, "Oh my God, those girls were working so hard. Send them to the main roster immediately!" I laugh thinking about how naive we were, but I loved that we were so hungry together.

That was the thing about our developmental system. The reason so many people from FCW succeeded in WWE wasn't because it was fancy, or because we had this state-of the art facility. It was because we all loved the business we were trying to break in to.

Roman Reigns, Sheamus, Bray Wyatt, Kofi Kingston, Xavier Woods, Jey and Jimmy Uso, Dean Ambrose, Big E, myself, TJ, Drew McIntyre, the Bellas, and so many others came from FCW and boosted WWE's product for years after.

When we started, we only had two rings, and they were still building the place as we were learning. There were stacks of canned goods to sit on, and no air-conditioning in the insanely hot and humid Florida weather. And the work was hard. It was as much a survival camp as it was a wrestling camp.

But the training was amazing. I still use much of what I was taught there today.

The lessons I learned about keeping your head above water and navigating the politics of WWE, I still rely on almost two decades in. I will always remember Dr. Tom saying, "Guys, if you make it to the main roster, you will only have one match at any television taping, if you're lucky. It'll only be five, ten, fifteen, maybe twenty minutes maximum. But what you do at a show, during the hours and hours you spend backstage not wrestling, those are the moments where you learn how to survive and thrive in WWE."

What Tom was really saying was that how you carried yourself and treated people, how well you learned and integrated the rules of the road in this industry, would dictate a lot. Especially when the industry at the highest level could be a political shark tank. To succeed, I needed to learn how to swim with the sharks and stay alive.

I felt I was ready to see if I could do just that.

But that next step, as with every step before it, wasn't going to be easy.

LOSING MYSELF

"Don't forget who you are, Nattie."

That's what my dad said to me when I dropped by my parents' house in Tampa after my first day in FCW. If anyone knew what it was like to lose sight of who you are, it was my dad. But while I heard his words, at the time I didn't really listen. Or maybe I didn't understand. On the surface it sounded like any other generic advice a parent would give, like "Be careful" or "You've got this!" But my dad was saying something to me that was very specific to where I found myself. He knew one of the biggest obstacles in wrestling is figuring a way to be unique.

"You don't want to stand out so much that you don't fit in, but you want to stand out just enough that you're different—while being the same," he continued.

Confused? Yeah, I was too.

I had no idea how to be *me*, but also more like the other women at the same time. And as I know now, that's a place where many people in wrestling find themselves—and it's where many people lose themselves too.

Time and time again, hopeful wrestlers have created a version of themselves that they felt a booker wanted, or the audience wanted, or that they themselves wanted to be. And over time they've slowly changed from the person they were when they left home into the person they've created on the road.

I think what made my dad worried wasn't that I'd get lost in a character, but in a system. And he was right.

A big part of being in developmental was working these little local shows that would kind of mimic WWE live events, where you'd go out there in front of a (much smaller) audience and get a feel for what was working and fine-tune what wasn't. Sometimes they were at armories, sometimes nightclubs, sometimes malls or high school gymnasiums.

Anywhere we could draw two to two hundred people to perform in front of, we were there.

TJ would kill it in front of the small crowds, and he used that time to hone the WWE style of wrestling to give himself a greater chance of making it to the main roster. He was on fire, and I could see he was learning so much and developing so fast—just like I knew he would.

Wrestling was what made him tick. It was his heart. It was his soul. It was his flesh and blood, and his passion. He was also so naturally good at wrestling. Everything in the ring came easily to him. He could springboard on any set of ropes anywhere in the world under any condition and do it effortlessly. He could work with anyone and make a match good to great to fucking magic no matter what his opponent's skill level was.

My cousin Harry, like me, was a third-generation talent, and he went into WWE with the heavy expectations that came with being the British Bulldog's son. I'd known Harry since he was a little kid, and he was always one of the more reserved members of the family—but even more so after losing his dad tragically when he was fifteen. It was like, when Davey died, something inside of him died too. Yet in the ring, Harry always came very alive. Wrestling was also his heartbeat.

While we were all in Florida at FCW, Harry lived with me and TJ in our one-bedroom apartment. He'd sleep on the air mattress in the living room, while TJ and I finally graduated to an actual bed. We all loved sharing that space together, talking about our dreams every morning over breakfast, and after practice, all going to work out.

Harry was super talented, but he also had things that he wanted to work on. We all knew how important it was to refine our "act" off-off-off-off Broadway in case we were lucky enough to get a call to join the main show, because there was no room to fuck up in front of the ever-present Vince McMahon.

The three of us were all so appreciative of where we were, and the shot we'd be given. We weren't in Stampede Wrestling anymore. We weren't getting booked by our family anymore. We weren't wrestling in front of nine people in the middle of Cold Lake, Alberta anymore.

We were wrestling in front of forty people in Florida instead!

The *huge* difference, of course, was that we were doing it because we had our foot in the door of the biggest wrestling company in the world. We'd all been through the wringer; we'd faced a lot of shit to make it. And the fact that we all got to WWE together made us very, very happy for each other.

But while the two guys were mainly working on the craft of wrestling, I had other hurdles to jump if I wanted to join WWE's women's division. While TJ and Harry were out there in front of live crowds getting better at the WWE style of wrestling, I found myself out there in front of audiences in "best body contests" and "diva dance-off" competitions. Stuff I hated doing.

The guys' job was to become the best wrestlers they could be, while mine was to go out there and shake my ass. And that personal nightmare of mine was made even worse by the fact I had no idea how to dance. I certainly didn't know how to dance in that stripper-y type way the company wanted from the girls. The only strip club I knew of, for that matter, was the one in Calgary by the name of Misty's that you had to drive past to get to the Hart House.

I would come home from practice and watch WWE's live TV shows, *Raw* and *SmackDown*, every week and see Dawn Marie or Stacey Kiebler or Torrie Wilson switch their sexy on with the flick of their hair or a pop of their hips. And I knew I didn't know how to do any of those things. When *they* hit sexy mode, they looked like they were professional dancers with this extra sultry edge to them, while when *I* tried that mode, I looked like I was being electrocuted while forgetting the Macarena. Envision my dad, a three-hundred-pound man, dancing in high heels. I was worse. I was the absolute shits. And praying to God no one noticed.

I knew suplexes.

I knew hammerlocks.

I knew clotheslines.

And I knew I was fucked.

I went through the few clothes I had time and time again to try to find something that would make me look like I was in the same universe as these stunning women. I'd try to cover what I didn't like about myself, while trying in vain to find things I did like. I would also overdo it with spray tanner trying to feel thinner and "sexier," because in the words of "The Enforcer" turned WWE producer, Arn Anderson, "Fat looks better with a tan."

TJ was amazing, as supportive as ever, but for this particular chapter of my life, I needed help of a different kind. If I needed to know who won what match in some random territory in the 1960s, TJ was my man. But he also thought "bronzer" and "concealer" were a tag team. I needed a woman's help.

Once again, Nikki and Brie Bella came to the rescue. They were like cellmates who understood the rules of the prison and thrived in that environment.

"Okay, show us what you've got," they said before my first "best body" competition, prospective buyers looking over a clapped-out car in some random armory in the heart of Florida.

I sheepishly opened my coat and showed off my $10 Walmart bikini. And do you know what no woman in any part of the world wants to see when they reveal themselves in a bikini? Wincing. The Bellas winced. Together. In concert. Double gut punch. Then came their head tilt that said, *It was a good effort*, before they darted looks toward each other that said, *Yeah, but no*.

Then they swarmed me in a frenzy of hair product, makeup, and the most rhinestones I'd ever seen in my life.

A few short minutes later, we stood at the curtain that divided us from the tiny crowd waiting to see our show. "I don't know how to do this," I said to them.

"Well, then you have to pretend," they said with the hard kindness a person needs in a crisis.

They were right. This was the most "fake it till you make it" moment of my life so far.

Then it was midway through the matches, and we women were up to do our thing. At least the Bellas were going out there with me. Because let me tell you, nothing makes a girl feel sexier than walking out into the shitty fluorescent glare of an old armory and letting it all hang out, while twenty children and grandparents sit in silence as you bend over through the ring ropes to get into a sweaty, grimy wrestling ring.

But I did it. And not only did I do it, I managed to totally disconnect from the situation and slap as many hands as I could on the way down to the ring. I winked at people, smiled at others; I worked the crowd until they cheered for me. I'm pretty sure I kissed a little old man on the cheek in the front row too. Whatever the hell it takes, I said!

And it was awful.

I hated myself.

I was smiling because that was my job, but twenty minutes later I was alone in my car, crying. I felt so stupid, so ugly, and so out of place. And like such a fraud.

For the first time, I understood what my dad was talking about. I was so far from home, and so far from myself, that when I caught a glimpse of my face in my rearview mirror, I didn't really know who was looking back. And at that moment I felt the pull to run. To leave FCW, and my shot at WWE.

But even if I didn't know who I was, I knew what I wasn't: a quitter.

So the next day, I got up, swallowed down my shame and insecurities, and decided to do all I knew how to do—which was to practice, practice, practice, until I got better at what WWE seemed to want.

Which NEVER FUCKING HAPPENED.

I never got better at stripper dancing. My body just refuses to move that way. Even after practicing for weeks, I still looked like the most unsexy woman in history out there.

But I got through it. I sucked it up, and I smiled, and I just pushed through. Because I didn't want to fail. I didn't want to go home, I didn't want to leave TJ.

And I wanted hang in there until I got my shot to be a *wrestler*.

FINDING MYSELF

In June 2007 I got my first real match in FCW, which was a triple-threat match against two talented independent wrestlers, Krissy Vaine and Shantelle Taylor, who I'd "wrestled" before in my tryout match. After waiting so long for my shot to shine, I can still remember how that first match made me feel: worse.

I remember winning, but more than that I remember feeling, immediately after that match, like Shantelle and Krissy didn't really accept me out there—and that wasn't on them. After spending so much time second-guessing my look, and living so deep in my physical insecurities, I'd begun to doubt everything about myself, even the stuff I knew I was good at—like wrestling.

In my head, I was like, *I'm in WWE now and I've got to be pretty, and I've got to be skinny, and I've got to be sexy.* I suddenly couldn't do a damn thing without thinking *What would Vince think?* And that made me really insecure, which made me try so hard that I lost the flow in my work. I was rigid, overthinking, looking for perfection and falling way short—and I knew the other girls who could wrestle could see that. They weren't wrong for feeling that way either. To them I was trying to be a model, and to the models I was a wrestler.

I started to get in my head about people not liking me, so I tried hard to be everyone's friend, which I'm sure had the opposite effect. I couldn't help but feel like I was back in high school again—only this time in a clearance-special Walmart bikini.

I painted a smile on my face, but underneath, I was really starting to struggle. I wanted this more than anything, but was *this* even the same thing anymore? Was *this* what my grandfather had done, or my uncles, or my dad? I was beginning to worry that my dream—being a wrestler at the highest level—was something completely different than I thought it was, now that I was within reaching distance of it.

I thought that once I got in the ring, all these insecurities would magically go away, but I'd just had my first match, and all my worst thoughts had just intensified. I couldn't help but despair. If my first match hadn't sparked something in me, then what would?

Well, as it turns out, it wasn't *my* first match that would light a fire in me again. It was the Bella Twins'.

One day after practice, Dr. Tom pulled me aside and apologized about all the body contests, saying it wasn't him or Steve who were booking them—that was coming directly from Vince. But now, he said, it was time to show what I had. Tom and Steve had booked a tag-team match where Krissy Vaine and I would take on the Bellas in the twins' first-ever match in front of a live crowd.

"The office is really high on the Bellas, so we're going to really need you to step up," Tom said. "We need you to be a leader in that ring and remember what brought you to the dance."

I was a little hurt that I wasn't the focal point, but I knew this was my chance to stand out. My dad's voice was clear in my head: I needed to remember who the fuck I was. If I couldn't pull my head out of my ass to help *myself*, then maybe I could do it to help someone else. For the first time in FCW, my assignment felt very natural. This was something I knew I could do and do well. So, on a handshake, the match was made. My chance to shine was back on the board.

And I could feel the surge of passion return.

On the night itself, there were a hundred people packed into a small armory—including the Bellas' mom, who flew in to see their first match—and the place was rocking. I remember the "locker room" we were in backstage was like a small closet with horrible lighting; it felt like we were all changing in the dark. I'm not sure how all of us girls fit into it. There was a cockroach crawling on the ceiling and the smell of mildew in the air. There was no toilet available, so if we needed to go to the bathroom, heaven forbid, we had to run across the street to a porta-potty, because the bathrooms the fans used were off limits. It was not glamorous by any means, but we always made it work. Bitching about it together was half the fun.

I knew this wasn't going to be the best match I'd ever have, but that wasn't the point. The point was to see if I could lead a couple of new wrestlers the company was clearly high on through their first outing. I would have to use my training and experience to wrestle my own match while at the same time guiding, directing, and protecting Brie and Nikki on the fly.

Krissy was a great tag partner for me that night. The match went off without a hitch, and backstage afterward, Tom told the whole FCW group what a good leader I was out there.

I could feel a change in myself almost immediately. I suddenly had purpose and direction.

Seeing the Bellas so relieved and excited backstage made me happier than I could have imagined. They said they were forever indebted to me, but they had no idea how much the opposite was true. We needed each other, and I think that's what we proved that night. If you get the mix right between the steak and the sizzle of the wrestling business, then you get something that can lift everyone up.

In the next months, Tom and Steve had me lead more and more in matches. They knew it didn't matter what hot, new, green prospect

WWE wanted to vet; I could handle anyone on the fly and make it work in the ring, both for myself and whoever I was in there with.

And all of my hard work paid off when WWE rolled its *Monday Night Raw* show into Tampa and I was one of four FCW talents picked as a "guest of the show." That meant I got to go to *Monday Night Raw* and be backstage and see how the magic was made.

When I got there, I was blown away by the size of everything, and the sheer number of people and trucks that producing a live TV show took.

I wasn't at Stampede Wrestling or Butlins anymore, and it was intoxicating to experience it in person. Cameras were everywhere. Crew members whizzed around running miles of wires and hanging thousands of lights near backstage sets with WWE logos on everything. And alone in the middle of the arena stood one big, beautiful ring.

This was the stage I wanted to perform on. That was the ring I wanted to wrestle in. This was the place I wanted to be more than anything in the world.

I knew the point of the invitation was to let the decision makers in the company interact with developmental talent, to shake their hands and get a look at them up close. Vince McMahon himself was down at ringside where the other guests and I were going, running through moments and matches with the talent scheduled for that night's show.

As we sat down ringside in the otherwise-empty arena before showtime, I watched Vince in action—a billionaire who could have been literally anywhere in the world, doing anything else he wanted, instead here in Tampa (just like he was in every other city his company ran TV), pulling all the strings and making all the decisions. I always compare Vince to the Wizard of Oz. Vince worked harder day to day than anyone I've ever met, and it was common knowledge to everyone who worked for Vince that he expected anyone he employed to be a workhorse just like him.

The ring that night was surrounded by all these huge, larger-than-life personalities that I'd seen on TV. John Cena, Shane McMahon, Shawn Michaels, Triple H, and many more were there going over their segments, rehearsing promos, and talking to writers. Mingling among them all were producers, an elite club of retired greats like Jerry Brisco, Arn Anderson, and Fit Finlay who were passing on their knowledge to help the next generation succeed.

And there I was, dressed in my best outfit, with my makeup done up the best I could, my hair curled, and my tan on, just trying my absolute hardest to be what they wanted me to be. I saw Torrie Wilson, who was even more stunning in person than on TV, and I wanted to hide in a lighting rig box before anyone saw me.

Then Vince walked past us with his headset on, on his way to the monitor they had set up so he could see the framing of the shots. Until suddenly he stopped and turned back to look me right in the face.

My heart dropped as he singled me out. *Oh, shit, he's going to recognize me as the niece of the guy who knocked him out.* Or maybe he wouldn't know me at all. That was even worse. *He might not know me.*

"I've been hearing very, very good things about you," he said. "Keep working hard."

My first reaction was like an excited little kid's: *Vince knows who I am!*

But my next reaction was, *Now I know who I am.*

If I wasn't going to be a leading lady in WWE's eyes, then maybe I could create a career as the character actress they would call to make any "scene" better.

If Vince didn't see me as the star, he might just see me as the star maker.

PART THREE

DEBUT

"Don't fuck this up," Dr. Tom told me as he delivered the news: I was going on the November 2007 European tour with WWE. The company liked to bring talent they were interested in to non-televised live events first, to see how they'd do in a bigger, more intense environment. Getting the chance to work with some of the main roster was a great way for management to see if you could meet their expectations in a more controlled setting than live TV.

And now it was my turn.

I was so excited I could burst, but I was also so nervous too. I knew that high up in the company there were still questions around me, my family name, and my look. But I also got the feeling I was seen as a workhorse, someone safe to guide all the less wrestling-savvy women through matches on live TV. And that was a role I was extremely proud to step into.

I just had to make sure I took Dr. Tom's advice and didn't let him down. This was going to be a situation where I'd be given either enough professional room to succeed, or enough professional rope to hang. A very scary thought indeed.

So, I left TJ and FCW for Europe. I remember not having much to pack. When you're on $500 a week, and you need to pay taxes, eat clean, buy wrestling gear, pay rent and utilities, run a car, and buy beauty products, the money doesn't go that far.

As I was boarding the plane, I felt like I had in school after my dad lost his job in WWE and we were wearing thrift store clothes and living on auction food. It's hard to wrap your head around how pretty, handsome, and charismatic the WWE roster—any WWE roster—is. These are people who get paid to stay in top condition, so every face was camera ready, and everybody was chiseled from stone. And here I came with my squeaky-wheeled secondhand luggage that I'm sure was originally on clearance at TJ Maxx, and every cent I owned in a hand-me-down Betsey Johnson purse from the Bellas.

I sat down in my assigned middle-row seat in the back of the plane near the toilets and did my best to look happy and approachable. The main thing I needed to achieve on this trip was to show the company I could gel with the other women on the roster—and then I'd be free from developmental jail forever. WWE was looking at me for the *SmackDown* side of the roster, if I did a good job on this tour, so I'd be in the same division as the likes of Michelle McCool and Torrie Wilson and Victoria, to name a few.

All the way across the Atlantic I was mumbling Dr. Tom's mantra to myself: "Don't fuck it up, don't fuck it up."

And then came showtime. I could see backstage that Michelle had a lot of respect from the women's locker room. Even though she had been discovered through the WWE reality TV competition *Diva Search*, where aspiring models competed for a WWE contract, Michelle very much wanted to be taken seriously as a wrestler. She was training with her then boyfriend (now husband) The Undertaker, and she took her role as the top women's wrestler on *SmackDown* very seriously, so I knew she was the one I needed to impress.

Gel with the women and keep my nose out of trouble.

Seemed straightforward.

Speaking of noses, I ended up breaking Michelle's.

First tour. Blood everywhere. Everyone side-eyeing me like I'm an asshole.

FUCK!

I felt like such an idiot and a failure. And once I got back to FCW after the tour, WWE didn't let me know right away if I was in limbo, in trouble, or waiting to be fired. Nothing. Just silence—until five months later, in April 2008, when I got a call from the 203 area code. It was legendary ring announcer Howard Finkel—Vince McMahon's first-ever hire back in the '80s—calling with my travel arrangements.

"What travel arrangements?" I asked him.

"Oh, you're coming to *SmackDown*," he replied.

"I am?!"

"Yes, you're going to debut on the main roster next week, after *WrestleMania*."

Howard was so sweet to me through my obvious shock. He gave me a lovely introduction to WWE, and wished me well in my new career. And just like that I was going to be a WWE Superstar!

Holy shit.

I thought I was done after breaking Michelle's nose, so to hear that I was going on WWE TV was surreal. From what I understood, they were bringing in this new women's championship, called the Divas Championship, and they wanted a really strong competitor for . . . Michelle.

Holy shit, indeed.

I wanted to make it up to her and prove that I could do this. That I wasn't her enemy. That I could be someone she could count on. I wanted her to like me so much. I hoped I could change her mind about me.

WWE told me they were tearing up my old contract for $24,000 a year and giving me a new deal for $70,000 a year guaranteed. Back then, everyone had a number that was their "downside guarantee," or the least amount they could expect to make. However, I would also get "bonus" checks for merchandise sales, and PPV appearances, and doing extra shows that exceeded my downside deal, as part of the company's profit participation model.

I also learned they were going to pay for my rental car and hotel for the first three months until I figured out how it all worked.

I was ecstatic, because at $24,000 a year, I didn't have money to buy proper, TV-ready wrestling gear. I was going to thrift shops and cutting up outfits I bought at Walmart or old clothes the Bellas had given me and trying to make it work, hoping no noticed I was making my own wrestling gear. Now that I was on the main roster, I finally had money for gear from a professional seamstress and to get my hair done properly by a professional hairdresser. Of course, it would take a week or two for my first check to hit my account. In the meantime, I was just enjoying the feeling of getting a new contract and taking some steps, making progress.

TJ was even more excited for me than I was for myself. He'd believed in me from day one. It was a weird feeling to be moving up without him, but I knew it would only be temporary. TJ was so talented; I knew it wouldn't be long until he joined me on the main roster.

My first TV taping with the company was such a whirlwind. I couldn't sleep the night before, and I couldn't focus because I was so anxious about my debut.

The next day when I got to the building before the show was even more of a blur as I shook hands, met everyone, and oriented myself to the new system and the new people. It was all just so massive and intimidating: hundreds of crew members, thousands of equipment boxes rolling in off several trucks. Cabling everywhere. And everyone was using shorthand that a newbie like me could only try to tune in to.

Then a passing voice, whom I presumed to be a writer, told me,

"Vince wants to rehearse your segment and take a look at your wrestling gear."

Oh, shit. Don't fuck this up.

I got changed into my gear, and walked from backstage through the curtain at the top of the ramp. Below, Vince was in the ring going through the show with all the talent. I had seen this huge set on TV so many times, but standing there in the fan-less building at the mouth of the set where everyone makes their entrance was such a rush. Even though I was new, intimidated, and disoriented, I still felt like a WWE *Superstar*.

"Vince doesn't like your wrestling gear," another passing voice said.

Well, that was nice while it lasted.

"He doesn't like my gear?" I asked, but the person attached to the voice was already gone.

My wrestling gear was pink and black, the colors my dad and the rest of the Hart family wore in WWE, but I was debuting as a heel that night and Vince wanted me all in black. Except I didn't have all-black wrestling gear. I'd brought the one piece of gear I had, the only piece I could afford!

Vince had spotted me the second I walked through the curtain, and immediately made his thoughts known. I came to find out that he seldom had to say anything directly. He just had to mutter his like or dislike of something and it would magically go from his lips to your ears in seconds.

Well, shit, do I go down to him now in a costume he doesn't like, or go try to find some other gear somewhere and make him wait?

But he was standing there looking at me, so I hurried down to the ring for rehearsal, still hopped up on pure adrenaline—I'd have to try to make my costume situation work afterward.

The script that night called for me to debut by teaming with the

Villainous Victoria to attack Michelle McCool and her sweetheart sidekick Cherry, who I was meeting for the first time that day. And when I got to the ring, Vince was trying to figure out exactly what I would do with the attack. He didn't know if I should slap Cherry or put the boots to her, so he told us to walk through both options so he could see them.

OK, I thought, *here we go. Slap up first.*

I knew Vince already hated my gear, so I needed this to go well. I needed to hit a home run. I was already so nervous in the ring with him and Cherry—I could feel Michelle right there burning a hole in my back too. I was overthinking everything.

"Practice how you're going to do it," Vince said.

This was new to me, because in developmental at that time, we didn't have rehearsals, because we didn't have television.

Vince could see I was reluctant. "You're a heel. You're mean. You're nasty. Just do it whatever way feels right!" he said.

I felt anxious and nervous and overly eager to please.

So, I hauled back and slapped Cherry so hard it sounded like a gun went off.

She was stunned. Everybody at ringside was just speechless. And I could see Michelle shoot Cherry a look, sort of like *I told you about this fucking girl.*

I was as stunned as poor Cherry. I'd fired off the shot on instinct, and it landed way harder than I thought it would.

"It's just a walk-through," Vince said gruffly, shaking his head.

"I'm so sorry," I said to Cherry. "I didn't mean to . . . I was trying to do it the way . . ." I couldn't implicate Vince; he was standing right there.

I felt so small—even more so because she was so sweet about it.

"I know what it's like on your first day," she said reassuringly, almost like she didn't mind that I'd just slapped her so hard. Like she could sense that I was trying way too hard to please and fit in, which I was.

Cherry and I became best friends that day. She lives just down the street from me now, and all these years later, we hang out all the time. But that day I just wanted the ring to swallow me whole.

Vince took me aside, and he was stern, but also kind of laughing, like, *Fuck, she means business*. I'm happy he saw I wasn't there to mess around; I just wish it hadn't been at Cherry's expense.

What a start to my first day. And I still had my actual debut to go, for which Vince had nixed my ring gear. I'd have to go out there in street clothes.

Before I left Florida, the Bella Twins had been kind enough to give me a suitcase of clothes "just in case," and thank God they did. I pieced together what I hoped was a professional-looking outfit from Bebe Sport—basically fancy workout gear—and tried to make it work. But wrestling is physical, and things move.

My thong, which was never meant to make an appearance, decided it wanted to debut, too, that night, and I later found out that Vince was furious about it. He didn't want the camera on me in general because he didn't like how my gear looked, and my wardrobe malfunction on top of that sent him over the edge.

"We need to get her some different clothes. Different gear. Everything," he told his producers, who then hurried to tell me.

So, in my very brief time on the main roster, I'd somehow managed to break Michelle's nose, nearly concuss Cherry in rehearsal, flash my underwear to the world, and piss Vince off—all before my first match even aired.

I learned that night that the old saying is wrong. I got *several* chances to make a first impression, and all of them were terrible.

DIVAS TITLE

In July 2008, Michelle and I were building to the inaugural Divas title match at *The Great American Bash* PayPerView in Uniondale, New York. The company wanted to establish her as the first-ever Divas champion, and 99 percent of the reason I got called up to the main roster was to give her someone to beat on her way.

I understood my role, and on a professional level, I wanted to give Michelle something special to give her momentum as champion. But on a personal level, we weren't hitting it off.

Apart from me still feeling just terrible about breaking her nose, I began to pick up on a competitive, protective barrier around Michelle. I completely understand it now—she'd worked hard to get to her position and didn't want what looked like a nepotism hire coming in and taking her TV time. (Little did she know what "the office" thought about me!) I think she felt like people thought she got to the top because of her connections as Undertaker's girlfriend. But I knew she worked her ass off and fought for every inch she got. She didn't want to go out there and be anything other than the woman who stole the show in the ring, doing what we both loved to do more than anything: wrestle.

We might not have seen it then, but Michelle and I were fighting similar perceptions. A lot of those same people who thought she was only there because she was dating Undertaker thought I got hired in

WWE because of my family being the Harts. But it took a while for us to realize the best way to prove those people wrong was to work together.

Now that I'm a veteran and considered a leader in the locker room, it does still take me a minute sometimes to warm up to people. A lot of people come and go in our business, and sometimes they genuinely love our business, and sometimes they're disrespectful to it. It can take a while to see which somebody new is. So I empathize in some ways with Michelle. She wanted me to prove myself to her—to prove I belonged. I get that now.

Also, the women's division in WWE was on shaky ground at that point, in terms of getting time to tell its stories, and making those stories the kinds of interesting, layered journeys the men had gotten since wrestling began. If a segment ran long anywhere in the show, or time was needed on the fly in a live TV environment, it was nearly always the women's segment that was cut.

When you're down in those kinds of trenches, fighting for scraps, the competition for airtime can feel like life and death. We all knew that if you weren't in the one "women's story" on TV, then you were legit in catering, making conversation with one of the writers about an idea you had (and praying to God they'd like it and would pass it along, or that they even just took the time to listen) and waiting for your turn, which might never come.

As for me, if I'm being brutally honest, I was way more worried about getting *any* TV time at all than Michelle should have been about me taking hers.

Immediately after my debut, I was pulled aside and told I was being called "the dumpy Diva" by top management, and that Vince wasn't happy with my look at all. I got a pit in my stomach hearing this. All the things I'd been fearing in my head were coming true.

The constant remarks on my looks were beginning to get to me. I knew what I was getting into when I went to WWE, but constantly being told you stand out for how *not* beautiful you are can emotionally wear a person down after a while. So I knew this Divas title match was either going to make me or break me right out of the gate. If I wasn't the hot new model–dancer "It" girl in the company (and it was clear to everyone I was not), then I needed to be the wrestling machine. If I wasn't going to be called on when they wanted a model, then I needed to be the one they called when they wanted a machine.

When it came to screen time, the big positive Michelle and I had going for us was that, with the inaugural Divas title match being on Pay-PerView, we would be allotted plenty of time on that card to put on the great match we both needed for different reasons.

The business model in wrestling since the 1980s has been that you build your stories on weekly TV, and the prime stories that come from that make it to PPV, where fans have to pay to see the outcome. With so few matches slotted on PPV, it's a real honor to make it there, no matter where you are on the card.

I didn't care about winning—I still don't—I just wanted us to go out there and tell an amazing story. I wanted us to lay a path for other women to get their time too. I thought if we blew everyone away with our *wrestling* talent, then the argument could be made for giving us more time in the ring, on TV and PPV, as a division.

And maybe I wouldn't be seen as dumpy, but as a professional wrestler.

We were blessed to be assigned the legendary wrestler-turned-visionary producer Fit Finlay for our match. If anyone in WWE was championing our division, it was Fit. He was as responsible as any woman on screen for all the success our division would have many years later.

But that night, our division was only starting its journey, and I was giddy with excitement backstage, because I knew we'd come up with something special. All day I'd been going through the story of the match in my head. I wanted to make an impression on management. I wanted to make an impression on Michelle. I wanted us to make a statement for the new division, and I wanted to . . . wait, what's that? Our match has been cut to four minutes?

Just like that, our time was chopped.

Fit Finlay came to both of us before our match with a stoic look on his face to deliver the bad news: "Vince said if the girls can get it done faster, get it done faster." Fit looked as sad as Michelle and I felt. Deflated.

He was standing beside us fighting for the women to mean more, to *wrestle*.

But that wasn't going to happen that night.

It didn't matter that we were the only women's match on the card, or that it was the inaugural match for what was essentially our division's world title . . . even on PPV, we weren't safe from the axe coming down on us.

But we were pros, so Michelle and I cut as much of the stuff we didn't need as we could and kept what we absolutely couldn't part with, and we hit that ring and went as hard as we could in our allotted time. I can still remember how beautifully Michelle went up for my surfboard submission and the ankle lock she did reversing out of it.

The fans in the sold-out Nassau Coliseum were just starting to get into the match—and then it was over.

Michelle was rightfully so happy at the end of our match to become the first-ever Divas champion, but I was left feeling worried because I knew we could have done so much better if we hadn't had to rush the story.

Weirdly, having that happen bonded Michelle and me a little more. It reminded us we were both navigating the same minefield. I realized that she was somebody that was fighting a war in our division, and she realized that I was just trying to keep my head above the choppy waters I found myself in: *Okay, Nattie's not the enemy, she's just somebody that's new here and just trying to fit in.*

We both saw that the threat to our visibility on the show wasn't each other. Michelle wanted the girls to have more, and she wanted to wrestle. And when she realized I was the same way, we became friends, and remain friends to this day. We even went on to make history together a couple more times before she retired in 2011.

But right after our first PPV match, despite the tension dying down between us, I still felt very alone in the new company. Back in the locker room, I looked at myself in the mirror, and in the reflection looking back at me, I could see how much I was second-guessing myself. I was almost unrecognizable, because I'd dyed my hair red, and I was wearing a dark blue outfit because I thought that would look glamorous. Without the Bellas beside me, I had no idea what I was doing in the style department, and without TJ beside me, I was losing confidence in my ring work too.

I knew I needed my people around me, but they were still in FCW.

And with my title match over, and my dumpiness still here, I had no idea what was ahead of me in WWE, if anything at all. I knew I needed backup before I slipped into the unknown.

"YOU GOTTA FIND YOUR VOICE"

After *The Great American Bash*, I ended up treading the WWE creative waters for months. While my on-screen career didn't explode the way I'd hoped, I'd thankfully gotten better at making friends, like Beth Phoenix. Beth and I had weirdly "met" years before on MySpace (Facebook before Facebook) as two women both looking to break into the wrestling business. Beth had signed her developmental deal with WWE a couple of years before I did, and afterward had messaged me saying my family had inspired her to become a wrestler. We continued to message each other all the time as she went through training and made the main roster, and when I went through the same process Beth let me pick her brain and gave me great tips about how to navigate the competitive environment.

Another woman I became very close to was someone who was basically assigned to me by Vince McMahon. Eve Torres, a model from Denver, had been fast-tracked as an on-screen personality without going through developmental like everyone else. If I was the boss of a company—any company—I'd hire Eve in a heartbeat. There was nothing *not* to like. She was intelligent, funny, reliable, hardworking, eager to learn, and easy to get along with. But when it came time to make her in-ring debut, she literally had no training and would have to learn in front of the world, in a weekly mix of live events and live TV.

"I'm not going to put her in developmental," Vince told me. "She can get her in-house developmental right here with you."

I guess that was a compliment to me, and at that point, I'd take any of those I could get.

Eve was a stunning girl and very smart, with a degree in industrial engineering, but knew fuck-all about wrestling when she started. I was so honored that she put her trust in me, even as I was running the gauntlet of being the new girl myself. I was still figuring out my way on the main roster, and all of a sudden it was my job help the *new* new girl figure out her way in the ring. But Eve always made me feel so appreciated for helping her learn the basics.

After months of slowly sinking, I was beginning to understand that making it to the main roster didn't mean for one second that I was out of the woods. All it did was put me closer to Vince's all-seeing eye. Not only was I "born" into WWE with the original sin of being a Hart, I was also carrying the unforgivable stigma of being unsexy. The more time passed, the more I began to see that if I were going to have a role, it was as the frumpy best friend in the rom-com who got the hot girl ready to be prom queen.

But again, just like I did in developmental, I took that role as a way to give myself a fighting chance. If I could be useful, I could survive long enough to figure out how to make this whole thing work for me. And then maybe I could make some history, like the rest of my family.

Eve and I began to work untelevised live events where I could help with her in-ring development—and I really ended up loving it. I remember at one of our matches, at a show in Pisgah, Alabama, Arn Anderson was our producer and going into great detail about what could make me a better heel. Arn was always kind of charmingly sadistic, and he said in the most serious low tone, "Tonight in your match with

Eve, I want you to stomp on her so hard it's like you're squishing the guts out of a worm!" I never got that visual out of my head. From then on in my matches with Eve I would stomp on her and yell, "Worm!" And we would both always burst out laughing in the ring.

I became good friends with Eve, who I would ride with, eat with, and split rooms with all over the country. And while I had a lot to teach her, she had a lot to teach me too.

Eve was extremely organized. Every time we went somewhere for a live event or a TV taping, she'd make sure we found the best hotel, or the place that had the best price, and then she'd find the best gym, or a place that would let us work out for free, and then she'd find the best coffee shop, and the best restaurant, and the best grocery store.

Town by town, city by city, Eve had the whole country scouted for us before we even got there. And when you're starting out, and money on the road isn't that plentiful, saving every cent you can while still finding good places to fuel your body and great gyms to get yourself camera ready is a must. Eve always had her shit together, and traveling with her showed me that if I was going to live a major part of my life on the road, then I'd have to be organized like she was.

While I'd grown up in the Wild West chaos of the Hart family, Eve was very well educated, and came from a really nice family. She had a focus and determination about her that came from being raised outside the business.

A lot of broken people get involved in wrestling. A lot of us come from chaotic homes or childhood trauma, because wrestling can help you get out and away from the situation you grew up in. It's like running away with the circus, except you live off scraps and have to scratch and claw and fight to make it from town to town. Our business can be cutthroat, because that's how some people progress up the card, so to a certain extent I've always got my guard up.

But somebody like Eve, she was like this little purebred kitten, and her wholesomeness caught me off guard. She was always reminding me about the little things in life, like, "Hey, it's not always about wrestling—don't forget to enjoy a nice cup of coffee."

It honestly had never crossed my trauma-dented mind to *enjoy* what I was doing—to savor a drink, or a bird overhead, or a sunset in a desert town. I was so tightly, anxiously clenched since I first stepped into a wrestling ring that it never even occurred to me that there was a world outside of those ropes that I might want to find happiness in.

My relationship with Eve reminded me of my relationship in FCW with the Bella Twins. They were all women who had come from outside the business, and at first I took their lack of familiarity with wrestling as a weakness, until I realized it was their strength. Their fresh eyes exposed me to different worldviews that I wasn't used to.

And those worldviews helped expand my own and made me a better person.

I decided that, while I could learn to appreciate the coffee or nature, the thing that would make this journey happier for me personally was family.

I grew up sharing beds with my sisters, meals with my cousins, stories with my uncles, and summertime with my grandparents. I figured, if I was ever going to get some of that feeling back, it was time to test my fledgling relationship with Vince, and ask for something that would make business sense to WWE, but also personal sense to me.

Down in FCW, Harry and TJ were a tag team, and I was floating around on the main roster on my own. Maybe we were a better package together than struggling apart. So, around the holidays in 2008, while on the road with Eve, I started practicing a speech that I was going to present to Vince. It was my first time pitching him, and I knew he either had to love it or would add another black mark to my already failing WWE report card.

Speaking up wasn't easy for me. I knew I had no power in the company, and it wasn't something I was naturally comfortable with doing. So, I'm not exaggerating when I say that waiting outside Vince's office in Nashville was one of the most terrifying times of my life. But I knew he would love what I was about to lay out, so I waited three hours outside his door for him to be free, even though every fiber of my being wanted me to run. And when I got my shot, I pitched him the idea I'd been rehearsing in the car with Eve for a few weeks: me, Harry, and TJ teaming up to become a faction in the company called the Hart Dynasty.

When I'd run the pitch past my dad, it was for us to use Bret and my dad's old tag-team name, the Hart Foundation, but my dad said that Harry, TJ, and I were "part of a dynasty" instead. He was so excited when I took his idea.

But my dad was a much easier audience than Vince.

If you pitched Vince well, it could change the whole trajectory of your career. But if it went the other way, he could fire you the next day.

That's why, inside his office, I was very passionate, very considerate of his time, and hit all the reasons why this would be great for all of us. And I fucking nailed it. Like, *nailed it* nailed it.

"What do you think?" I asked, trying to hide how proud of myself I was.

"Well, I think it's a terrible idea," he replied, finishing the large steak he was eating at his desk without even looking up at me.

Now, I once fell crotch first from the top turnbuckle onto the top rope, and the pain of that was nothing compared to the pain of this.

In my shock at the bluntness of his reply, I forgot to leave. And he didn't seem to notice. He just kept chewing as I stood there, unsure whether he wanted me to say something else. Then, after about two minutes of me being mute and frozen, Vince finished his meal, then his thought. "I don't just dislike it," he said before taking a gulp of water, "I hate it." He stood for his next meeting. "I have my own vision for

Harry, and I see TJ as a singles wrestler. I don't see you guys as a team at all."

"No, I get it," I meekly offered. It was a long shot and—

"But I'll give it a chance," he said as he cleaned his hands with disinfectant.

I tried to read his face, because I thought my ears had failed me. "You're going to do it?" I asked him.

"Since you had the courage to come in here, and since you're so passionate about the idea," he replied, "I'll give it a chance."

I didn't know this about Vince at the beginning, but a good thing about him was he was willing to try out creative suggestions even if he didn't believe they'd work.

"Thank you," I said, turning for the door before I outstayed my welcome.

"Nattie," he said, "you gotta find your voice around here."

I nodded and smiled as I left like I knew what he was saying, but I had no idea what "find your voice" meant.

It wasn't long before I did.

VOICE FOUND

"Um, sure," I said when I was asked to chaperone the next WWE Superstar marked for glory. Except this time it wasn't a hot model from Denver, it was a giant from India.

And I'm not using that term loosely.

The Great Khali was seven feet tall, and during his run in WWE weighed 345 pounds. He was a former police officer who had stood out in Hollywood in movies like *The Longest Yard* and *Get Smart*, and he had wrestled in other promotions like New Japan.

But the man was so big he couldn't drive a normal car by himself, so I was asked to do it. As per Vince's promise, TJ had debuted in February 2009, and then Harry joined us in May, making us the Hart Dynasty in WWE, and it was actually TJ and I who were asked to drive Khali. But TJ and Harry were pulled from that tour when their opponents got injured, leaving only me to drive.

Back in the '80s, Andre the Giant had referee Tim White as driver and travel partner because Andre faced the same hardships just getting around that Khali faced, being a similar size. Mark Carrano, the head of talent relations at that time, said that if I did this for WWE, then I'd get free travel and a free hotel while I was doing it.

Free was always appealing and it would give me a little extra money to buy new wrestling gear. So even without TJ and Harry along for the trip, I was in.

I met Khali at the airport in San Diego on a Friday morning, and while waiting for him in baggage claim, I could see what an attraction he was, and not just for WWE fans in the arenas. Everybody there wanted to talk to him and get a picture. I wondered if he felt like an animal at the zoo, but he didn't seem to mind stopping. He made time for everyone, which was lovely, but meant it took us nearly three hours to get from the goddamn baggage claim to our car! So I knew from the jump this was going to be an adventurous weekend.

The tour—or loop, as we call it—started that same day, and we had shows on Friday, Saturday, and Sunday nights, and then Monday was *Raw*. But before I even pulled out of the parking lot, Khali said, "I've got a friend."

Now, that sentence left hanging like that can be quite unnerving. I didn't know if he meant at home, in the trunk, or in his head. So I asked, "What friend, Khali?"

His English was broken, but easy to understand. "Here in San Diego. My friend owns a restaurant," he said.

Phew.

Oh, and free food. Hell yeah.

"It's an Indian restaurant here with authentic Indian cuisine," he said.

"No problem, we'll get there after the show."

But Khali was hungry *now*.

"Well, how about we go to the gym and then go see your friend before the show," I said.

This was acceptable to my huge, hungry, polite, and now happy new friend. So we went to the gym first, and I was so impressed by the pretty intense workout a guy his size knocked out in there. I don't think the lat-pulldown machine had ever had so much action. Khali was dripping sweat on the way out of Gold's Gym, and I know this because I walked nose first into his moist lower back when he stopped suddenly in the doorway.

"You think that would fit?" he mumbled to no one in particular.

I couldn't see what he was talking about because I was wiping a giant man's sweat from my eyeballs with my gym bag.

Then Khali reached over the counter and took an extra-small Gold's Gym T-shirt from the back wall and studied it, before deciding it would indeed fit his humongous frame. Now, the shirt he had in his Kong-like hands would have struggled to fit me, never mind him. But, with considerable effort, Khali slid that bad boy on over his wet hair and dragged it down over his body. Not gonna lie—I was seriously impressed with the quality of the fabric as it held together under such monumental duress. But it refused to go any further than Khali's sixty-five-inch chest.

"Nattie," he said, not panicked. "Help."

Oh, he was *stuck* stuck.

The more I tried to help, the more he struggled, and the more he struggled, the more attention we got from fellow customers.

Now he was panicking.

You ever see those videos where people are trying to remove a bear's head from a bucket? Well, that was us in Gold's Gym. Until eventually we managed to get this shirt meant for a kindergartner back off this giant man. And then, as I stood there with his sopping wet T-shirt in my hand, the whole gym watching, he said, totally calm again, "I'm hungry now."

So, with plenty of time left to make our live event that night, I paid for the shirt so neither of us got in trouble, and we went to his friend's restaurant for a late lunch.

When we arrived, he was treated like a god. And I do mean like a god. Khali was a national icon back home, and the owner of the restaurant treated him as such.

We were seated in the nicest area of the dining room, and before we even pulled our seats in, the parade of food began. Spicy, colorful, flavorful, joyous, wonderful, beautiful food. Tons of it. Enough to feed a large wedding—or a giant, I suppose.

Now, I heard back in the day that Timmy White once made the mistake of actually trying to finish all the rounds of drinks Andre bought them and barely lived to tell the tale. This was my giant-consumption moment, but with curry instead of red wine.

Plate for plate, dish for dish, Khali and his most gracious host wanted me to taste and sample everything Khali was having too. This is maybe what Vince meant when he said I needed to find my voice, because instead of saying "no thanks" at a certain point, I kept eating, because I didn't want to offend anybody. All that rice, chicken, naan, dosa, tikka, biryani, and grilled, spiced paneer—I was going round for round with a super heavyweight just because I couldn't say no.

The food was amazing, but I truly felt like I was going to fucking explode.

And I had to wrestle Layla in just under a few hours at the live event.

"We gotta go, Khali," I said, rolling myself to the door just in time to make the drive to the show.

Khali packed up all the food we didn't eat and brought it with him in the car. And although I wanted to puke at even the mere smell of more food, I was kind of okay with it, because I figured it meant I wouldn't have to stop after the show to find him more stuff to eat— I could just flop straight into my bed at the hotel.

When we got the building, I reminded myself of Khali trying to fit into the Gold's Gym T-shirt as I tried to fit into my wrestling gear. I was incapacitated with heartburn and running through the upcoming match in my head, trying to figure out how to stop Layla from slamming me, chopping me, diving on me, and generally touching me in any way so I wouldn't explode. I sure as hell wasn't about to take a hip toss.

Mid-match, I got the sweats from all the strong flavors and spices I had ingested earlier, and had to tense every muscle fiber in my body just to make it out of there without ruining my career, and probably my gear, too—Spandex is thinner than people know. But I made it. I got through the match, and the crowd didn't notice any difference—though I'm sure there were some backstage suddenly wondering if I had a drug problem with the way I was huffing and sweating just walking around.

In the parking lot after, I saw Khali's giant frame waiting for me, but without his food parcels from before.

"Did you give away your food?" I asked him, already dreaming of my pillow.

"No, I ate it," he said.

"That's a shame," I replied, hoping he'd still be full.

"No, we're going back there now," he said with a smile.

Find your voice, Nattie. Find your fucking voice.

"Okay," I said, smiling back, but secretly wanting to bawl at the thought of any more food, no matter how delicious it was. But I was tough, I told myself, and I could get through another couple of hours of Khali eating as long as I knew my comfortable hotel bed in the next town was waiting for me at the end of it.

So back we went.

Except this time, it was the restaurant owner's house we were going to. Apparently the restaurant was long closed and the owners wanted more one-on-one time with Khali.

And even though the house was very small, the spread was even bigger than the lunch had been. It was already midnight, it was a four-hour drive to our hotel, and the amount of food laid out was bottomless, much like my new giant friend's stomach.

Fuck, this was going to be an all-nighter.

"Are you okay, Nattie?" Khali asked, mesmerized by the banquet in front of him. His eyes were lit up like a child at Christmas. He was homesick and every dish clearly made him feel closer to home. Who was I to ruin that for him?

"Of course," I said, stomping down my inner monologue. "Maybe just a couple of hours, okay?"

It was a two-bedroom house, and because word had gotten out Khali was coming, it was populated by about twenty people. There were dogs roaming around and children crying in diapers in the background. It was a hectic scene, with Khali sitting in the middle of the room on a big velvet recliner sofa like a king on a throne. And he was eating everything brought to him while holding court speaking his native language, as I tried to make conversation in a language I did not speak while looking for a bathroom.

Then Khali whispered to me, "Do you like this house?"

"Huh?"

"The house, do you like it?"

"Why, are we buying it?"

"Do you like these people?"

"Khali, it's one in the morning and we got a four-hour drive to the next town—"

"That's why I'm asking," he said. "We'll stay here tonight."

And I'd love to say I found my voice, but I spent that night in the king-size bed of the restaurant owner and his wife after just meeting them a couple of hours before. Where were they, you ask? Well, they slept on their living room floor with their children, and the remaining guests, and the dogs, while Khali slept on the kids' bedroom floor because he couldn't fit in the bed.

"TJ," I whispered into my phone under the parents' covers. "I'm . . . I'm. I don't know where the fuck I am, but I'm not in danger or anything."

"What?!"

I quickly explained to TJ what happened, and that I didn't know what the fuck I was doing. "I don't know anyone here except Khali, I've never been so bloated in my whole life, and I'm just exhausted from eating, wrestling, and driving."

"Why didn't you say anything? What are you doing? Why do you get yourself into situations like this?" TJ asked.

"Because . . ." I couldn't finish the sentence. I just wanted to do a good job because the company asked me to, and Khali was such a sweetheart that I had a hard time speaking up.

I stayed awake all night, just lying there—until I smelled more food being cooked in the morning, and something snapped inside me. I went out to the living room and everyone was up and eating a meal that was even bigger than one from the night before.

And Khali was in the middle of it, again inhaling everything that wasn't nailed down.

I walked over to him while smiling at everyone else. "Khali, get in the fucking car," I whispered to him, before thanking our wonderful hosts and walking out the front door.

A few moments later, Khali popped his giant head out the front window. "Is something wrong?" he asked as I stood waiting outside by the car.

"Get in the fucking car this minute, or I swear to God I'm going punch you in the nuts."

"What?"

"I mean it," I said. "I'm going to uppercut you right in your nuts if you're not in this fucking car in five minutes. And don't even think about waiting around for food to bring. You hear me?"

I could tell by the look on his face that Khali was half-scared, half-impressed. I'm not even sure he understood everything I had said, but he must have gotten the gist of it because we were on the road within five minutes.

As Khali snuck some prawn crackers from his pocket into his mouth,

I couldn't help thinking that maybe I was a new woman now. Maybe I would be able to put my own needs over others' from now on. Maybe I would put my foot down more and stop trying to people-please all the time.

Maybe I'd found my voice.

Or maybe not, because an hour later Khali and I were already stopped to find him something to eat again. And two hours after that because he saw a Waffle House. Once my fleeting temper faded, I couldn't help but laugh at the amount of food this man could put away and how much I enjoyed being his travel partner, even though he also drove me nuts.

When WWE asked if I wanted to stay Khali's travel buddy, I jumped at the chance, and over the next six months we ended up becoming really good friends. Khali confided a lot to me, and we bonded over how much we both really loved wrestling. I got to see a very human side of this gentle giant who always made time for everyone, wasn't too proud to sleep on the floor, and missed home.

But holy shit, he loved his Indian food.

It can happen in wrestling that strangers become family, and family become strangers, because we're on the road so much. And sometimes it's the ones you least expect that you end up bonding with the most.

I learned that weekend that finding my voice wasn't going to happen overnight. But it *was* still there, under many layers of childhood conditioning. I just needed to set it free.

DIVAS CHAMPION

Sometimes in wrestling you get the spotlight because it's your time, and sometimes you get it because it's not someone else's. WWE always keeps a deep bench for that very reason—when one Superstar goes down, there's always another to take their place. Perseverance is a key trait if you want to survive the long-term grind of being a WWE Superstar.

It's easier being away from your family and making all the towns if you're being featured on TV every week and making lots of money. It's so much harder when you feel invisible—or worse, when you sense that you're just not what they're looking for. But I'd seen enough with my family over the years to know that, if you just hang in there, and do good, consistent work when it seems like nobody is watching, then *sometimes* an opportunity will come your way.

Even then, though, you have to fight to make it happen.

For female wrestlers—or "Divas," as we were branded then—2010 was a frustrating time. We were given two or three minutes for our matches on TV (if we were lucky), and we weren't allowed to do anything that looked violent—which, as you can imagine, if you're trying to put on a wrestling match, was quite limiting. The directive handed down from Vince was no punches from the women; we had to slap each other instead. And while the men's world titles were steeped in gold and history, our Divas Championship was this bright pink butterfly-shaped belt that screamed *This is a toy, not a title.*

We were still a long way from the women's evolution that was to come in WWE, but there was already a group of women forming backstage who wanted more than pillow fights and musical-chair segments. Women like Beth Phoenix, Melina, Maryse, Mickey James, Victoria, Cherry, Michelle McCool, Layla, Eve, the Bella Twins, and Gail Kim were all pushing for longer matches and more serious storylines, frustrated that the emphasis was still so much on keeping us "feminine" and "pretty" when all we wanted to do was kick each other's asses and put on a show. But we didn't have the stroke to complain too loudly; we just had to let our work speak for itself, and keep persevering.

In my own corner of WWE at that time, the Hart Dynasty—me, TJ, and Harry—had just been dissolved. Since, true to his word, Vince didn't love the team, TJ and Harry were just used to make *other* teams look like stars—which led TJ to pitch the breakup because everyone stood more chance of success apart than together. The Hart Dynasty might not have worked the way I'd hoped on screen, but it did get both guys to the main roster, where we could all now look for new opportunities on the big stage.

And for me, the next opportunity came much sooner than I expected.

My friend Beth Phoenix had been out with a torn ACL, but as *Survivor Series* came around that year, management wanted her to come back early and win the title that night. Beth wasn't ready. So she did something I'll never forget: she gave me a heads-up that Vince wanted to move the title to somebody new, and told me that I should go to him and make the case that the title should go to me, because she believed I deserved that opportunity.

But I wasn't sure at all.

I had conditioned myself to think that I was there to *make* champions, not *be* one. But Beth was insistent. She said Vince would never see me as a champion if I didn't present myself as one—if I didn't fight for it.

When I told TJ, he said that everything in WWE, for every*one* in WWE, hinged on their relationship with Vince. "At the end of the day, Nattie, this is all make-believe. If Vince sees the passion in your eyes, and hears you make a better case than the one he had in his head, then you have the same shot as everyone else."

One of the most valuable lessons I've learned in WWE was just dawning on me. Some people get handed opportunities, and some people make opportunities. If I didn't make my opportunities happen, I was going to get nothing. So, a few weeks before *Survivor Series*, I went into Vince's office, shaking with nerves, where I laid it all out for him—how I'd been working since 2001 to be a champion, how I hadn't come to WWE to be mediocre, how I knew I could make a great champion. I could feel this was going to be my moment.

I'd never spoken up for myself like this in my whole life, where I made the case for why I was good enough for something special to happen for me—not for the boys, but for *me*. But I wanted Vince to see that I'd found my voice just like he said I should, and—

"No," he said. "I don't want you to be champion. I want Beth to be champion, not you."

Okay then.

I left feeling like an idiot for even thinking Vince would see me that way. He would rather have an injured Beth be his champion than a healthy Nattie. Well, there was no coming back from that. I'd have to wrestle as a luchador from now on, because I never wanted to show my face again.

I know TJ said it was all just make-believe, but I couldn't help thinking it was a rejection of me personally instead of it being a storyline thing or a timing issue. After that meeting, I started looking at myself closer in the mirror and noticing things I wanted to change about myself. I was beginning to wonder if getting a little nip here and a tuck there would be a good move for me and my career. Plenty of other women in our locker room were doing it to keep "TV ready." Plenty of the guys, too, were doing everything they could—naturally and otherwise—to make sure they always looked like a star. And inside, I felt like I wasn't enough. Not even close.

I was at sea and looking for a way to find land. But in WWE, no plan was ever the final plan until it was actually implemented.

A few weeks after I pitched my idea to Vince, Fit Finlay, who was now the primary agent for women's matches, pulled me aside with news: they wanted me to challenge Michelle and Layla for the title.

"*Me?*" I said, in shock.

"Yes, you, Nattie." Fit seemed confused as to why I was so stunned. He saw in me the potential I didn't yet see in myself. "And Vince wants you to win it."

"Win what?" I hadn't heard that sentence much—that I was going to win.

"The match!"

"But that means I'd be champion," I replied, like nobody else in the company had thought of that.

"Exactly!"

Oh shit.

I was going to be a champion.

And that thought was still ringing in my head on November 21, 2010—two years after being called up to the main roster—when I wrestled in the Divas Championship match at the *Survivor Series* PPV, knowing it was my time.

Just like in my first PPV, standing across the ring from me was Michelle McCool—only this time with a new partner, Layla, as both women, who were the "villains" in the match, tried to beat me in a two-on-one handicap match.

In our storyline, "Laycool"—as the two women were collectively known—were co-champions and had "terrorized" me for weeks on television before the match, mocking my family heritage and snapping my dad's signature sunglasses that he wore to the ring, leading to us facing off on PayPerView.

Standing in the ring that night, I couldn't help but reflect on how far I'd come with Michelle in particular. She worked hard to create moments where *I* could shine, going above and beyond to make sure I looked strong and had my moment.

And I did.

Winning a match like this—the biggest match in my career by far—meant Vince wanted to feature me. He wanted to center the division around me. He believed in me. He believed in my ability to tell stories, and he believed in my ability in the ring.

It meant he had faith in me to represent his company.

Being a champion never meant you were the toughest or the fastest or the strongest. It meant Vince trusted you enough to pass you the baton to move your division forward. That you could handle the live events, the extra media tours, the meet-and-greets, the live TV and PPV schedule—and do it all with media savvy and grace while making WWE look good.

Growing up, I wanted to be a champion because I wanted to be able to say that I did what my family has done in every company they've been in. But if I'm honest, as an adult, getting that title had more to do with wanting Vince's approval, and no longer feeling like I was the ugly duckling or the supporting actress.

And maybe being champion would finally make me feel like I was enough. I didn't know if it would, but I was excited to find out.

So I was now the Divas champion—but thanks to a new black cloud that was hanging over me, I had a feeling it wouldn't be for long.

CONTROL VERSUS CHAOS

Walking through the curtain to the backstage area after winning the Divas Championship, I experienced this new feeling I was unfamiliar with—pure euphoria. It was a burst of elation that the tightly woven childhood trauma around me had never let me experience before.

Becoming champion, and doing it at *Survivor Series*—one of WWE's "big four" PPVs, along with *Royal Rumble*, *SummerSlam*, and *WrestleMania*—was *such* a high that I forgot to feel uneasy. I forgot to feel anxious. It was the moment that I was craving, the one that verified I was enough.

Once the cameras were off me, and I was tucked safely away from the crowd, I suddenly became emotional when Beth hugged me, and the other girls from the match joined in. Waiting his turn was Fit, who locked me into this strong, proud-dad-like hug, and seeing his genuine pride in me made me feel so good about myself. For that moment I felt safe in his strong embrace. It reminded me of the way my grandfather would hug me so tight and tell me just how proud he was of me.

But once he let go, and the adrenaline and euphoria lowered a fraction, in marched fucking imposter syndrome to sit on my head.

All this love, and the well-wishes—did I deserve them? *What if I'm not good enough?*

I couldn't enjoy it anymore; my elation was replaced by dread. It felt like my days as champion were numbered—and not just because of me, but because of my dad.

What if they don't want to keep the title on me with everything about my dad now in the news?

A couple of months before I won the title, I was backstage at *Raw* when I read on Twitter that my dad had been arrested and charged with two counts of possession of a controlled substance, two counts of trafficking a controlled substance, one count of grand theft, and one count of burglary of an occupied dwelling.

He was arrested in Thonotosassa, Florida, after causing a scene at a gas station. When deputies arrived to calm him down, they searched him and found twenty-eight methadone tablets and ninety-five Oxy-Contin pills, along with pill bottles with names on them that weren't his.

Before I could even put my phone down, someone from WWE management pulled me aside to see if I was okay. They asked what was going on, but I had no information other than what I was reading online.

Turns out Daddy was taking out loans against my mom's ten-dollar-an-hour paycheck to buy other people's prescription drugs. But when he was caught, the people that sold him their prescriptions said he stole them, and because of the number of pills he had on him, my dad was now in serious trouble for "trafficking" as they didn't believe the large quantity was for "personal use."

They clearly didn't know my dad.

When he got picked up, I was the only one available to bail him out. My mom was visiting her family in Canada, on a short vacation from working in a fabric store to make ends meet, and my sisters didn't have the relationship I had with him because they didn't want to deal with him anymore.

Over the years they'd distanced themselves from him because they were angry and hurt and frustrated at his behavior. I could relate to him a little more because we shared the common bond of wrestling, so as I got older, I took on a lot of the responsibility for trying to help him get on track and help the family navigate his issues. My mom wanted him to get his shit together, but no matter what she did, she couldn't stop him or change him, and it was exhausting for her. She eventually stopped fighting because she had nothing left.

So I stepped in to help prevent my dad from "doing drugs and fucking up." But when I heard the news he'd been arrested, I knew I was as powerless to change his behavior as my mom was before me. TJ and I hurried home to Florida, where, after bailing my dad out of jail, we brought him to an attorney.

In Florida, the mandatory minimum jail time for trafficking that many prescription drugs was twenty-five years and a $500,000 fine, so we had to get some serious representation to help him try to fight this. My dad wasn't selling drugs and had no intent to. He couldn't get enough for himself, never mind selling what he did have to someone else. The attorney gave us a deal because we knew a friend of a friend, but we still spent $25,000 on legal fees in hopes my dad wouldn't go to jail.

I had seen him in bad shape before—locking himself away for days, exploding out of nowhere, not talking for weeks—but nothing like this. It was clear to me that while my dad was very much an addict, there was something far more severe going on with him too. I watched him sitting with his head down in our car as we drove back from the attorney, and he was so obviously out of control. And seeing him that way made me feel out of control too.

It was in that moment that the hard truth hit me—I had lived my whole life in fear of a man I loved.

I feared what he might do to himself.

Feared what his behavior might do to our family.

Feared what was coming next.

Because it was clear to me, sitting in the front seat as an adult now, that my dad was hurtling toward someplace dark and inevitable, and there was nothing I could do to stop it from happening.

Even if we could get him help on these charges, there was going to be something else down the road. There was always going to be a next time. His brain had deteriorated so much that he would take something for his pain, not remember, and so take something again, and not remember that either. I didn't feel like a helpless child; I felt like a helpless parent.

And then he broke the silence. "Remember when you held my title above your head when you were a kid, Nattie?"

"I do, Daddy."

"One day you'll do that for real," he said. "With your own title."

Once I'd gotten my dad home and he'd fallen asleep, TJ and I sat in silence. On top of wondering what this all meant for my dad, I began to wonder what this all meant for me. I was suddenly really worried that I was going to get in trouble at work, that I was going to be punished: pulled off TV and sent home because WWE would be mad at my dad and, by association, at me.

I felt ashamed at the thought of going in to work, and terrible about what my dad had done, and I was riddled with anxiety about it all.

And anxiety did as anxiety does: as the days and weeks passed, I started thinking that, because of my dad, maybe I would even be fired.

I found myself going over all the times Vince and everyone else backstage asked how my dad was, and I told them how great he was doing, because I always held out hope that maybe there was something more my dad could do in the company, and maybe it would help my mom if my dad made a little bit of money here and there. And then when the news broke about the drugs and the drug trafficking and the theft, it just made me look like a fucking liar.

I knew he wasn't doing okay, but I always wanted to protect him and put him on a pedestal for the rest of the world, so that other people would think he was great, and maybe he would start to feel better about himself too.

Even if *I* was angry at him because he never had any money, and that my mom had no money because of him—even though she worked so hard—I didn't want anyone else to be. Even if *I* was angry at him that it was up to me, in only my second year on the main roster, when I wasn't making much money, and had huge road expenses and taxes of my own, to now take care of all these legal fees and charges and make sure that he didn't go to jail, I didn't want anyone else to be.

If I'm honest, there was a lot I was angry about, those days.

But most of all, I was angry at my dad because I could never find peace.

I could never lie down at night and not worry about him.

I could never get in the ring and not worry about him.

Fortunately, my dad's lawyer managed to convince the courts to show leniency if he got help.

"You won't have to go to jail if you go to treatment," I explained to him. "You *have to* go or it's prison time. They want to press major charges against you, but they're willing to work with you if you go into rehab, Daddy."

But while my family were elated that he didn't have to go to jail, my dad was just incensed by the court making him do *anything*. And it turned him against me, because it looked to him like I was turning against him. Like I was siding with "them" over him because in his mind, nothing was his fault. How could I agree with "them" that he had a problem when he was so convinced he didn't?

That's why two months after his arrest, when WWE had just made me their Divas champion, I was even more worried about my dad's behavior coming back to haunt me. Maybe he'd walk from rehab and end up in jail. Or maybe he'd relapse and do something even worse the next time.

That's what my head was full of when I walked toward the locker room, my new title over my shoulder. I got so scared that I'd be punished for what might happen that I went and found a small corner of the building, near where they set up props in the loading dock, and cried, because I knew this was the pinnacle of my career, and not only could I not share that with my dad, but I also couldn't get the sickness in the pit in my stomach to go away because of what was happening with him.

Daddy was right, I did hold the title above my head, just like he held his up before me. But he missed it because, while he was doing his stint in rehab, he wouldn't talk to me.

I broke his heart, and he broke mine.

I guess in Narcotics Anonymous they would say he was in denial, but even back then, I felt it was more than that. I could see my dad was losing himself, and his addictions were just dragging him quicker into the abyss.

DROPPING THE TITLE

With everything happening with my dad, I was ashamed going to work. My head was full of scenarios of what people were saying behind closed doors, or when my back was turned. The only thing I could control *somewhat* was how I performed between the ropes. Under Vince, every second of TV was controlled, but during non-televised live events, I could do what I naturally did best, and I would do it with anyone on the roster for as long or as short as they needed. I would wrestle those with no experience and those with tons.

Because I couldn't shake the voice in my head warning they'd strip me of the title, I did what Harts do—I wrestled. And wrestled. And wrestled.

I didn't want to be at home. I wanted to be on the road. I wanted to be in the ring, like TJ was, and my dad and uncles were before me, and my grandfather before us all. So I threw myself into the work, into the matches. I didn't know what else to do to prove my worth.

But I soon got my shot, one month after winning the title, at WWE's next PPV. The event was Tables, Ladders, and Chairs, and it was going to be me and the returning Beth Phoenix versus Laycool in the first-ever women's tag-team tables match—where the only way to win was to slam your opponent through a table.

When Fit told me this was going to be my first PPV match as

champion, I immediately thought this was my chance to cement my place as the face of the division—to prove I belonged. It was the kind of match that only the men had gotten to participate in before, so it was a huge deal—for me, the other participants, and the whole division—that we made this as good as anything the audience had seen before.

Fit and ex–cruiserweight great Jamie Noble immediately began to work with us on the match, mapping out how we would wow the crowd and steal the show. Fit was a legitimate shooter who could genuinely beat the hell out of anyone, so his input always brought a level of seriousness to our matches. He knew that with a specialized match like this, we were able to do so much more than we had been allowed to do in normal matches—and he was as determined as we were to show the world what we could do.

Fit was always trying to do stuff that would help the girls tell better stories and help connect us more with the audience using the little screen real estate we had. And he especially wanted this match to feel more special and more meaningful. He even got our merchandise guy, Joe Hickey, to paint a beautiful custom table for the match. The table was pink—the Hart family color—with Michelle and Layla depicted as witches on it. He was making them the biggest heels he could.

Joe (who still works in WWE today) personally painted the table, but it was Vince who agreed to let us have the painted table and use it as the table that I'd put Michelle and Layla through for the finish of the match.

It really felt like there was a buzz around our match, not only from the fans but from fellow wrestlers too. Triple H (who is now Chief Content Officer at WWE) contributed by suggesting I try doing my submission finishing move on both Laycool members at the same time, by stacking Layla on top of Michelle. I wasn't even sure it could be done, but we nailed it on the first try and knew it had to be part of our match, as nobody had ever done that before.

With the date quickly arriving, the whole match was coming together, full of spots that would put us on par with the guys—finishers off the top rope and brutal bumps to the concrete outside. Fit and Jamie had created this masterpiece of violence and storytelling that pushed boundaries to make us feel special to an audience who at that point hadn't seen our division let loose too often.

We were feeling great—right up until the rehearsal before the show, when Michelle and I nearly crashed from the top rope and were caught by former Four Horseman Arn Anderson, who, at the last second, broke our fall to avoid a spill that would have badly hurt us both.

All I could think of as I rolled back into the ring was: *Vince saw that.* He always watched rehearsals. I was already on thin ice because of my dad, and I knew I needed this match to go like clockwork or I was on borrowed time as champion.

So later that night, when the match began, I was amped to make this the best match I could. I knew, looking around the ring at the other women in there with me, that their mindset was the exact same as mine: *let's show the world what we can do.*

The only direction that we got from Vince was, "You guys have a total of fifteen minutes with entrances. Natalie over." (Vince always called me Natalie.) And that was it. Entrances would take five minutes, so we'd have ten minutes bell-to-bell in ring, and "Natalie over" meant I was winning the match.

Maybe he did want me to stay on top after all? I needed to get out of my own head and realize Vince really believed in me.

Ding ding.

The bell rang, and we went to work.

And we were kicking ass, pulling off everything on time and to plan . . . until Beth went to take a bump through the ropes as rehearsed, but the knee brace she wore for her torn ACL caught the ropes, stopping her momentum dead and dropping her head first onto the lightly padded concrete below—folding her into an accordion and compressing her neck.

We didn't know it at the time, but Vince was backstage livid at the spot, as he thought we were taking unnecessary risks. He'd seen us fall in rehearsal, and now thought Beth had really hurt herself. He was growing more concerned as the match kept going.

In the arena, though, the crowd were on their feet and with us every step of the way. So we just kept turning the tempo up. We never went off script, never tried anything that wasn't rehearsed and agreed, but we were all out there filling the plan with life and passion—and improvising when we had to. All four of us were firing on all cylinders. Everything came together beautifully and actually better than what we'd planned.

Like the end.

I was on the top turnbuckle, where Michelle and Layla were trying to suplex me through the pink table waiting underneath us. The finish we had planned was for me to push Michelle and Layla through the table, but when I did, the damn thing didn't break. Even though we'd scored it to make it easier to snap, both women together were still too light to break the table in half. Suddenly I heard Vince screaming through the headset: "Tell her to jump! Tell her to jump!" So there I was, Nattie Neidhart, who had barely done a move from the top rope since my debut in Matrats, getting ready to launch myself onto both of them to finally break that table. Like a flying fucking squirrel. Here we go.

I jumped, and the crowd in Nassau Coliseum erupted as I drove both of them through the table. The crowd hit their feet. We'd just delivered a groundbreaking match for our division and the people were into it. I was thrilled. I felt like things were finally going to change. This was the big break that I needed—that we needed—and we nailed it.

Cody Rhodes (as I write this, the current WWE Champion) told me

I'd become a star that night. But backstage, Vince barely looked at us. Just a quick, firm handshake and he was gone. No praise, no criticism, nothing.

Fit, however, pulled us in, and told us how proud he was, and how we'd given a match just like the guys would. But when I wasn't booked on *Raw* the next night, I knew Vince saw it differently. To him, we were just lady wrestlers being too violent. He didn't *want* us having matches just like the guys would. So even though we followed the script, did the match as it was laid out, and had the match of the night, there was no follow-up on the live TV shows in the week that followed. Our match was swept under the rug, and all the goodwill and rising fan interest faded from lack of momentum.

When Fit asked about the match in production meetings, Vince's only comment was that it was scary watching his women wrestle like that, and he didn't want his girls being like that in the future.

A month later at the *Royal Rumble*, I dropped the title to Eve Torres. Eve was worthy of being a champion, but I couldn't help but feel like it was happening because I'd failed. Like there was something about me Vince just didn't like.

Eve clearly represented what Vince wanted—pretty, sexy, someone who could do a moonsault but didn't live and breathe wrestling. In many ways, I envied that she didn't love wrestling with all her heart. I wished I could just let it go and not care so much, because it didn't matter how good I was or how much the crowd got behind me. The audience that mattered was an audience of one—Vince McMahon.

I felt like I was failing and out of control. Maybe it was my family drama, or maybe Vince just didn't see me as long-term champion material. Whatever it was, I just felt so defeated, because my chance to break out actually ended up setting me back.

DIVAS OF DOOM

After the Tables match and me dropping the title at *Royal Rumble*, Eve, Michelle, Layla, and Beth continued to get screen time, but I ended up in creative limbo. I was in the bad books, it seemed. WWE wasn't my company; I didn't make the rules. And it wasn't just a strange time for me, it was a strange time for all three of us who made it from Stu's ring to WWE.

Even though TJ and Harry had been tag champs with the Hart Dynasty, Harry's contract wasn't renewed in 2011 and he left WWE. That left TJ and me bouncing around separately on different WWE shows, which meant we saw each other less and less, and I think it's fair to say that neither of us liked where our careers were heading.

I was learning that in WWE you live and die on a thousand decisions that other people make for you. And things like your entrance music, aesthetic, placement on the card, exposure, merchandise, media reach—and most importantly, your weekly live TV bookings—were controlled by someone else: Vince McMahon.

You would arrive at the arena, find out how Vince wanted you to be used that day—if at all—and then your job was to implement his vision. That meant sometimes you would be doing something meaningful and juicy, and sometimes you'd travel across the country to find out you weren't on the show at all. Those days were the toughest, because you'd spend your day watching your friends and colleagues busily planning out their TV segments while you waited to never be called. And that could happen for days, weeks, or months. For some it happened until their contract ran out and the company let them go.

And even though I was now at the bottom of the Diva ladder again, I was determined to make sure that wasn't me. Vince knew that whatever WWE gave me to do on a show I would do, and that approach soon landed me a middle ground where I was on TV, but without a clear direction or purpose—I was someone who was just there, floating, not meaning much.

This led me to being paired with a bunch of random people to make teams that didn't make sense in any of the storylines. Even though I enjoyed my rotating partners personally, none of our team-ups lasted or went anywhere in terms of a storyline.

With WWE creative making it clear my singles run was over for the foreseeable future, I figured if I was going to be a part of a team, my smartest path was to find someone *I* thought I could make a viable, formidable, sustainable tag team with.

And with TJ and me working different live events, and therefore not traveling together, I found my new tag-team partner in my new travel partner—Beth Phoenix.

Now, Beth was an amazing road wife, but how did I know we'd have chemistry or play well off each other when the pressure was on?

Well, one day Beth and I—or Debbie Desperado and Cheri Hatchet, as we called ourselves on the road—arrived at the Dallas Love Field Airport, which wouldn't have been a problem if our flights weren't leaving from Dallas *Fort Worth* Airport instead. By the time Beth and I realized our mistake and made it to our designated airport—checked our bags, and sprinted sweating and panicked to our boarding gate—it was thirty minutes before takeoff.

Score!

Or it would have been if we hadn't been informed by the fake, overly chipper airline lady that passengers must board *forty-five* minutes before takeoff. We could see our plane sitting there, and our bags—with our wrestling gear (that we never should have checked!)—were being transported to its hull. So we did what any self-respecting wrestlers would do. We begged. And begged.

But the very chipper airline lady held her painted-on smile as she stood in our way.

Now, missing a booking is a cardinal sin for anyone in WWE, but for someone who was already lost creatively, it was career suicide.

So I did the only thing I could think to do, and shouted at Beth, "It's all your fault! You missed the turnoff and now I'm going to lose my job! What about my children? Huh? You know what their father is like. He's a deadbeat. Poor little Sonny. What will I tell him?" I reached for the airline lady's hand as if to keep me from fainting. "What have you done, Beth?!" I howled. "What have you done?!"

And this is when I knew we'd be an amazing tag team, because Beth didn't miss a beat before she dropped her head and began to bawl. Like, real fucking tears. "Please help me fix this," she sobbed in appeal to the airline lady's better angels. "I'd never forgive myself if they took her house."

Brick by brick, layer on layer, Beth and I built my tragic situation up, breaking the lady's smile for the first time—until eventually, with Beth fanning me, the airline lady relented.

"I'll make sure your bags are on board," she said as she left to go call someone.

And with a rush of pure adrenaline, rattling with nerves, excitement, and disbelief, I began to laugh so hard that I couldn't stop. Not even with Beth shaking me to snap me out of it while nervously watching the airline lady's every move in case she saw me.

"Beth?"

I was wheezing. She was pissed.

"What, Nattie?"

"I just peed myself a little."

That's all it took for Beth to join me laughing like two sinners at the back of church—each dragging the other further into hysterics the more we tried to stop it.

We arrived at the building for the night's match just in time for rehearsal. And our producer, Arn Anderson, complimented how the scarf I usually wore around my neck was now wrapped around my waist.

That day, as we had our dinner of pistachios and diet orange soda backstage, we began talking about our aspirations and dreams. We began to spitball things we could pitch, and how to break out of the boxes we felt Vince and the company had put us in.

Even with Beth, I knew it would be an uphill battle for me. She was someone the company was clearly behind in terms of her booking. She'd come back from her ACL tear, killed it in our tag-team Tables match, and now was just waiting for her shot in the spotlight.

The shot we'd both been waiting for came in the summer of 2011, when I turned heel on AJ Lee. Now Beth and I were on the same show, and on the same side of the good/bad divide.

"We should sell ourselves as a team," Beth said.

"A strong team with a strong name," I returned, riffing right along with her idea. "Make them see that we're more than pillow fights and lingerie matches."

"Mhmm."

"But how?"

All we had coming up was a "sexy" photoshoot that WWE had lined up for most of the Divas division.

"Maybe that's it," I mused.

"What's it?"

"The photoshoot. Maybe we look for ways to make things happen in the company *off* TV, first."

"Make our own path."

"Exactly."

So when the photoshoot came, Beth and I were prepared and had our complementary outfits ready to go. We figured if we could plant the seed of us as a team by looking similar, then we had a shot at Vince or someone else up high thinking it was their idea to put us together full time.

We put our best into that shoot, working extra hard to get the angles right and the poses down, but it was near the end of it when our real opportunity came.

"Before you go, we need you to do something for Twitter," one of the WWE digital guys said.

"What's Twitter?" I asked.

"It's a new thing . . . it's like this . . . there's a small character limit . . . and . . . uh . . . it's on the internet and you can put videos on it," he replied sheepishly.

Beth and I looked at each other. It was one thing to look like we were a team. What if we could verbalize that too?

So when the "Twitter cameras" began rolling, we worked in that we were the "Divas of Doom" and hoped something might spring from it. The next we heard about it, Michael Cole—WWE's lead TV commentator—began using "Divas of Doom" to describe us on TV too. And we were ecstatic, until we heard Vince put out an edict that "You don't fucking call them Divas of Doom. It's too much like Legion of Doom" (the legendary tag team we took the name from). "They're Divas! They need to be feminine!"

But this new Twitter thing did its job, and "Divas of Doom" started trending.

Well, now we were happy, and also worried, because we knew we couldn't rock the boat with Vince too much, or he'd pull the whole thing and bury us to prove who was boss. Still, we figured this whole thing started with a photoshoot, so why not take a chance and do another one?

We found a little gym in the next arena we were at, grabbed a camera crew, some weights, and some five-inch heels and short skirts, and filmed a vignette of us being beautiful and feminine just like Vince wanted—but while weightlifting and looking powerful to embrace who we are too.

We were both determined to show Vince who we were before he got the chance to show us who *he* thought we were.

Now, Beth is one of the strongest women I've ever met, so to measure up to her I decided I'd squat 300 pounds in high heels—but as soon as I started to descend I realized I was in trouble. *I'm either going to blow a fucking ankle out, or give myself a hernia. But as long as I look fabulous, what's a few internal stitches between friends?*

Of course, when I looked over to Beth, I saw she was benching a Buick's worth of weight with ease.

Bitch.

But the visual was worth it.

We were trying to be what WWE wanted us to be—but also different. Ourselves. We both loved working out and looking our best, and we wanted to represent that on-screen, and not just be blonde Barbie girls.

Vince never really ran with it, though. I guess we were ready for the women's revolution in WWE before it was ready for us.

Beth and I did stay together as a team, but it was on Vince's terms. We feuded with some fun teams, did some cool stuff, and had a solid little run together—but it became apparent pretty fast why Vince didn't want to go all in on us as a team. Vince wanted Beth to be the Divas champion, and if anyone deserved it, it was her. Beth was (and still is) one of the true greats in our division—the total package of looks, charm, strength, poise, and talent. So I couldn't get mad at the decision.

But it did make me worried about what Vince saw for me—if anything.

Vince spent a lot of time laying out that Beth was the star of our team, and I was the sidekick. That Beth would get the wins, and I would take the losses. Beth didn't want it like that at all, but that's the way it was written, so that's the way we both played it.

Thankfully, before I had too much of a chance to worry about my spot in the company, word came that Vince had a huge idea in mind for me too.

Me? Vince never has ideas for me.

I was so excited!

Maybe my boss—the man who held my career in his hands—really saw who I was after all. It finally felt like my time in WWE was about to arrive.

VINCE'S BIG IDEA

"Hey, Nattie, you got a second?"

I was backstage, and Ed Koski—now WWE's head writer, then a writer on the rise and someone in Vince's inner circle—approached me.

Oh shit, this must be it. This must be Vince's idea.

"Oh, sure," I replied, cool as could be despite feeling like I was going to burst from excitement. But as he ushered me to a quieter spot backstage, my excitement suddenly gave way to dread.

Hang on, has my dad done something again? Maybe it's not the idea. Maybe it's my dad.

"We have an idea for you," Ed said.

"Oh, thank God."

"What?"

"Nothing."

"Well, *Vince* has an idea for you," he said more specifically.

Vince himself?! Eeeeeek!

"What's he thinking?" I asked, downplaying my exhilaration. I'd never been singled out by Vince before for this kind of attention, so I'm not going to lie, it was kind of cool.

"Well, it's this . . . he loves this idea, by the way. *Vince* does. It's from *Vince, not me.*"

It's from Vince, I get it.

"Well, it's really good," Ed continued, almost like he was stalling for time, or looking for the right words to get to the meat of the idea. "It's just—um, well, *Vince* has this idea that, you know, he wants to do with you, and it's his baby and it's important to him, but he really wants you to have this character where you . . . pass gas."

Ed and I just blinked at each other for thirty seconds.

"Like you have, like, terrible flatulence," he eventually offered, like that part needed to be clarified.

What the fuck do I say now?

Throughout 2011, I felt like I was bouncing around the roster like a loose nickel in a spin cycle, and I didn't want 2012 to be the same. For the past seven months the spotlight had been firmly on Beth as the new Divas Champion, and she was knocking it out of the park. But now that we weren't tag-teaming anymore, I needed something creatively for myself. So when Ed pulled me aside, I have to admit I quickly prayed, *Please, God, let this be my moment.*

Turns out God hates me.

"Vince wants me to do what now?"

"Fart. Basically."

"Why?"

"He wants it to be your character. Ongoing. Like every week. Natalya Neidfart."

I smiled, though I felt my lip quivering. I hoped if I could tease a smile from Ed in return it would let me know this was all a rib. But his poker face remained.

"What's the payoff? I do this and where does it go?"

"Vince just said he has a *big* payoff for you."

I could tell by the way Ed was explaining it to me that he was just doing his job. Vince wanted him to relay the message, and Ed, who is a nice person, was just doing what he was told. "Listen," he said in a quieter, more consoling tone, "Vince knows that you're always willing to play ball, and you always take everything you're given and try to make it great."

Now, I can't imagine that too many people have been in this exact situation before, where their boss wants them to pretend to pass gas as part of their job, but the only way I could even begin to approach this was to try to make it work for me. Politically, I could see a situation where, if I did this, I *might* be able to ask Vince for a creative favor in return for my next storyline. But if I said no, I would either continue my stint in Diva purgatory or be looked at as difficult and "hard to work with" and maybe even let go.

And with Harry gone and TJ bouncing around, same as me, I wanted to try to use this awful situation to better my and TJ's positions if I could. So I did what I've done a lot in my life and smiled when I wanted to cry.

"Sounds like a great idea," I lied.

"It'll be great," he lied back, and patted my shoulder as he left.

Alone backstage, my first reaction was to look for somewhere to be sick, or cry, or both. But I stopped myself, and calmed myself down. I couldn't let my paranoid thoughts take over. I may have thought of myself as a *wrestler*, but Vince thought of us as *performers*. *This is going to be a performance and nothing more*, I told myself. But try as I might to believe that, I couldn't shake the fact that this was Vince punishing me for something—I just couldn't pinpoint exactly what.

At least that's what I thought until I saw just how hands-on he was when my flatulence segments began to tape backstage at TV every week. I mean, the man's eyes were alive with creativity. He was like a tortured artist high on his greatest work—but instead of capturing the Mona Lisa or hand-carving Zeus at Olympia, he was picking fart sounds he liked.

I thought there was no way the owner of a multibillion-dollar company was going to take the time out of their day for this. But boy, was I wrong.

"More, Nattie!" came McMahon's booming voice off camera the first week.

More what, exactly? Does he think I'm really *letting them rip here?*

But it was more enthusiasm he was looking for. Enthusiasm that matched his. It was then, when I saw Vince's wide eyes off screen setting up the scene, so happy and boisterous about the whole thing, that I realized, this wasn't punishment. It really was his baby.

I mean, Vince *really* wanted this to work, and it wasn't intended to humiliate me, it was intended to get me sympathy.

"This is a big babyface character for you, Nattie," he explained, laying out his vision. "You're always perceived as this serious wrestler, so when we kind of give you this different layer and make it comedy, it will lead to a big babyface run."

Ed had told me Vince had a big payoff, and now it sounded like Vince was saying the same thing, so I just rolled with it. I mean, how could I not? Vince was Spielberg-ing this thing so hard. He was into the nuts and bolts of the motivation behind the farting and reactions to it. And he was so nice to me while doing it, spending so much time working with me in the backstage vignettes and complimenting my performance.

This was his opus, and I was his muse.

Or something.

But there was always room for improvement when creating art.

"Nattie, I want your face to be like this. I want you to, you know, sell the effort of it," came my direction.

"The *effort* of it?"

"Yeah, like this," he said, cocking his leg and making farting sounds.

Do I wish he'd have spent that time doing literally anything else with my character? Sure. But I felt like I had to take whatever spotlight I was being given, because in WWE, that kind of attention and focus on storylines was never easy for me to come by. While other women in the locker room dined on weekly banquets of TV time, my career was about thriving off the scraps.

I was an expert at turning lemons into vodka-fucking-lemonade. And that's what I did.

Even when they had me pretend to fart on Eve Torres. That's right, *on* her. Even when they had me pretend to fart in the ring during matches. Even when they had me pretend to fart in hallways where someone was knocked out from the smell, or got sick because of the odor, I kept going. I just, ahem, held my nose and did what was written for me to do, until the day, about six weeks after the whole thing started, when one of the writers guided me into a corner to finally talk about where things were headed.

Vince wasn't there, which seemed odd, but I couldn't have been more excited to see what he had planned to make this whole humiliating journey worth it. Then the writer said, "Vince wants us to build to you passing gas so hard you actually shit yourself."

At first, I thought he wasn't serious. But he was.

"But what's the big payoff?" I asked. And there was a pause long enough for me to answer my own question. "Oh," I said, finally catching on. "That *is* his big payoff."

"Yeah."

I wasn't going to be redeemed, or get a big match, or be "rewarded" with something more substantial or less degrading. I was going to shit myself on national television.

"But . . . I don't . . . I don't feel right doing that," I mumbled. I really didn't want to do it, but I also didn't want to seem "hard to work with" either, so I meekly offered, "I can do what we've been doing, but I don't want to . . ."

The writer squeezed my shoulder and left me to my unfinished thoughts. He knew Vince was dead set on this, and any issues I had with it were between the boss and me.

So there I was, dressed in the prettiest, most sparkly dress that I could wear, taping another farting segment and feeling stupid for believing this was all going somewhere better.

But I got wiser about everything that day.

And just as I was beginning to panic about how to get myself out of the "big payoff," the following week, it was all canceled. Just like that.

"What happened?" I asked the writer who had delivered the news.

"Vince is stopping it because the online feedback that we're getting is that this isn't very empowering to women and that it's not a good look for the women of WWE to be doing stuff like this."

You fucking think?!

"Oh, I guess that makes sense," I replied as calmly as I could.

I managed to wait until I got into the women's bathroom before dancing and silently screaming like a woman who'd just won the lottery. It was the best thing that could have happened, because I was out of that storyline without having to say I *wanted* out.

I wasn't the one who ended Vince's masterpiece, it was the fans.

That meant I could still go to him as the good soldier with some creative capital stored and pitch my own idea to him.

Which I did, less than a week later.

"I know our story didn't work out the way you wanted, Vince. Me either," I said. "But I have another idea I'd like to try."

For the first time since I got to WWE, I felt Vince was immediately engaged in something I had to say, because we'd spent all those weeks together and gotten to know each other. "What is it?" he asked.

No matter how bad the last few months had been, I knew now they would help me get to the place I'd always wanted to get to on-screen: with TJ.

ALL VINCE'S SIDES

I had a very good relationship with Vince—in many ways he was a father figure to me and I loved him—but Vince was a hard person to read, and I think he liked it that way. He liked keeping the talent and people in general on their toes with his unexpected reactions to everyday things. I know others have highlighted before how little Vince slept, but what they don't talk about is how tired I think he was because of it. People paint Vince like Superman sometimes, and I think making him into a mythological character does nobody any favors. Yes, he operated on very little sleep, and yes, he did work harder and for longer than anyone else in the entire company—or anyone else I've ever known, for that matter. I've never seen a person work more relentlessly than Vince. But he was human, just like the rest of us. And I think, especially as WWE grew exponentially and Vince kept working like crazy, that decades-long sleep deprivation manifested in a pendulum of extremes at work.

Vince was complex. Vince was decent. Vince was generous. Vince was very kind and he could be very cold at the same time. He was human. He was very nice to me. He was the devil to others. He was a man who was obsessed with cleanliness but loved toilet humor. He revered the old-school macho approach of never showing fear or pain or "weak" emotions, but he cried regularly when talking about his family. He wanted his shows to feel "raw" and edgy and like "anything could happen," but he was a control freak who obsessed over every line and every detail of every segment to the point there wasn't a single second left for spontaneity. He got genuinely excited about being pitched a good idea, only to change everything about it.

I brought him many ideas in our shared time at WWE, and when he liked an idea, it left me on such a high after I'd felt his approval. He wanted talent to "step up and grab the brass ring," to "show him something," but sometimes he made it terrifying to step out of line in any way. I never wanted to disappoint him. I always wanted every performance to be perfect, even though in our world—in any world—perfection every hour of the day isn't realistic.

Working for Vince changed my entire life. He did bad things to my family, and he did the most amazing things for my family too.

The year Vince inducted my dad into the WWE Hall of Fame, I wanted to do something special for him that showed how grateful I was for him honoring my dad. I found a picture of a young Vince and his dad, Vince, Sr., together backstage at Madison Square Garden. I put it in a frame and gave it to Vince backstage after my dad's induction. Vince opened the box the frame was in and he couldn't speak. He just looked at it, put it back in the box, and quietly cried while pretending to watch the next Hall of Fame inductee on the television monitor.

As much as he could go off on people, Vince always listened to me. He always made time for me. Always. And I've never, ever forgotten it. I hope it was partly because Vince liked me as a person, but I also think it was because he admired my grandfather Stu so much.

Stu sounded, looked, and conducted himself in the very manner Vince admired—like an old, grizzled tough guy who lived his whole life on a handshake. Vince loved mimicking Stu's voice and cadence whenever he was around me and always did it from a place of love and respect. I think it was that respect for where I came from, and the fact I used his ear very, very sparingly, that allowed me to pitch to him personally.

So, in 2012, after the farting storyline died, and when it was clear to me that neither Vince nor his creative team knew what to do with me or with TJ, I asked Vince to let me accompany TJ to ringside as his on-screen manager. That way we could travel together and be on the shows together, and I could get involved in the matches from time to time if the situation called for it.

Much to my surprise, Vince agreed on the spot, and TJ and I soon found ourselves in a storyline with the late, great Mr. Perfect's son, Joe Henning, where Joe mocked TJ (known on-screen as Tyson Kidd) for his lack of wrestling heritage, driving the knife in further by publicly claiming that TJ "would never be a true Hart."

It was during that storyline I got to see flashes of Vince's extremes up close and personal. In one backstage segment, I was at the costume and makeup station when Joe—billed as Curtis Axel—approached me and tried to slime his way in with me since we were both third-generation wrestlers in WWE. I didn't take the bait and left. Then, later in the show, Joe appeared with my bra, taken without my knowledge from the costume area, and sniffed it on screen like a creep.

In reality Joe couldn't have been more of a gentleman, but on screen he wanted his character to be so sleazy that when TJ finally caught up to him, the audience would be salivating to see Joe get his ass kicked. Being raised in the wrestling business taught Joe that anything you can do as a heel to make the audience crave your comeuppance, you do it.

But when Vince saw Joe sniff my bra on screen, he lost his mind. And I mean Vince exploded so much that Joe thought he'd be fired on the spot.

We were all confused, as it was written for Joe to take my gear and sniff it, but Vince's issue seemed to be that Joe sniffed it with too much gusto—that he should have been more subtle with the sniff! Of all the crazy things that have happened on television at WWE in the past, this particular act was somehow over the line to Vince. He wanted to push the envelope, but not so blatantly that it would get him shit from the network.

And moments like that made me scared to rock the boat.

Back then WWE wasn't run like a typical corporate entity. Vince was in charge of everything. Vince was WWE and WWE was Vince.

Vince himself was an intimidating figure, but what made it scarier was that he had your career—your livelihood—in his hands. WWE had come from the Wild West of regional wrestling, where there were no unions, no healthcare, no loyalty, and no regulations. Vince took a small family-run organization and grew it into a global juggernaut. And while every other area of the company had changed and evolved to match its growth, the one part that hadn't was that every decision went through Vince. And I'm talking *every single decision*, from billion-dollar TV deals to whether we had too many sequins on our costumes. He would literally call talent in the middle of the night to discuss their hair color with them.

Vince is the most unique person I've ever met. His eccentricities were many. He was constantly surrounded by steaks and hand sanitizer, so he could avoid both carbs and germs. I remember one extra talent for a match who went to shake Vince's hand backstage afterward, smelling like he had left his unwashed ring gear in his car all day in the baking-hot sun. He smelled like a dead animal! Vince was polite and shook the guy's hand and thanked him for the match, but then grabbed a huge bottle of Febreze that was left nearby and sprayed the guy down like he was a shoe or something. I'll never forget the visual of my billionaire boss doing that!

Even if you smelled fine, a handshake was a dicey proposition because Vince didn't like it when people didn't shake his hand hard enough. He really liked a firm handshake—but not too firm. I remember one time my cousin Harry shook Vince's hand really hard and Vince looked really pissed. But then again, if you gave him a light handshake, he would be pissed too.

Everything about a person was a test to Vince. If somebody had gray hair, it was almost personally insulting to Vince, because he hated to be reminded that people get old. I think he hated thinking about his own mortality because it was something he couldn't control.

When Bret came back for *WrestleMania* and he had some gray in his hair, Vince was adamant that I go talk to Bret about dying his hair jet black. I tried. "Fuck no. I don't want to look like Wayne Newton," was Bret's response to that one.

Vince was obsessed with smiling. He loved when heels smiled, he loved when babyfaces smiled. He always wanted you smiling on your entrance if you were a heel or smiling even bigger if you were a babyface.

But the thing he loved most of all was dancing. If you could dance, you had Vince's heart. And dance is how I got to see and hear Vince's other side—the childlike, fun-loving side.

TJ and I didn't last long together on WWE TV for reasons I don't know. It wasn't like they broke us up into something else more meaningful. We were just destined to go back to blowing around in the creative winds, I guess.

And blow around I did for a few months, until one of my random pairings on WWE TV brought me back into contact with my old friend, the Great Khali, for a dance segment on TV.

As you may remember, I took to dancing like a piano takes to water. But Khali wanted to show me how to dance like he did back home. He was really kind and understanding about my reservations, but felt he could really help me. So one day we took up residence backstage to rehearse me murdering Khali's number, and from behind us I heard an unmistakable voice—my grandfather Stu.

I turned to see Vince standing there, impersonating Grampy while clapping along. He was smiling as wide as an ocean, his hips moving side to side in the rhythm and pattern Khali was showing me.

"Keep going!" he insisted.

And so we did—the world's stiffest Canadian, the world's largest dance instructor, and the world's richest groupie, all throwing shapes like three TikTok dancers fishing for likes.

Vince had this enthusiasm for dance that bordered on scary—like he moved in a possessed way that made you lurch from being morbidly curious to medically worried for him. He was so "into it" that his movements were both fluid and violent at the same time. And he'd keep eye contact the whole way. Just lock right in and fire those hips around like bullets trapped in a drum.

And for one minute on that one day, he didn't act like the boss—he acted like someone who'd gotten dragged onstage of their favorite show. Like that person that's been waiting their whole life for the one moment, and they were going to take it with everything they had. That was Vince.

"We gotta keep this going with you two," he said as he finally danced through us and shimmed his way around the corner and out of sight, his cackling disappearing in the distance.

And true to Vince's word, Khali and I did end up on TV together—and on the road together again. I loved that time with Khali, and we made the most of anything we were given. But I wanted to do what I came to WWE to do: to be a part of something meaningful in my own right.

Luckily, that something meaningful was already in motion. It was a project *about* being in WWE, but it wasn't going to air on WWE TV. It was a reality show that E! and WWE were calling *Total Divas*.

TOTAL DIVAS

On our first week back on the road in January 2013, Triple H asked me if I had a minute. Everybody knows Hunter Hearst Helmsley as one of the best heel main event talents of all time, but as his in-ring career was winding down, his power within the corporate and creative side of WWE was growing.

Hunter might have been Vince's son-in-law, but anybody who observed his strategic approach to the business could see this would have been the path for him regardless. He was called "The Game" on TV because of his knowledge, passion, and love for the history of the business, along with his understanding of the storylines, character development, and athleticism that moved it all forward.

And those days, when he said he needed a word, it was usually a message directly from Vince.

He got straight to the point. "There's this new show that we're doing and it's going to be about the life of female Superstars in and out of the ring, and it's going to be called *Total Divas*," he said. "We think you'd be great for it, and want to put you forward for the show."

I was stunned—and nervous. I knew there had been whispers, and I'd wanted to get a shot, but now it was real. A project like this felt like the chance I was looking for to show myself more outside the ring so that I could maybe get more opportunities inside it.

But what worried me was knowing that my life outside the ring was a hot mess more often than not, and I wondered just how much access a show like this would want.

"We'll give you more information on it, but Vince wanted me to give you a heads-up that this is something that we're thinking about for you."

After that short conversation, things happened quickly. Word spread fast and wide that others were auditioning, or had already auditioned, to be on the show too. But once I got word that I was to fly out to LA for a photoshoot, and to meet everyone at E!, I knew I was cast.

I was speechless. None of the big opportunities in our division had come my way before—and certainly not anything so public facing. My self-doubt kicked in and I eventually asked someone from upper management, "Why me?"

"Honestly?" he replied. "Nobody wanted you on the show, Nattie. Nobody from WWE and nobody from E!. There was one voice in those meetings who insisted it be you, and that was Vince."

I was so confused. Vince clearly didn't see me as a centerpiece of the women's division. But he did seem to see me as an ambassador—someone he could trust to put the division's best foot forward in public.

Over the years, how I saw myself within WWE—and the entertainment business in general—swung so wildly that I would spend days and weeks awake at night wondering why I wasn't good enough. I worked harder, traveled more, trained anyone they'd ask me to, and tackled any segment or character I was given with everything I had. I tried to be kinder, more considerate, more available. More sizzle than steak. I changed how I looked, got breast enhancements, Botox, lip injections. I watched my weight, had standing appointments at the hair salon, trained other WWE Superstars on my days off. I tried, and tried, and tried to be what I thought WWE—and Vince—wanted me to be.

Fortunately, along the way I also found the woman that *I* wanted to be, and as I walked into the E! building that day in Hollywood, with its large doors and polished floors, only one thought ran through my mind: *Oh shit, is that Khloe Kardashian?*

I nearly dislocated both my eyeballs to find out as I kept my head forward but ordered my eyes to dart to my extreme right. And yes, it was her striding out as I was walking in. This caused me to have two further thoughts: *That's cool.* And. *Oh, I could easily suplex her.*

I was still in the dark about who else made it on to the cast as I was ushered past offices, smiling faces, and people dressed in business casual crisscrossing each other with scripts in hand. I knew Vince wanted me in; now all I had to do was impress the E! side of the partnership and I was a lock. You always have the job until you don't have the job. It's definitely yours until it's not. And that thought made me even more anxious, because I didn't want to go back to WWE having not gotten the job, after Vince went out on a limb for me.

I was brought into a very nice office where a man called Jeff Jenkins waited to greet me. Jeff was the mind behind *The Simple Life with Paris Hilton and Nicole Richie* and *Keeping Up with the Kardashians.*

He was warm, focused, and super professional, but he had that Hollywood producer energy—like he was ready to sum you up in ten seconds flat. We talked about my time in the ring, my family, and my frustrations about sometimes feeling overlooked in the women's division. I told him how I was tired of scratching and clawing for every inch of airtime—how I felt the fans hadn't really gotten to see me in a proper storyline that showcased my personality.

When our conversation ended, he had this huge grin on his face. "You nailed it," he said, standing up and extending a hand. "You're fascinating. You're open, you're honest, and you clearly have a unique life story. I love, love, love the energy you brought. We absolutely want you on the show."

I tried not to show my relief, but inside, I felt like screaming. I was so happy. For once, something big was happening *for* me rather than *around* me.

My next stop was a photoshoot at the other side of the building, where I finally got to meet my fellow castmates. I knew some of them from backstage chatter, like Trinity and Ariane (Cameron from the Funkadactyls). But the real shock was seeing Brie and Nikki Bella walk in.

They'd taken almost a year off from WWE because they were frustrated by their lack of opportunities on the main roster, so I had no clue they'd be returning—especially not to star in a reality show. But it immediately made sense, as they had the name value, media savvy, and unique look and personalities to really help us stand out as a new show.

Then Jeff, the producer, told us all that WWE and E! were adding two newcomers, Eva Marie and JoJo Offerman, who knew nothing about wrestling, so that they could film their fish-out-of-water reactions to our crazy world of slams, backstage politics, and 5 AM workouts. The producers loved the idea of blending established personalities and up-and-coming performers to help build storylines that fans would love.

"Listen, we're planning an eight-episode show," Jeff told us as we were getting our pictures taken, "but we're only going to shoot a pilot to see how it goes. If it does well, then we'll do more, but you guys have to hit a home run with this."

All of us girls had been in pressure situations our whole careers. We knew what the network needed, and we knew we'd have to pour our hearts into it to give them the material. And that's what we wanted. We wanted this show to go mainstream.

But we couldn't do it alone.

We'd have to rely on the people in our lives to help us get it there.

I had no idea what was happening in everyone else's lives, but I knew in my chaotic life there would be no end to the drama reality TV loves, and I was worried because that wasn't something I could sanitize and control. Because reality TV, for all its glitz, can expose every flaw and amplify every argument. I knew we'd all be stepping into each other's personal business—and bringing along a camera crew while we did it.

All these kinds of reality shows leaned heavily on the cast's personal relationships, and the producers loved that Brie and Nikki were in relationships with two main-event WWE guys, Daniel Bryan and John Cena. Trinity was with John Fatu—the tag-team legend known as Jimmy Uso—and Ariane, at that time, was dating someone who wasn't in the wrestling business at all.

On my end, TJ and I had been living together since we were teenagers, and had known each other longer than that, which in a show full of short- and medium-length relationships made our dynamic unique—especially in a business where bonds can be tested by constant travel, injuries, and creative ups and downs.

So, between the seven of us and our significant others, all the ingredients were there for those raw moments the camera needed: arguments, emotional breakdowns, humor, big announcements, and more.

As I stepped away from the lights of the shoot for a second, I took in where I was and what we were about to do. The world was in the middle of a cultural shift when it came to women's sports, and the women in WWE had felt it too. It was the topic of not just our conversations but also those in the mainstream media. Female stars were making serious names for themselves in tennis and gymnastics and soccer and basketball and a bunch of other sports, and lots of organizations and leagues were finally noticing.

We could all see that something was changing, but this was the first time it felt like WWE and Vince saw it too. The world wanted to see more women highlighted.

And that's the moment it sank in: we had to make this show count—not just for us as individuals, but for every female wrestler who'd ever been told her segment was "too long" or that fans only cared about the guys. If we could succeed here, maybe we'd kick open some doors that had been closed for far too long. Maybe we'd usher in a new era.

Or maybe we'd crash and burn.

Either way, we were going to give it everything we had to find out.

MY WEDDING

TJ and I just wanted a normal wedding.

Well, as normal as you can get on a reality TV show.

Well, as normal as you can get on a reality TV show when you have a family like mine.

Actually, we never wanted a normal wedding at all.

We never wanted *any* wedding.

But in the spring of 2013, Russell Jay, one of the *Total Divas* producers, asked us if a summer wedding in Florida was something we'd consider.

We'd been filming the show for a few months at that point, and E! was so happy with the footage they were getting that they extended our first season to fourteen episodes before the first ones even aired. Russell was looking for the perfect finale to the season, and he thought it was fascinating that TJ and I still just kinda hung out together like we did when we were teenagers, and never took that last step that most long-term couples do.

"What do you guys think?" Russell asked. "We'd pay for everything, and make sure you guys got the best wedding you could imagine. If it's something that's on your radar anyway, why not let us take care of it?" Russell's offer was very generous.

When TJ and I sat down and talked about it, it wasn't really from

He quickly pocketed the gummies when he saw me coming, and scurried into the mansion.

"No, wait!" I was in hot pursuit! "Daddy?!"

As I hurried to the front door, I kind of felt a weird sense of pride that it was *only* gummies, compared to what else he could have been buying on my special day. Like, for my dad, this was his best behavior.

I quickly entered the house . . . and immediately slipped into the splits.

Oh my God. What is that on the floor!?

My dad peered around the corner to see what the commotion was, his mouth already full of gummies.

"Where's . . . your shoes?" I was going to ask about his dealer, but in the five seconds it had taken to catch up to him, he'd somehow managed to get barefooted.

"I don't know. Can you find them for me?" he asked, munching on his THC like a confused bull chewing cud over a fence.

But my attention was pulled to the developing scene behind him—crew members hurrying around with disinfectant spray and wipes.

"Is everything okay?" I asked them.

"It's the cat. The house is like a crime scene."

"What's the cat?" I asked.

In the show, our cats had been stealing all my scenes, so Russell had the idea that my cat, Gismo, should come along to our wedding and be my ring bearer. They even sent a last-second limo service to my house to get him. Thing was, I didn't know this at the time, but poor Gismo wasn't well. He had an upset stomach and terrible diarrhea and everyone kept insisting on picking him up, which was making matters worse.

Oh, that's what I slipped in.

"Where is he now?" I asked as I hurried toward the back of the house, but nobody seemed to know.

our point of view that we looked at it. We never felt like we needed to take more steps—we were each other's person, and neither of us is the traditional type, needing a ring or a name change to prove our love for the other. But as we fleshed it out, we talked about how much fun it had been for my dad to be on the show in the past, and how much he'd love being father of the bride in the big season finale.

At this point E! was convinced *Total Divas* would be a hit for them, and it was important to me that the show be as big as it could be because it would let WWE know that women on their roster could draw audiences to watch them, just like their male talent did. But on a more personal level, having the show succeed would allow me to feature my dad in my scenes, which helped him feel like he mattered again. I could see him light up when the cameras were on him, and I loved that so much for him. Just being back in the creative mix really helped him find meaning in his life after wrestling had moved on from him. And to see him find purpose again was a gift to my whole family that I wanted to keep going as long as I could.

So a wedding it was.

TJ and I loved each other and planned on spending the rest of our lives together anyway, so we figured why not just do it? If someone else was willing to arrange it and pay for it, then it'd just be a stress-free party surrounded by friends and family in the beautiful Florida sunshine.

At least that's what we thought.

The day started off perfectly as I drove up to the twenty-million-dollar mansion E! had rented for the big day in Sarasota. The sun was warm, the sky blue. I felt a sense of calm that . . . suddenly disappeared when I saw my dad standing outside the front door holding a bag of THC gummies.

"Daddy!" I whisper shouted at him as I stumbled out of my car. "There's cameras everywhere!"

I strode from room to room, passing by thousands of dollars of my favorite flowers, peonies, courtesy of E!, and saw my mom laughing hysterically outside the bathroom, where my younger sister was stuck inside thanks to a faulty lock. "Can you help Daddy find his shoes?" I asked her as I continued toward the back to find Gismo.

He must be with TJ.

Russell passed by quickly, looking flustered. "There's a hurricane coming this way, so we need to get everyone ready ASAP." Then he slipped as he made his way back around the corner.

Gismo had let loose on every flat surface in the house.

I hurried from window to window looking outside for TJ. I was a little worried about him in a tuxedo in the Florida heat. He's so muscular that nothing seems to fit him quite right and he hates wearing clothes on the best of days, and this day it was super muggy both inside and out.

And then I saw him, my soon-to-be husband, under our beautifully decorated arbor getting the Heimlich maneuver.

"TJ!" I shouted as I sprinted outside towards him.

As I got close, I heard the unmistakable pop of a chiropractic adjustment. And I recognized the other man as my dad's long-time best friend, Doug.

"Have you met our justice of the peace?" TJ asked, as Doug released him.

Doug waved.

"What the fuck?"

Turns out my dad had asked Doug, who was a chiropractor and had been giving out adjustments to all of our guests, to officiate our wedding based on certification he got from the internet. I love Doug. But with the day I was having, I didn't have a lot of love to spare.

"I think I'm going to die," TJ said as I pulled him aside. "It's so hot out here."

"*You're* going to die? Gismo has the stomach flu, my sister is locked in the bathroom, my dad is stoned and shoeless, there's a hurricane coming, and I'm getting married by my dad's fucking *chiropractor*!"

But we weren't done yet.

"OH, FOR GOD'S SAKE!" came a yell from inside the house.

And that's how I met the homeowner, carrying Gismo at arm's length like he was a bomb about to explode. Then I looked down at the man's suit and saw Gismo already had.

"He just went all over my bed too!" the exasperated homeowner announced.

As he approached, I pulled TJ into his path to handle it and just slipped away. I hadn't been expecting much from the day, in that I didn't feel like TJ and I needed it. But now that it was here, I certainly wanted it to be going a lot better than it was.

As I walked back through the house, I found my dad. I don't know whether it was the THC, or something he'd taken before he got to the house, but he was now not only shoeless, but shirtless and sweating profusely, with his head wrapped in my sister's Louis Vuitton scarf.

I couldn't take any more.

I turned on my heel, slipped, caught myself, then walked through the front door to get my dress from my car because, disaster or not, I was a pro, and this wedding was going to happen.

I found a little room upstairs to get changed and just sat there in silence, fighting tears, as the rumbles from the crew and my family organizing themselves got more frantic-sounding under my feet. I thought a wedding that was going to be handled by someone else would be a little more stress-free, but between the cat mess, the lost shoes, Doug, and the hurricane, I just needed a minute on my own.

And that's when a familiar voice came through the door to steady my thinking and settle my breathing. "I'm sorry, Nattie. But everything's going to be all right from here on," TJ whispered through the crack.

It reminded me of all the times he waited outside the bathroom at my grandparents' house while I purged my food in secret. It also reminded me that, TV show or not, this was the person I wanted to spend my life with.

"Okay," he continued, "maybe it won't be all right, but it won't be more than we can handle."

He was right. We'd lived through a lot together, but never more than we could handle. And his words, as usual, made me swing from being stressed out to just not worrying so much. Even if it all went up in flames, at least it would make good TV.

Suddenly, I went from not caring about us getting married to that being all I cared about. Let the hurricane come—we'd still be together when it was gone.

By the time I put on my wedding dress and opened the door, somehow everything had gelled. My dad found his shoes and clothes, Gismo was fully emptied and ready for showtime, and Doug performed a surprisingly great ceremony.

Somehow, everything was all right.

But it was the reception where everything really came together. That was where everything went from chaos to closeness as my dad and I danced together, the cameras catching every moment. He was relaxed, smiling, and completely in his element—drinking his favorite drink, Jack Daniel's straight up, surrounded by people making a fuss over him. For a brief moment, it wasn't about the show or the ratings or his injuries or our differences.

It was just me and him, enjoying a moment I'll never forget.

I remember taking it in, as a woman who'd never felt surrounded by happiness and family like this before. I knew it was a rare thing for us. But on that day, in that moment, I felt happier and more loved than I ever had before.

Looking back, I'm glad I was wise enough to savor that memory. Because even back then, I couldn't shake the feeling that we'd never be as happy again, all together as a family.

Unfortunately, I was right.

PART FOUR

TAKEOVER

The wrestling business has a habit of repeating. If you look close enough at the talent and their journeys, you begin to see patterns, or types. If you're one of the very few lucky enough to survive the churn, you might even see someone who reminds you of yourself. Or, to be more precise, someone whose journey reminds you of your own.

For me, that person was Charlotte Flair.

And when I met her, she told me that's how she felt about me too.

As much as I loved doing *Total Divas*, I was a wrestler, not a reality TV star. I wanted to remind the world what I could do in that ring more than anything. And my shot came from Triple H and the work he was doing in building a third brand after *Raw* and *SmackDown*, called *NXT*.

The name *NXT* had been with WWE in different guises over the years, but this iteration of the name referred to WWE's new in-house developmental brand, which aimed to find the best new talent in the world and give them a place to cultivate their talent "off Broadway."

NXT wasn't just a show, it was also a state-of-the-art facility in Florida called the Performance Center that housed a gym, wrestling rings, trainers, and medical facilities. It was kinda similar to the developmental program I started out in—but much more elaborate, cutting edge, and structured. This was a no-expense-spared developmental system modeled after how other major sports franchises developed their future talent.

With this new developmental brand came a weekly TV show, and a monthly PPV, in front of a live audience that sought to replicate, at a much smaller scale, the feel of being on WWE's main roster. And within that TV show and developmental system, the *NXT* women's roster was making serious waves for themselves. Importantly, they were doing it by being treated differently than the main roster women—and by differently, I mean equally. Equal time, equal storylines, and equal opportunities to main event talent as any of the guys.

And the one that stood out from the pack for WWE was another daughter of a legend—Ric Flair's daughter Charlotte.

Charlotte had that second-generation aura—she carried the famous Flair name—while also forging her own path. And to cement her rise through the ranks, Triple H wanted a credible, familiar veteran to take her on at a time when everyone could see she was poised to become a major star.

When Hunter approached me about a match with Charlotte to crown the first-ever *NXT* women's champion on their inaugural *Take-Over* PPV, I jumped at the opportunity. I'd been paying close attention to *NXT*, and how the women there were getting more ring time—Paige and Emma had already put on a solid fifteen-minute match that turned a lot of heads. It showed me there was hope for more meaningful women's wrestling, and I was hungry for exactly that. So when Hunter said, "We want you to face Charlotte to crown our first women's champion," I was ecstatic. This might have been a developmental territory, but I knew the match could be special.

The word on Charlotte was that she had the athleticism but, only a year into her professional wrestling career, could still get rattled in high-pressure spots, and that's why Hunter had thought of me—I was the type of veteran who'd rather make the match great than just "get my stuff in." It was a chance to highlight Charlotte's potential while giving me a spotlight in a brand that was on the rise.

The idea was to frame our match as a generational clash, paying homage to our legendary wrestling families. We were the daughters of legacy, Charlotte and I, and having two legacy wrestlers facing off for a championship would add a layer of prestige to what was already shaping up to be a landmark *NXT* match. Hunter wanted each of us to have a family representative in their corner. For me that night, it was Bret Hart; for Charlotte, it was Ric Flair.

I'd wanted my dad there, but about a week before the event, he suffered a massive seizure that lasted fifteen minutes—what they call a "grand mal"—that turned him purple and left him in a coma for two days. While we wouldn't realize it until later, after my dad died, that seizure was another symptom of the hippocampal sclerosis that had been quietly ravaging his brain for years. So were the memory loss, difficulty learning new information, confusion, and mood swings my dad had been struggling with.

That week I rushed between hospital visits and planning sessions for *NXT*, worried people would think I was distracted. Seeing my dad in a coma was horrifying, but I was trying to keep it together; I didn't want the company to pull me from the match. This was the big opportunity I'd been waiting for in WWE, and I didn't want to lose the chance to prove myself. So I carried the stress silently and poured my heart into the match, hoping I could make my dad proud when he came back around.

We had one rehearsal for the match at the Performance Center where I really got to see where Charlotte was at in her development. I love to get in the ring with new opponents to move around and talk with them—to hear their ideas and bring my own ideas to the table. I wanted to lock up with her, to feel her reaction, and to learn how she moved, how she danced in the ring. I can tell so much about a person's ability by how they lock up with me.

And right away, when we locked up, I knew this could be special.

We had great chemistry. But what I really liked about her was that she was very respectful to the process and let me lead in the veteran role. She was wide open to all of my ideas, and she listened intently to why I was suggesting we do what we do, and when to do it.

I could see she was just very eager to learn.

I could also see the vulnerability in her that a great wrestler needs, to be able to connect with audiences in a deeper way.

We'd first met months before, when she was brand new to the system. As she was introducing herself, she talked about how much we had in common and immediately opened up to me about feeling like she wasn't good enough, or pretty enough, or overall *enough*. And I remember telling her that those are totally normal things to feel, coming from such a huge family name and legacy. I knew intimately what she was going through and what she was feeling, because our starting points and paths were so similar.

That initial meeting bonded us, and when we met again months later to do this match, I could see her vulnerability was still there, but she also had a growing confidence, which made me so happy to see.

During the rehearsal we had for the match, Charlotte was such a pleasure to work with. I never told her what was happening in my life, but the whole experience really helped me take my mind off my dad for a little while. I knew she was going through a tough time herself, with her brother Reid having passed away the year before from a drug overdose, and I hope it did the same for her.

I knew that no matter what was going on in our personal lives, we were both determined to tear the house down when we hit that ring.

On the day of the match, I couldn't help but wish I'd been able to have my dad there with me, since Charlotte's dad Ric—one of the greatest ever—was going to be ringside. Luckily for me, my family pool is deep in this business, so I was honestly thrilled to have Bret in my corner, although in my heart, I wished my dad could be there.

Whenever Bret is around, I'm extra motivated to deliver. He has such high standards for everyone's work—especially his own—that it makes me want to reach or surpass his expectations. Knowing he'd be watching from ringside, I felt the urge to make him proud. But that pride also came with a mountain of nerves.

Ric, meanwhile, was clearly so proud of his daughter, but just as clearly still in deep mourning from losing his son. Just minutes before our match, I saw Charlotte and Ric crying together backstage, overcome by memories of Reid. Charlotte's makeup was streaking; Ric was very teary-eyed.

Hunter pulled me aside and said, "Please help keep her calm. Keep this train on the tracks." His trust in me to guide her through the emotional storm and ensure we didn't implode from the weight of everything was a lot of pressure, but I was moved that he believed in my ability to lead.

Backstage, the atmosphere was electric. *NXT TakeOver* events were a newer concept then, but you could already tell they meant something special. Everyone was dressed up, from talent to management, and there was a certain pride in the air. Hunter brought in legends like Pat Patterson to watch and give feedback. Bret and Ric were pacing around from nerves and excitement, while Charlotte and I tweaked spots in our heads to make sure we had the finish perfect.

Just before I went out, I asked Hunter how long we had for the match; I wanted to be sure we weren't about to get cut for time. He looked at me and said, "You don't have a time limit. Just paint the story you want to paint. We trust your judgment. Take as long as you need." In all my years, nobody had ever said that to me. Usually, it was

"You've got two minutes," or "Your match is cut in half because we ran over on the last segment." Knowing I had the freedom to let the match breathe was both exhilarating and terrifying. I had to make the most of it.

I knew my role, and Hunter had given us the tools we needed to deliver. Charlotte was new, gifted, and athletic; she just needed someone to guide the narrative. And I took pride in that role. I saw what she brought to the table—raw energy, genuine emotion, and that intangible "it" factor. And my job was to harness her spark as we told the story of a hungry rookie feeling the weight of a massive legacy and a veteran desperate to show she could still headline a major match. For me, it was a *WrestleMania* moment, but in front of just a couple hundred fans.

We both came in with something to prove, and we poured every ounce of that emotion into the match. Charlotte had pitched a brilliant spot for the match where she'd put me in the Sharpshooter, facing Bret. It oozed drama—Ric Flair's daughter stealing a signature move right in front of the man who made it famous. That moment exemplified what we wanted: a clash of two families, but also two individuals blazing their own trails.

The match was more than a collection of moves—it was pure emotion. Charlotte carried the grief and determination of someone who'd just lost her brother. I brought the frustration and eagerness of a wrestler who'd spent her career chained to two-minute segments, dance-offs, and frivolous gimmick matches, and the pain of someone who was scared for her father's life.

We both had our own very personal reasons for wanting to show that women could wrestle full-length, deeply personal stories. And we wanted the fans to feel our passion, the raw grit, and the sense we both had that this match really mattered.

Nobody expected a women's match to steal the show, but we were determined to do it anyway. *NXT* was the perfect platform, because Hunter believed in giving women time and trust—two things we rarely got on the main roster. I knew this match had a chance to make a statement.

And it did.

We did.

The second we walked backstage after the match, there was this rush of energy. Everyone—management, the crew, other wrestlers—was clapping and cheering. Charlotte was swept into a whirlwind of tears, hugs, and interviews. It was her moment, and I was proud of her. She was no longer just Ric Flair's kid—she was well on her way to becoming her own icon.

I have to admit I felt a bit invisible in the celebration, but I was also thrilled we'd delivered something people wouldn't forget. Charlotte and I had told an unforgettable story together.

I slipped away for a second in the middle of the hug fest to find Bret; I needed his reaction more than anyone else's. He smiled, gave me a hug, and said, "That was great"—which might not sound like much, but from Bret, it's pure gold.

Looking back, that match stands as one of the most important of my career. It proved I could be the ring general I'd always wanted to be. It also marked a shift in women's wrestling, especially in WWE. It was more proof that women could wrestle more than a few novelty spots. We could captivate an audience and deliver a match layered with history and emotion.

For me, that night will always be the one where I said, *Here I am. I can do this.* Even though I'd wrestled on bigger stages, nothing felt as monumental as stepping into that ring at *NXT TakeOver*, with Bret and Ric on either side, and telling the crowd, *We deserve to be here.* It was more than a match. It was a proclamation.

Though WWE remained reluctant to push it, something really

interesting was beginning to stir when it came to the women's division, and I was just glad I'd managed to hang on long enough to ride the wave that I could feel swelling.

Women around the world were suddenly box office and ratings draws, in a host of other sports and entertainment fields. The timing was right for WWE on its main roster shows to finally give women their chance to be equal, and I was ready to do my part.

Fortunately, the fans were too.

My grandfather Stu as a young wrestler. He hand-beaded the belt he's wearing.

A rare photo of Stu wrestling.

Stu wrestling Eddie King for Toots Mondt in New York City in 1948.

My grandmother Helen, the original Queen of Harts, in her younger years. No one was more charming, smart, or beautiful than she was.

Stu and Helen Hart in the 1940s.

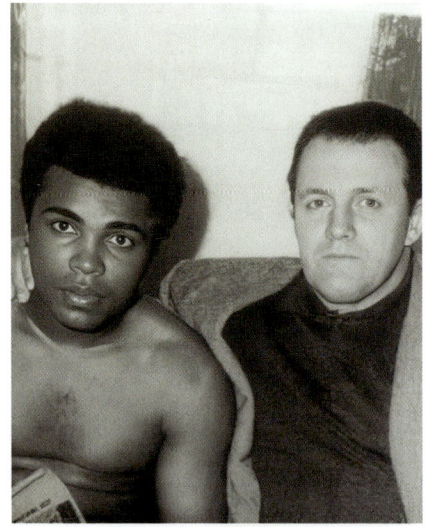

Stu with Gorgeous George and his wife Betty. George and Stu were very good friends.

Stu and Muhammad Ali in 1972 in Calgary. Stu was one of the first wrestling promoters that Ali met, and they had a really great connection and mutual respect.

The first photo ever taken of the Hart House, featuring soldiers who stayed at the house during World War I.

The Hart House as it stands today. People travel from all over the world to drive by the house and see what it looks like.

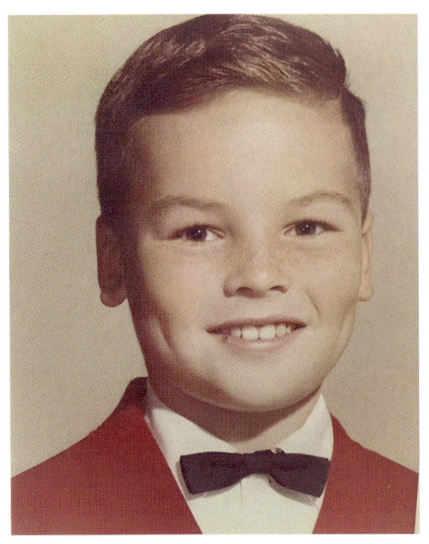

My dad at eight years old. I always thought we looked alike!

My dad at fifteen, when he was playing football in high school.

My dad (middle) during his shot put days, when he was ranked the number one shot-putter in the nation and number five in the world. My dad was a world-class athlete!

RESUMÉ

JIM NEIDHART
3972 Jewell S-308
San Diego, California 92109
(714) 272-6979

Age — 24
Height — 5'11½"
Weight — 275 lbs.
Birthdate — Feb 8, 1955
Eyes — Brown
Hair — Red

ATHLETIC HISTORY

High School - Newport Harbour High 1973
    Football - All County, All-State and All America Tackle
    Track - Shotput 1973 United States National Champion (69'3¾")
        All-America Track Team

College - UCLA (1973 - 1977)
    Track - Shotput - ranked 5th in world (1975)

Professional Football - Defensive tackle Super Bowl Champion Dallas Cowboys 1978
    (among last cuts)

Professional Wrestling - 1978 to present. Outstanding heavyweight wrestler on
    Western Canadian and California circuits

STRENGTH

Weightlifting Totals

Bench Press — 570 lbs.
Squat   — 689 lbs.
Power Clean — 405 lbs.
Incline Bench — 485 lbs.
Power Snatch — 300 lbs.

* Neidhart is considered to be the strongest man in professional football
   (NFL or CFL) and will challenge any football player in strength or power-
   lifting contests

SPEED

40 yard dash - 4.7 sec.
1½ mile run - 11 min. 50 sec.

MEDICAL

clean, no significant athletic injuries ever

My dad's résumé from 1980, shortly after he started wrestling.

My mom and dad three months after they met. My mom is wearing a shirt that my dad gave her from when he played for the Oakland Raiders.

My mom and dad on a fishing trip during the good 1980s. I love this picture of them in happy times.

My sisters and me on a staircase inside the Hart House, holding a doll of my dad that my mom made, during the summer of 1988.

My sisters and me with my mom at a dance recital. I really loved performing even at a young age.

Our childhood home in Land O' Lakes, Florida. It always looked like a spaceship to me when I was young!

My dad smiling during happier times with a bottle of champagne and his favorite Rolex watch. He loved drinking Moët & Chandon.

My sisters and me with Brutus Beefcake, who was a close friend of my dad.

My dad posing with Big Bird, aka Rick Rude, one of my dad's best friends.

Randy Savage visiting our house when we were kids, pictured here with my mom and dad and my aunt Georgia. We always had really fun houseguests growing up.

Me with all of my cousins and my grandparents
at the Hart House for Sunday dinner.

The wrestling ring on the Hart House lawn. In this photo,
TJ and my cousin Harry are practicing for a match.

TJ and my cousins Matt, Annie, and Angie in the kitchen of the Hart House.

TJ, pictured with my cousin Ted, at ten years old, the year TJ first met our family.

My cousin Matt, pictured on the lawn of the Hart House just a few months before he tragically passed away. Matt was so handsome.

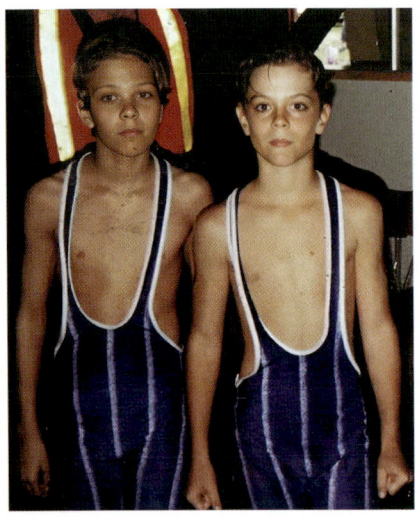

TJ and Harry in 1995. This was TJ's very first match.

Me and TJ during our Matrats days.

TJ training with world-famous wrestling coach Tokyo Joe in the Dungeon in 2004.

My dad and Bret in their early Hart Foundation years in WWE.

My dad and Bret high-fiving each other. My dad loved Bret like a brother.

My dad, Bret, and Owen in the ring right after the infamous Montreal Screwjob in 1997.

My uncles Davey, Owen, and Bret and my dad—four of the very best— during a photo shoot for WWE.

My dad and me the night we teamed up together in 2005, before I got signed by WWE.

Backstage at the Saddledome in 1997, during the WWE *In Your House* PPV, with my sisters and Vince McMahon.

Me and Dr. Tom at his wrestling school in Knoxville, Tennessee. Tom taught me so much about wrestling and how to be my best both in and out of the ring.

Me with Fit Finlay, who has been a huge influence in my life and has a heart of gold.

Me with Nicole and Brie, the Bella Twins, while we were filming *Total Divas*.

Me and Cherry now. She is still one of my best friends today.

From my infamous road trip/ dinner with the Great Khali. What a great friend.

Doing a surfboard submission on Michelle McCool in the first-ever Divas Championship match in 2008.

I loved wrestling Eve Torres, and I loved our time on the road together. I was always the villain in our matches together, but that didn't mean we weren't having the best time ever competing in the ring.

Putting Michelle and Layla in a Sharpshooter at the same time during the first-ever women's table match in 2010. This match was so fun!

The night that I won the Divas Championship in 2010, celebrating with Beth Phoenix. Beth has helped me so much in my career.

Wrestling Charlotte Flair in 2014 at WWE's first *NXT TakeOver* event—one of my favorite matches.

Hugging Lacey Evans during the first-ever women's performance of any kind in Saudi Arabia in 2019— a truly transcendent moment for women in sports across the globe.

Backstage as champion on *Smackdown*. I love those girls and I was so proud of how far we had all come in the women's division!

Me and Ronda Rousey locking up a year before she came to WWE. We've always had a special connection in and out of the ring.

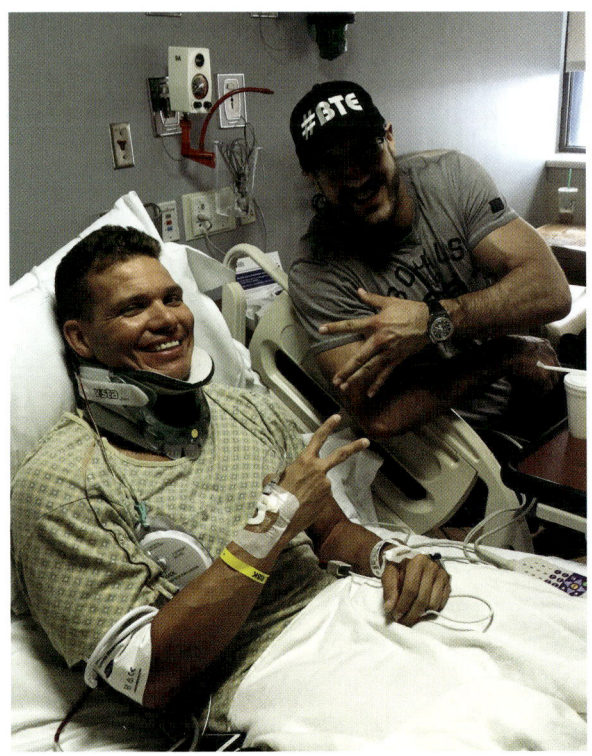

TJ and Cesaro right after TJ's spinal fusion surgery. Cesaro was there for him during his darkest hours.

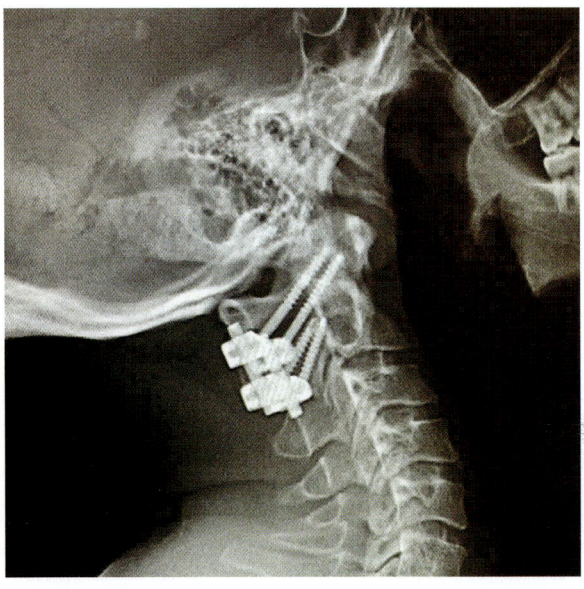

An x-ray of TJ's neck after C1–C2 spinal fusion surgery.

I love this picture of my dad and me in happier times.

My dad with his grandsons (my nephews) Lachlan and Maddox.

My dad and me with Billy Corgan a week before my dad passed away. It was the last thing we did together, and my dad was so alive that night. My dad really loved Billy's music, and Billy is a close friend who believed in me from the start.

My dad and Bret at the last *Wrestlemania* that my dad would attend. I remember taking this photo of them and knowing just how special it would be.

Me and Bret inducting the Hart Foundation into the WWE Hall of Fame in 2019. This was taken *after* Bret had gotten attacked onstage during his speech.

With my mom, who is my rock. She's truly the best and has never let me down.

With my mom and my sisters. I'm so proud of them. We make the best team, since day one.

With Bret, who's always had my back, in Calgary.

With Lachlan and Maddox, my two beautiful nephews. They mean the world to me.

With my favorite person, TJ, backstage at WWE.

HASHTAG

Women's wrestling in WWE was building steam, even if the upper management failed to see it. My match with Charlotte was being talked about in the same glowing terms as any of the men's matches that year in terms of quality and drama, entertainment, and athleticism. But to anyone paying attention to *NXT*, it wasn't so surprising, as a lot of the women's matches there had been building quite the buzz too.

The fans were finally getting to see and enjoy the results of what our division could do when we were given the space and time to deliver, and boy, were they vocal about it online.

Thanks to the rise of social media, fans were better able than ever to both voice their support when they saw something they loved and sound the alarm when they saw something they didn't. All of a sudden it wasn't just fans in the stands who could make their voices heard at the top levels of the company—it was also fans online.

I saw the decision makers in WWE, one by one, start to spend more and more time on their phones at TV tapings and live events. They were getting immediate customer feedback on every match, segment, and show. And it just drove momentum for our cause as women wrestlers.

In early 2015, the Bella Twins went up against the two women who the fans had seen tear the house down in *NXT* about a year before—Emma and Paige. But that night these four women weren't given time and space to create magic. Instead, they were given just thirty seconds on a three-hour show to rush through a "match."

When the four women came back to the locker room, they were clearly livid. The look in their eyes just told you they'd been pushed over the line. They were sent out on live TV with no time to wrestle, or tell a story, or get heat, or do a comeback. Essentially, they were set up to fail, because no wrestler in the world can make something good out of such a short amount of time.

The question began to reverberate around our locker room: How could we get the people to care about us, when they got no time to connect to us?

I knew from working on *Total Divas* that when we're allowed time to build stories, and to develop personalities, we can bring eyeballs to the product. Our ratings proved that past any emotional or moral argument. It was just facts. But we were put out there, time and time again, in short, meaningless segments—because upper management made the mistake of thinking that if they didn't care about women's wrestling, then neither did their fanbase.

But they were wrong.

Very, very wrong.

Because the fans were enraged.

Within minutes of the Bellas, Emma, and Paige coming back to the locker room, the hashtag #GiveDivasAChance trended worldwide for days, with stats on how our division was featured compared to the men's roster being posted and reposted. Fans began to go back through our programming and tabulate how many matches per three-hour *Raw* and two-hour *SmackDown* our division was getting, and it was almost always just one, usually a two- or three-minute "cool down" match in between "important" men's matches.

With the increase in great women's matches in *NXT*, and the stagnation of opportunities on the main roster, suddenly the dam broke.

Current and former women's wrestlers posted their support of the movement, too, talking about their experiences of getting the same ratings as the guys, selling the same amount of merchandise as the guys, but not getting the same opportunities as the guys.

This wasn't an "us versus them" scenario with our male colleagues—they were just doing what they were told, same as us—but it was an "us versus them" in term of WWE's creative direction.

We just want to be treated equally.

In WWE in 2015, everyone got paid a downside guarantee, which was the lowest number you could expect to make in a year—just like they did when I first started out in 2008. But the women's downside wasn't anywhere near what the guys made.

Now, WWE is an attraction business, and none of the women expected to make what John Cena was making. He was simply pulling in more money for the company in PPV, tickets, and merchandise sales than anyone else, by a huge margin.

But it's hard to make money if you're not featured, and you can't be featured unless the company who employs you features you.

My downside was $150,000 a year—somewhere in the middle of the women's range—which meant that after I paid for taxes, my rental cars, gas, insurance, hotels, food on the road, gym memberships, hair treatments, costumes, and tanning I would take home $75,000 for four to five days a week on the road.

And because we had very little merchandise compared to the guys, the only way to top up our guarantee was to try to get on every show the company had, because you'd get a per-appearance bonus for each live event or PPV. And if you were a woman wrestler, you'd have to fight like hell just to get on those shows, because out of ten matches, our whole division would get only one.

That left us all fighting over that one match, because our salary depended on it.

I remember my very first *WrestleMania*, I got a check for $75, because prior to that appearance, they'd forgotten to take out tax from an Australian event I worked. But even with the taxes they took out, I would have only made $2,075—which is a small number for *WrestleMania* to begin with. In the mid-2010s, the guys on that show would get anywhere from $50,000 to $500,000 depending on their place on the card. My "usual" range for *WrestleMania* payments was $5,000 to $15,000.

Back then, WWE was a billion-dollar company, and between downside guarantees, merchandise payments, live event payoffs, and PPV bonuses, a lot of wrestlers were making millions because of it—but none of them were women.

A lot of us over many different years and eras had been putting the work in to make a moment like #GiveDivasAChance to surface. And with the fans firmly behind us, a lot of women began to become more defiant—to rage against the machine a little more.

Even Vince's daughter, Stephanie—then the chief brand officer of WWE, and someone who had genuinely been trying to change the culture from the inside—publicly acknowledged the outcry, tweeting her support of the fans using their voices in such a powerful and organized way.

But as the steam built, and the momentum continued, I couldn't help but feel a little scared of it all. These women who were leading the charge, I thought they were really brave to stand up to Vince. I'd had so much fear instilled in me growing up, from watching my dad lose what he loved and seeing the effect it had on him, that I always felt like I had to be the perfect company girl. I felt so much pressure to show WWE that I wasn't like my dad, and I was never going to miss a show, and I was always going to do what the promoter wanted, that I stayed silent.

If I spoke up, would I be let go? I was financially supporting myself and my mom and dad too. Would I get a call randomly on some Friday afternoon from someone in talent relations saying, "Sorry, Nattie, it's just budget cuts"? I knew what happened when someone was made jobless and homeless and suddenly without the thing that gave them purpose, and it wasn't something I ever wanted to live again.

I guess deep down I never felt good enough to be in WWE, and I was afraid that if I stood too tall, WWE would notice that too.

I genuinely wish I'd had the courage to say something publicly. I wish I'd been more ballsy, and had gone out there and talked about my experiences and stood up for myself and the women's division.

I'm still like that today; I sometimes settle for less than I know I'm worth because I don't want to make any waves. I don't want to put a foot out of place or do anything I'll end up regretting, and the fear of doing something wrong paralyzes me.

So, in that moment, women like me needed women like Paige and the Bella Twins and AJ Lee, who were now saying, *No, we need more*. Women who'd had enough, and who stood up and were like, *Fuck it, you guys want to cut all of our time? Well, we're going to go out there and do your thirty-second match, and then we're going to let everybody know how sick and tired we are of having our hands cuffed!*

Ronda Rousey had proven she was the biggest draw in combat sports when she was a UFC champion. The Women's FIFA World Cup broke records for attendance and viewership, with the US women's team winning the tournament. Serena Williams was at the peak of her career, and women athletes in many sports were breaking glass ceilings one after the other in the noisiest way possible.

Culturally, women were starting to demand more for themselves in sports and entertainment in general, and women's pay and representation were becoming a hot topic across all sports programming.

So, in a way, WWE *had* to do something. Vince had worked hard to take his company from being the ugly stepchild of the entertainment business to a mainstream, socially accepted franchise; if there was an empowering movement disrupting other organizations, then he wasn't going to be left behind. And even though the hashtag was a product of his own attitude toward women's wrestling, Vince the storyteller and marketer could also see the feel-good story waiting to happen, if he gave the people what they wanted.

He may have helped cause the current frustration among the fans, but that didn't mean he couldn't take their money fixing it too.

WWE even went public and asked the fans for their patience while they made adjustments to their approach to women's wrestling, through calling up some of the women who had been blowing the roof off *NXT* and retooling the amount of time and opportunities per show our division got across all brands. And for the first time since I'd signed my first WWE contract eight years before, I felt that what I hoped and dreamed for would actually become a reality.

I'd gotten a taste of what could happen when we were afforded the time and space in *NXT* with Charlotte, and now it looked like those same opportunities were coming to the main roster.

WWE called it the Women's Revolution. And it was made for someone like me.

But when it did arrive, I was left out of it.

I guess it was because of what happened to TJ.

THE DARK MATCH

June 1, 2015, was a pretty standard day. About six months before, TJ had started tagging with another amazing wrestler called Cesaro. I then joined their team as their on-screen manager, and the three of us began traveling together. That day, we were in San Antonio, and arrived at the AT&T Center at around 1 PM to find out that we weren't wrestling on the show that night. Instead, we were scheduled to film a TV advertisement for a national fast-food chain.

Both TJ and Cesaro were workhorses, so they always preferred to wrestle than to have a night off. But the Elimination Chamber PPV had been the day before, and TJ and Cesaro had a strong showing on that card, so TJ figured it might not be the worst thing ever to take a little time to recover.

After we filmed our commercial, I said I'd like us to get some pictures backstage to keep our group looking like a group. Cesaro had had special jackets made for us (which we still have to this day), white and black with red trim with "B.T.E." printed on the back. B.T.E. stood for "Best Team Ever," which is what we'd named our group. I mean *we* as in just us; it wasn't an official WWE thing. I wanted to use the power of social media to get our messaging out—especially since we wouldn't get the chance to do it live on TV that night. We all really believed in our team and wanted it to be featured in fans' minds even if they didn't see us on TV every week.

TJ made a coffee and left it in the dressing room near his bags to drink later, when he'd return to watch the show after humoring me with the pictures I wanted. But before we could go anywhere, a senior WWE producer came to TJ at around 6:10 PM and said Vince wanted TJ in the ring in twenty minutes. The non-televised matches started at 6:30 for the people live in the building—an opportunity that WWE used to assess talent they were interested in without the bright lights of TV shining on them. I always just called them "dark matches."

TJ immediately told the producer that there was no time. He wasn't in ring gear and hadn't warmed up, because they told him he wasn't going to be wrestling that night. But word came that Vince was adamant: he wanted to see the *NXT* standout, wrestling veteran Samoa Joe, in the ring that night, and he wanted TJ in there with him. It wasn't a surprise that he wanted TJ, because TJ made everyone look like a million bucks. He was that good.

TJ was upset, and not just because he was a perfectionist. He was well aware of what could happen to wrestlers who weren't warmed up—tears, fractures, pulled muscles, and worse. He was also annoyed because he'd never wrestled Joe before. TJ was a student of the game, so he knew *of* Joe, but didn't know him personally, so they'd need to talk to figure out what they were going to do out there. With so little time before the match, this would be a wrestler's version of flying blind—winging it, or "calling it in there," as we say.

But more messengers were sent to relay that it *had* to be TJ. It was clear to him that he wasn't getting out of this. So, with only fifteen minutes to bell time, TJ rushed to the locker room to put on his gear. He was so rushed that he even forgot to take off the cross he was wearing around his neck that day.

I remember TJ pulling his kick pads up, walking to the holding area just behind the curtain—a spot we call "Gorilla" after the late, great Gorilla Monsoon, who used to sit there overseeing the shows back in the day—and I could see he wasn't happy at all. He'd always had a very strict warmup routine of push-ups, jumping squats, and band work, along with taking a niacin supplement that helped keep his body warm by heating the blood.

That night, he got to do none of it.

It was in Gorilla—where Vince also ran the shows from his monitors—that TJ and Joe met for the first time and quickly tried to figure out what Joe wanted to do. TJ knew upper management's eyes were on Joe, and if it went well, Joe would get his start on the main WWE roster. That was something TJ wanted for Joe, so he really wanted the match to work out.

Everyone knew the point of the match was to make Joe look great, but as far as how to do that, Joe and TJ had just minutes to come up with some sort of game plan. A few months earlier, TJ had safely taken a version of Joe's finishing move from another wrestler, so he wasn't concerned about using it in the match. Joe was going to win, and they both agreed it made sense for him to do it with his Musclebuster finishing move. There wasn't time to worry about the move or planning anyway; as soon as TJ's music hit, he had to go through the curtain and just do the best he could with the limited time he had to prepare.

Cesaro and I came through the curtain behind TJ, and I watched him trying to warm up his various muscle groups as he walked to the ring in front of the crowd of about ten thousand people.

TJ was a pro, and he and Joe got through a great match, calling everything in the ring, like two skilled dancers putting together a whole routine on the fly. The guys were so into it at one point that word came back from someone in upper management, who was watching on the monitor in Gorilla, that they could see them talking to each other, and to hide it better. But this was a dark match, never to be seen on TV, and they had to communicate with each other somehow.

They moved into the finish of the match, where Joe would hoist TJ into a suplex position, then lock his hands behind TJ's knees, compressing TJ into the fetal position, before Joe did what he and TJ agreed he'd do—explode backwards, taking them both to the mat.

But when TJ hit the mat, he was instantly paralyzed.

TJ told me later that for about ten seconds, he couldn't feel or move anything on his body, and a blinding white light flashed across his eyes, before he felt an unbelievably crushing weight on his chest, like he had 2,000 pounds on top of his chest. He said the white light he saw when he hit the mat was the brightest thing he had ever seen.

I knew immediately TJ was hurt, and hurt badly. After watching him work for years, and being in the ring with him countless times myself, I knew from the way TJ was lying that he wasn't just "selling" a move.

He was lying on the canvas like a puppet with its strings cut. Cesaro reached under the bottom rope to grab TJ's leg—like they'd done as part of their act countless times before—but this time TJ shouted that nobody touch him. And then I heard him say the words that terrified me more than any words I'd heard in my life: "I can't move."

Cesaro and I immediately rushed into the ring, and as I got closer, I could see in TJ's eyes that he was furious and scared and confused all at once. I've seen TJ in matches since he was fifteen years old. There had been times when he'd been hit harder than usual, and I've seen him get his bell rung before, but this was different.

I felt frozen. I stood over his motionless body and put my hands over my ears. I was the most scared I'd ever been in my whole life. Everything moved in slow motion as the ref asked TJ if he was okay, and TJ just replied, "No."

TJ never said no. He was made of iron, always ready to brush off any nasty fall or injury. But this time was different.

TJ rolled to his side as his paralysis finally gave way to numbness. The ref asked again, and this time TJ answered, "I don't know." Then his hand went to the back of his neck. "No," he said, "I'm definitely not okay." Then the realization hit him, and he yelled, "I broke my fucking neck!"

His words shook me to my core. Time slowed down even more.

When TJ saw more referees coming to the ring to check on him, he pushed himself to his knees and hauled himself up using the ropes. "I don't want anyone without a medical license touching me," he said to the match referee. "Keep them away from me."

He grabbed the top rope to balance himself and looked for the "hard camera" in the stands—the camera that captures the wide shots for TV, and the camera that Vince watches the matches through—and he glared down the lens before turning to leave. "I just want to go home," he said before seesawing himself over the top rope and landing feet first on the floor.

Cesaro and I rolled out to meet him ringside.

"I thought you broke your neck?" Cesaro said.

"I did," TJ replied, limping away from the ring.

"Well, how did you do that?"

"I don't know."

TJ was in shock, and not thinking straight at all. As wrestlers, we'd seen other people break their necks in the ring before. We'd seen the aftermath, how the injured parties carried themselves and reacted. But TJ wasn't presenting himself like those other wrestlers. He was walking himself out of there, spitting fire, and wanting to go home.

"You want to head up the side ramp?" Cesaro asked TJ.

It was Cesaro's way of asking TJ if he wanted to avoid Gorilla, where Vince and the other producers were set up. Cesaro knew his tag partner would be walking straight into a situation that would lead to tensions escalating even higher for TJ.

"No, I *want* to see those fucks for the last time," TJ replied. "'Cause I know that was my last match ever."

He walked into Gorilla, where Joe tried to shake his hand. "This isn't about you right now," TJ said to him.

To this day, my heart also hurts for Samoa Joe, because the last thing in the world any of us want to do is have the person that we are wrestling get hurt, much less seriously injured.

Vince wasn't there in Gorilla, so TJ turned to the upper management instead. "I just broke my fucking neck, and I'm never going to be able to wrestle in this company ever again. You guys are so fucking stupid. The last thing I ever want from you is a flight home tonight. That's all I want. Just get me home." TJ was so angry because he was so scared.

Various levels of management and department heads tried to soothe TJ in Gorilla, but he just let them have it. He stood there cursing them all out over and over again, saying that he knew something bad was going to happen and repeatedly demanding a flight home.

When they just kept trying to soothe him, and not address his points, TJ stormed out of Gorilla, blowing past Hunter and Stephanie, who were going over a promo for the show. Two management guys followed behind, asking if TJ was okay, but he just ignored them, because it wasn't okay. And they were the same people who had encouraged him to wrestle that night despite his concerns.

When TJ got back to the locker room, Cesaro followed him in as I waited outside. TJ's now-cold coffee was still sitting there, and he sat down and slowly drank it. He knew his own body, and he knew whatever had just happened was the end for him; his career was over. He knew this was the last time he'd ever be in a wrestling dressing room as an active talent, so he took a few minutes in the eye of the storm to soak it in.

He just didn't know how severe it would turn out to be.

TJ loved the locker room. He felt it was an honor and a privilege to be among the tiny percentage of people who do what we do that actually make it to the big league. He knew he was respected there, and in turn he held that locker room in the highest respect. TJ didn't just like working as a wrestler. He *was* a wrestler. It was all he ever wanted to do since we met as kids. And he was amazing at it. He was a wrestler's wrestler. He was the guy that other wrestlers would talk about whenever the conversation turned to who they admired in their business. He'd fought hard to get to WWE and loved being part of the roster.

And now it was over.

As he sat there, his body turned from numbness to pain—like somebody had put a baseball through the top of his spine. He carefully took off his gear and made his way to the shower. Under the water, he wanted to crack his neck so bad for some relief, but he knew not to.

The pain kept intensifying.

One of the guys in upper management came into the dressing room when TJ hadn't reappeared in a while.

"Are you okay in there?" he shouted into the showers.

"Get the fuck out of here," TJ replied. "You guys didn't give a fuck about me before, so don't pretend you fucking care now. Just get me home."

Then Cesaro got in and played diplomat between TJ and management. He got them out of there, put a chair at the entrance to the showers, and sat there like he was TJ's personal security.

When TJ got out of the shower, the World's Strongest Man, Mark Henry, was there and told TJ that I was waiting for him in the hallway.

TJ just wanted to go. He didn't trust anyone in WWE to have his best intentions at heart. But when he got to the hallway, a representative from talent relations stopped him. He told TJ that if he didn't go to see the trainer, he'd never work at WWE again.

That just set TJ off again. "Are you an idiot?" he yelled back. "What the fuck are you doing threatening me with my own threat for? I told you I'm fucking done!"

And in stepped Cesaro again, to calm everything down. "You don't want to get on a flight like this. Let them check you so they can get you an ambulance."

When TJ left the dressing room, Cesaro and I convinced him to go to the trainer's room before getting on a flight. Because of how well they'd looked after other wrestlers with broken necks, we were sure that once WWE understood what bad shape TJ was in, he too would immediately receive the best medical care in the world.

But as with many other events that night, we had no idea just how close that decision would come to paralyzing TJ for life.

HANGMAN FRACTURE

In the trainers' room, they did a physical examination on TJ's head and neck, and TJ could barely move in any direction at all. His neck was on fire.

I had no idea why there were no paramedics there or what was happening—I just knew TJ needed help as soon as possible. So I hurried to the women's locker room in a state of shock and packed my bags as fast I could. Brie Bella and Summer Rae helped cram my things into any pocket or compartment that would take them.

TJ grabbed his stuff, too, and we both walked out to the big parking garage to my rental car.

The hospital was maybe six minutes from us. It felt like an hour's drive.

Every single bump, pothole, and red light was agony for TJ. I was so traumatized that I accidentally turned the wrong way down a one-way road. I had no idea where we were, or how to get to the hospital. I wasn't thinking right or seeing properly. I was just trying to make TJ's suffering stop. I couldn't stop crying no matter how hard I tried, but I was also trying hard to hide my tears so that TJ wouldn't feel more scared.

Eventually, we made it. I helped TJ out of the car to the check-in, where Cesaro was waiting. It was a smaller hospital, but they quickly admitted us to the emergency trauma section, where they did a CAT scan, then sat us in a small waiting room for what seemed like an eternity.

Then, out of nowhere, this SWAT team of EMTs burst in. "Sir," they said urgently, "we have to do an MRI and then transport you to a different hospital. Do you mind if we cut your shirt off?"

TJ replied, "I can take it off."

But their reaction to TJ's offer to remove his shirt scared me: they told him not to, in the same calm, steely tone that bomb experts use on civilians when one wrong move could kill them.

So we froze.

They asked me how we got to the hospital, and when I told them I drove, one of the EMTs replied, "Do you have any idea what could have happened?!"

"No," I said, "because we don't know what's wrong."

They immediately and very carefully put TJ in a neck collar and placed a brace in his mouth so he couldn't move a muscle.

With TJ a little more secure, they explained that typically there are three millimeters of space between the C1 and C2 vertebrae; TJ now had nine millimeters. Any movement at all could be extremely dangerous, especially because the gap was so high up his spine.

"Is he in danger of paralysis?" I quietly asked where TJ couldn't hear.

They said they needed to get him into an MRI machine to know more.

Later that night, the scans showed that the ligament that holds the C2 in place was ruptured. There was nothing holding those vertebrae in place, which meant TJ's head was being held in place by his neck muscles alone, and any movement in any direction could be catastrophic.

The transport ambulance took him immediately to the trauma center that could better deal with the issue. And that's where we waited, until a specialist in complex spinal injuries came to see us that morning after reading the MRI.

The first thing he said was, "We're going to have to do an emergency procedure and you'll never wrestle again. You need to find a new career."

TJ had told me the night before that he'd made peace with the fact that his wrestling days were done, but it was different hearing it so plainly from the doctor, though not without compassion. I saw Cesaro in the corner silently wipe a tear from his eye.

Seeing TJ so beaten down, tired, and scared made me step up. Since he'd landed on the mat the night before, a lot of decisions had been made on TJ's health and well-being that we had little or no say in. And I was growing sick of it.

"Are you the best?" I asked the doctor. "Because with what you're saying, as severe as this is, TJ needs the best."

"No, I wouldn't say I'm the best," he replied. No ego, just matter of fact. "I can do this procedure, but I wouldn't say I'm the best, no."

"Well then, no offense to you, but we need to find whoever is the best," I said. "We need to find the guy that you would go to if you found yourself or one of your family in our position today."

The doctor understood completely, and we were referred to Dr. Uribe, a leading spinal specialist, who just happened to be practicing in Tampa, where we lived. I was so relieved that the best was close to home. But the truth is, we would have gone anywhere if it meant getting the best care. We just had to wait for a medical airlift back to Florida, as there was no other way the hospital was comfortable transporting TJ.

So we sat there for three days, while TJ got more and more frustrated.

He wasn't on any painkillers, and he wasn't getting much sleep. The stress and fear and pressure just built and built until, on the third day of being stuck in that hospital room, and another day of no airlift coming—TJ began to plan his own way out.

He looked up a flight and told a hospital worker he was leaving. The guy pleaded with him to stay, but TJ was adamant that he could leave if he wanted to. He even said that he could drive the seventeen hours home, and that I could look after him there until he was called in for surgery.

I begged him to stay, too, until the best help became available, but TJ just wanted to run—to be home. He felt trapped in an unfamiliar place with no definite timeline on which this hell would end. So he was adamant he was leaving.

That was until a nurse told TJ exactly what he was dealing with. "You should have been paralyzed. You should have suffocated to death the second this injury happened because your C2 stabilizes your skull on your spine and your C1 plays a huge role in breathing," she said calmly. "You have what's known as the Hangman's Fracture. Your neck is the very same as someone who has been hung. Now, only five percent of people survive this type of injury, and of that five, ninety-nine percent end up quadriplegic, needing an air tube to breathe. But somehow you're alive and able to walk, which is a phenomenon. So please, just let us help you."

Her words were the most humbling ones TJ and I had ever heard.

We'd gotten the medical version—the technical version—already, but for some reason this was the version that hit home for us. TJ had a similar injury to the one that put Christopher "Superman" Reeve in a wheelchair and on a breathing tube after he fell from his horse. But for some reason, TJ was upright and moving. It seemed like the advice and training that Tokyo Joe had given us on building up the neck back when we were still in Calgary had saved TJ's life all these years later.

From that moment, TJ did whatever the medical professionals asked him to do. He told me that night that even though he knew he'd broken his neck, and he knew it was really bad, he also knew a lot of people in wrestling who had broken their necks and had been okay. You almost become a little desensitized. But this was entirely different. No one else in WWE had ever had a spinal fusion this high up, ever. TJ was in a boat all by himself.

He'd survived the fall; now he'd just have to survive the surgery.

Back in Tampa, Dr. Uribe explained to us that not only would he be trying to repair TJ's neck; he'd also have to work around an artery, and close to his spinal cord, to do it. "This surgery is very risky from a few different standpoints," he said.

But Dr. Uribe was not just a doctor, he was also a medical educator who trained other doctors to do this surgery—so we really had found the best person to take those risks with.

And that's all I would accept for TJ. I was like a lioness when it came to protecting him and making sure that he got the best care, because I could tell that his world was destroyed, and he couldn't protect or fight for himself just then. He didn't have the strength, mentally or physically. He needed me to do it for him.

So I fought, the way he'd fought for me so many times. I also felt a lot of fear inside for TJ. But I didn't want him to know. I held it in.

The morning of the surgery, eleven days after the match, I walked into TJ's room, but he wasn't there. My heart sunk; I thought I'd missed him somehow. But then I saw his bathroom door open. When I peered in, TJ was standing in front of the bathroom mirror with his neck brace off for the first time since the first hospital had put it on.

He was looking in the mirror, trying to make sense of it all.

When I saw he had no collar on, I froze, in case my presence made him flinch.

"My head feels like a bobblehead," he said, acknowledging I was there.

"Please put the collar back on, TJ," I begged.

He was so fragile that the doctors hadn't allowed him to leave our house in case something happened. And now he could see and feel just how much his neck had atrophied in eleven short days. His neck looked thin.

"I had to see it," he said. "I had to see what happened to me."

Now that he had, he carefully put the collar back on again. "I'm ready," he said.

As they wheeled him away, Dr. Uribe hung back and said to me, "Are you religious? Do you believe in God?"

"I do believe in God."

"Good," he said seriously. "Then let's pray together."

We'd been told there was a chance TJ wouldn't make it through the surgery, and even if he did, he might still end up paralyzed. I was so scared, I could barely clasp my hands together in prayer. I can only imagine what it was like for TJ at that moment.

"The surgery will only take about ninety minutes," the doctor told me beforehand. "We'll soon know everything."

But the operation ended up taking four hours.

I was freaking out in the waiting room for every minute past the ninety I'd been told it would be. Then Dr. Uribe finally appeared. He told me that TJ's injury was nearly an internal decapitation, so the process required to fix his neck was more intricate than it looked. TJ needed four screws, four rods, and sixteen staples just to stabilize it.

I later learned that wasn't the only reason for the extra time. Even atrophied, TJ's neck muscles were so thick and so dense and fibrous from years and years of specifically training that area that Dr. Uribe had a hard time getting through them.

"Can I see him?" I asked.

Dr. Uribe brought me into TJ's room just as he was waking up from anesthesia, and the doctor immediately began tapping TJ's legs and hands, asking if he could feel anything.

That second before TJ responded was a lifetime.

But he moved his arms and legs.

And then TJ started crying uncontrollably.

The stress, the worry, the wondering if he'd even wake up again—it all came pouring out.

Seeing TJ so relieved, so happy, but still in agony, made me lose it too. I was so scared one minute and so happy the next. My heart felt like it was on a roller coaster.

I hadn't known what version of TJ I was going to see in that room, if any version at all. But whatever I could get, I knew I would take in a heartbeat. I just wanted him back with me in any way I could have him.

But he wasn't dead, and he wasn't paralyzed.

So many things could have gone wrong . . . so many mistakes that could have been made, and any one of them could have killed or paralyzed him.

But none of them did.

We knew we still had a long, long road ahead of us. But at least we'd be on that road together.

Just not like before.

THE REVOLUTION

The women's division was rising, but I personally was sinking. After TJ's surgery, we were quickly reminded that life didn't stop or slow down just because we were going through hell. Commitments still had to be met and bills still had to be paid, so I needed to get back to work. But when I reached out, WWE sent word through their travel department that I suddenly wasn't needed—the first time they'd ever said that to me.

Back then, WWE would bring everyone to TV tapings just in case they needed someone at the last second, like they had with TJ in San Antonio. But after TJ got hurt, I was told not to come at all. The first week, I understood. The week of surgery, I understood too. The week after TJ's surgery, same. But then all of a sudden it had been five, six weeks of them saying, *We don't want you coming to TV*, and they weren't saying why.

Then I found a note on TJ's iPad where he was saying goodbye to everyone, and thanking us all for the great life he once had, and that's when I really got scared.

I gently confronted TJ, who got so mad at me for reading it. He promised he wasn't planning to kill himself, just writing down his feelings to process everything, but seeing it made me feel really powerless to help him. It felt like he was writing his goodbyes.

That childhood feeling of being out of control again only grew bigger. It began to haunt me and eat me up even more when, just a few months later, my dad took a nap one day in the middle of cooking some eggs while my mom was at work and nearly burned their rental house to the ground.

That was the second time he'd ruined that property—he'd already left the bath running and flooded the whole house—and this was the second time I'd had to pay to have it renovated (secretly, so that their landlord wouldn't kick them out for destroying the place again).

After the fire, I knew I couldn't risk him seriously hurting himself or my mom, so, when he resisted getting help, I legally signed him into involuntary rehab for four months under the Marchman Act, a Florida law that allows a person to petition the court to have a family member temporarily detained and treated for substance misuse issues.

He hated me for it—so much so that he had all these pictures of my sisters up on his wall in his room at rehab but none of me, because he'd ripped them all up and stuffed them in a drawer in his dresser, something I discovered when I found the pieces while helping him organize his clothes. I felt like the worst person in the world, but as a family, we had no idea how to handle him anymore.

My older sister Jenni lived in Canada, too far away to offer much help, and while my little sister Muffy was in Orlando, she was fiercely protective of her children and didn't want our dad around them when he was out of control. I can't say that I blame her. My mom had tried and tried and tried to help him, for decades, and it just went nowhere. Nothing was helping, and he was only getting worse.

I couldn't help my dad, and I couldn't do anything to help TJ, either, as he grieved the death of his purpose in life. TJ's identity was wrestling. That was gone now. And he didn't know who the hell he was anymore.

Everyone I loved was crumbling. I had to take back some power somewhere, and the only thing I could control was at least finding out where I stood in work. So I called a senior producer to try to find out what was going on.

No sense in small talk, I figured, so I got right to it. "You guys are buzzing about this thing that you're going to do for the women, and I've been here this whole time, and I've been waiting this whole time, doing whatever you guys needed. And now you're telling me that you don't need me at TV when this amazing thing for the women is about to start?"

WWE's plan was to bring in new female *NXT* talent and put them in factions with established main-roster women—a mix of both worlds, to give more women than ever screen time.

He said, "Well, we do have something in mind and, you know, we're thinking of maybe having you be with Emma and Bayley. Maybe. It's just an idea. We're not sure yet."

"Is this because TJ got injured?" I asked. His reply was something about picking the right moment for me and how my time to shine would come. So I tried again. "Is it because of what happened to TJ?"

"Not that I know of."

"So when are you going to bring me back?"

"Let me check on that for you."

At home TJ was of course struggling, but he was adamant that I not miss the opportunity I'd been waiting my whole career for. And I felt terrible for not wanting to miss it either. He had lost his dream, and I felt guilty that I hadn't lost mine too. We'd come into this business together, and I had no idea how to continue fighting for my dream in the same business where he lost his.

"I love having you home," TJ told me when we talked about it. "But there's nothing for you to do here. I've just gotta sit and wait to heal. But there's no point in both of us sitting here and moping around."

He was right. But I was afraid of leaving him.

"The longer you don't go back," he said, "the harder it will be."

TJ knew I needed to get back to work because what I saw happen to him had shaken me to my core. It played with my mind. Made me doubt myself. Made me overthink, and overanalyze every movement. And he knew as well as I did that if I didn't get back in that ring again soon, it would just get harder for me to do so.

Still, all I felt, when I finally got the call to come back, was guilt. I didn't want to leave TJ. But selfishly, I didn't want to lose my place either. In WWE, you stay employed by staying relevant. And the truth was, I didn't want the train to leave without me. I didn't want to miss the women's revolution that I had waited so long for. The women's division was finally changing and I really wanted to be a part of it.

So, for the first time since we started together as teenagers, I was leaving our house to wrestle, while TJ couldn't. And it was the hardest time I ever left my house; I cried all the way to the airport.

When I arrived to the TV taping in Atlanta, Vince and his creative team had the plan laid out—all the new factions were being excitedly whispered about backstage. And after tearing myself away from TJ, I was devastated to find out I wasn't in any of them.

On screen later that night, Stephanie McMahon introduced Charlotte Flair, Becky Lynch, and Sasha Banks to the main roster from *NXT*—but no Emma or Bayley, who had been discussed as my teammates.

It was official—the Women's Revolution had begun, and I was a spectator, not a participant.

When Sasha, Becky, and Charlotte came backstage, I was genuinely so happy for them. They'd been putting on amazing matches in *NXT*. But I'd be lying if I said I wasn't feeling left out and confused and guilt ridden and scared and lonely and pissed off too.

I'd been around WWE a long time. I could tell there was something different in the air—an excitement, the promise of something new—and I would have given anything to be included in it. Because if I *had* been included in something meaningful, then I might have despised myself a little less for being there when TJ wasn't.

I'll never forget how bad I felt, standing there after leaving TJ injured at home, applauding others for an opportunity I would have given anything for my whole career.

With everything that was going on in my life at that time, I really could have used a feel-good moment at work to take my mind off some of it. But I understood, that's not how it works. Dealing with disappointment at work is something we all have to navigate. And the feeling of not being good enough can visit us all. But at that point in my life, I thought those feelings might swallow me whole, because I was already so beaten down that I was afraid to look people in the eye for too long in case they saw how much I was struggling.

I just wanted to get home.

I wanted to make sure TJ was okay.

I wanted to be a better wife, and a better daughter.

But I also wanted to be included.

And I just wanted to not want it all so much.

But I couldn't help that I was born into wrestling, raised around wrestlers, loved a now-former wrestler, and wanted to wrestle. Wrestling was my identity too.

IGNORED AND FEATURED

The year 2016 rolled around, and nothing in my life felt settled or resolved.

My dad was in rehab for four months and got clean, but once he put some distance between himself and his drug use, we realized that he was still acting the same: weird, strange, out of it. We took him to several different doctors and got tests done, but they couldn't come up with anything conclusive. They said that it was more than likely that he was suffering from something like dementia or Alzheimer's, but they needed to do more tests and more CAT scans and more PET scans and more MRIs to know for sure. The more tests we got, the more the prognosis leaned toward Alzheimer's. So that's what we thought he had. We were also exhausted from searching for answers.

My dad was still angry with me for making him do rehab again, and I was angry with him because I was struggling to pay for everything he'd wrecked along the way. But as every new test pointed another arrow at him having some kind of brain deterioration, I knew I needed to have more compassion. If he wasn't on drugs and he was still behaving this way, then something else was definitely going on.

Back home, TJ was still recovering from his surgery, and even though it had been nine months since he was injured, he still hadn't heard anything from WWE, or Vince, about any restitution for his injury. TJ was no longer able to wrestle and now had a spinal fusion at the very highest vertebrae in his neck, which allowed him only half the movement he had before. It was a serious condition TJ would have for the rest of his life. Some feelers were sent out to see if TJ would like to go to NXT and "help out," but TJ didn't want to be coaching people on how to achieve their dreams a month or two after losing his. The idea of that hurt him too much, and I completely understood why.

Especially after the company had decided to pretend his injury never happened.

TJ wasn't waiting around for an invitation to stay with the company; he was waiting for a call, or text, from Vince. He was waiting for a simple apology. But it never came. Nothing did. Even back when he first checked his phone after waking up from surgery, it was full of best wishes from wrestlers at WWE and all around the world—but nothing from Vince.

There was no text.

No call.

Nothing from Vince asking if he was okay.

TJ thought, in WWE's eyes, it was like if they never mentioned it, then it never happened—but that just made TJ feel like he didn't matter to them. And that ate him up. We kept waiting, in the hope that Vince would reach out and acknowledge what had happened to TJ. I told TJ they'd eventually have a conversation with him and we could all work through this and figure out the next steps in his life. But TJ was tired of being forgotten and dismissed, and hope wasn't going to cut it anymore. So he hired someone to be a voice that Vince might respond to.

While TJ was healing physically from his injury, emotionally he wasn't healing at all. And so he wasn't strong enough to stand up to anyone, let alone Vince. He didn't have the same confidence he'd had before his injury. At all.

"All I want is an apology," TJ told his lawyer.

"That absolutely won't happen," his lawyer said in return, "because that would be admitting fault."

TJ didn't want to file a lawsuit at all. TJ just wanted Vince to address what happened to him in their ring. He agonized over it for months, because he didn't want the tension between himself and WWE to escalate, and neither did I. It was the last thing in the world I wanted. But after eight months of radio silence from Vince, TJ eventually decided to send Vince a letter.

In that correspondence, TJ said he wasn't okay with what had happened, and listed the series of events that led to his injury, as well as the dire medical implications it would incur for the rest of his life. He stated in the letter that he wanted to put it all in writing in case Vince wasn't aware of what had happened to him. TJ said that because of his injury, not only could he never wrestle again, he couldn't even move his head, and Vince hadn't reached out a single time to check if he was okay.

After the letter was sent, TJ received some calls from WWE management asking about his going to *NXT* again. TJ felt like they were offering him a job just so he'd move on—that the company was relying on his love of the business, and his reputation of being a good soldier, to make this all go away without having to actually address it.

It was painful watching TJ grieve the loss of his dreams and I was scared that losing his purpose would do to him what it did to my dad. Day by day I could see TJ sink a little lower, move a little further away from me, so I asked him if he'd like to come to *WrestleMania* with me and see all his friends. I told him we didn't have to see anyone in management; seeing the people who actually missed him, and loved him, and wanted him around would be so good for his mental health. It was WWE's biggest event of the year, and Cody Rhodes was having a big party. All the wrestlers would be there, and just being back in the world he loved would lift his spirits.

And just when I saw a little life come back into TJ's eyes at the thought of getting out of the house, a reply came from Vince's lawyer via letter, a month after TJ sent his.

Their account of what happened was completely different than TJ's. They denied everything and finished by saying that if I talked about TJ's injury at work or disparaged the company, they would trigger a clause in my contract and let me go.

I was in shock at their position, and TJ was now even more upset.

I had tried my best to walk the line of going back to work while also being there for TJ. I had never been a bad employee—as a matter of fact, I was probably too much of a pushover. But this was the moment when TJ and I decided we'd had enough of being nice and being quiet. I felt like I couldn't emotionally take much more.

We were trying to be reasonable, but sometimes trying to reason with a machine just doesn't work.

I ended up going to *WrestleMania* on my own, and that whole week I was there, I smiled and pretended that we hadn't just gotten a legal letter from the company denying TJ's account of what happened to him and threatening to fire me if I talked.

After years of trying to do everything right, and being a rock-solid company girl, I felt all of a sudden like I was walking around enemy territory . . . like I had to watch my every move and conversation. I felt scared to talk about TJ at all. I hadn't done anything wrong, and neither had TJ, yet we still felt very much on the defensive.

Even though what was happening with TJ took up most of the oxygen in our lives, the WWE juggernaut kept rolling, and along with it, their Women's Revolution. They were using the pre-show of that *WrestleMania* to announce that the Divas moniker was being retired, and our division would now simply be called the women's division—and that a new Women's Championship would be up for grabs later that night. The *NXT* influx of Charlotte Flair, Becky Lynch, and Sasha

Banks would take center stage and fight to become the inaugural Women's Champion.

And as I watched Charlotte win the match from backstage, a million miles from any revolution, I was suddenly told by someone in the creative team that the champion I was watching be crowned would need a new challenger, and that challenger was going to be . . . me.

To say I was shocked was an understatement.

Charlotte and I had just had a match at the Roadblock PPV, but I thought it was just one and done to get her ready for *WrestleMania*. The plan being laid out would expand and extend our rivalry into a big deal—a feud across several TV and PPV matches with the new face of the division.

To this day, I don't know whether Vince had planned that all along, or he put it together to show he wasn't mistreating me in case everything ended up in court. I really don't know if it was a coincidence or not. Uneasy, I called home to tell TJ, and asked him what he thought about it.

He told me that what was happening with him was separate from my career and he didn't want anything taking away the few-and-far-between opportunities that came my way. He was genuinely happy for me that I was getting my shot to show the world what I could do in a meaningful storyline. His excitement was contagious, and it made me feel less guilty about being excited too.

I knew he was heartbroken that he couldn't do what I was about to, but I knew he was also ecstatic for me. I could hear the difference in his voice—the sound of life in him again.

Still, those twisting feelings of guilt gnawed away at my stomach, knowing that Vince was about to feature me, while he continued to ignore TJ.

SORRY

I had to make myself do it. I had to make myself go through those ropes, and I had to do it before the other wrestlers arrived that night in Dallas. I'd been fighting this panic ever since I saw TJ get hurt, but I was too young and came from too great of a legacy to let my fear follow me around for the rest of my career.

I thought of my grandfather and how tough he seemed at all points of his life. I thought of my dad and how fearless he was, sometimes to his own detriment.

I stepped through.

As I walked from corner to corner inside the ring, my hands shook. It felt like the more I wanted them to stop, the less control I had over them.

I used to have nothing to be scared of. I was born into a tribe of people who had walked this road before me, then with me—until one by one our business sidelined them all.

I thought of my uncles, the British Bulldogs. Davey died at thirty-nine due to a heart attack, and Tom ended up in a wheelchair due to his in-ring injuries and died at sixty.

I thought of my other uncles—Bret, who at forty-two suffered a career-ending injury in the ring, and Owen, who at thirty-four died *in* the ring.

I thought of my dad and his brain injuries, most likely originating in football but exacerbated by wrestling, life, and the road.

And I thought of TJ, at home now, unable to move his head.

And it hit me that I was the only one left.

It shortened my breath, made my hands tremble worse.

When I was starting out, I was surrounded by my family. I had them to lean on, to help me, to guide me through one of the roughest sports and entertainment genres there was. I knew I had nothing to be scared of then, because there was nothing in this business they hadn't seen or done, and it felt like nothing bad could pierce through that fortress of experience and toughness.

But that night in Dallas, I realized all my old armor was gone, and I either needed to forge my own—or get out.

I had a huge segment later that night on *Raw*, which involved me confronting Charlotte Flair, the new Women's Champion, and giving her a piece of my mind. And one of the lines I had to say was, "I have the heart of a champion."

But I wasn't sure the segment would feel real, because I wasn't sure I believed that about myself anymore. I didn't feel tough or brave or even worthy. I was scared. I felt like a fraud.

Back in the empty ring, I ran and hit the ropes like my people had done before me, and like I'd done myself countless times. I knew if I wanted to continue in the wrestling business, then I needed to honor where I came from, but also carve out my own legacy.

I needed wrestling more than anything else in the world—it was my North Star when I was lost. So I knew that if I couldn't wrestle my way around this, then I needed to wrestle through it.

I finally had a storyline where I knew I would be given time and space to grow, and all the spotlight that came with it. But the best thing that could have happened to me happened at the worst time.

I just couldn't let that stop me.

I couldn't let anything stop me.

So I threw myself backward on the mat—the most fundamental bump a wrestler learns to take—and I felt that familiar jolt through my body. It was painful, but I was okay. Nothing broken, nothing damaged, nothing changed.

I looked up at the lights in the arena, and told myself that if nothing else, I was going to be a professional and put my personal life to the back of my mind.

Maybe this was a different kind of toughness. Maybe I was like my family after all.

Later that night, I went from being in that ring on my own to being in there with Charlotte, a live microphone in my hand, surrounded by thousands of fans in attendance, and being watched by millions more at home. I raised that microphone to my lips and said, "I have the heart of a champion."

It didn't matter to me right then whether I believed it or not. All that mattered was I made the fans believe I did. And their reaction to the line told me they were fully on board.

"Nattie, you see this Women's Championship on my arm?" the villainous Charlotte replied. "This proves my family will always be better than yours."

Now, I know it was scripted that way, and I knew it was coming, but with the place I was in my head, the line woke something in me; it made me react without having to think about it. It was theater on the page, but in my bones it was a fight for my family. I wanted to defend them, and protect them and all they'd done.

So I tackled Charlotte to the mat as the crowd cheered, and I twisted her into the finishing move my uncle Bret made famous in WWE, the Sharpshooter—only for her father Ric to slide into the ring and pull his arrogant daughter to safety before I locked it in.

And with that little piece of business, we were off to the races. I could feel myself returning. Match by match, minute by minute, I could feel myself reattaching to my passion—to my dream. The crowd was with us. Charlotte was an amazing opponent. Somewhere in those matches I began to emotionally shift from fear to gratitude, from panic to elation.

But I also felt guilty. As bad as I felt for doing what TJ couldn't do anymore, I felt even worse for enjoying it. This was all I ever wanted to do in life, and TJ was so happy for me, but I knew I wouldn't be able to find peace in it all until he found his too.

After all, I was finally being featured by the same company where my husband was being ignored.

Or at least he was, until a tech glitch opened a line of communication a few months later, at the beginning of 2017. WWE was developing its internal employee portal, where they could post schedules and updates, and talent could request time off from talent relations.

As the IT team beavered away building the infrastructure, TJ got a message to his phone that said the days off he'd requested had been approved—the exact number of days he had been out with his injury.

At first he thought nothing of it. Then it dawned on him that he didn't want it listed anywhere in WWE's corporate system that it was him who had requested time away from the company, when he was in fact injured.

So he called WWE, and was called back by Triple H, who said it was a mistake and that they'd rectify it right away. He told TJ they were still in the testing phase of the app, and that he was never supposed to get that message. "I'm so sorry about that," Hunter said.

And while their conversation started about one thing, it bled into another, as Hunter asked TJ how he was.

"Honestly," TJ told him, "I don't understand how I can get an apology about an app, but not about my neck."

Hunter fell silent. Maybe he knew it wasn't right. Then he asked, "Can you leave it with me?"

TJ knew that, at this point in Hunter's career, he wasn't the overall decision maker—he was just the person asked to relay messages from Vince. But TJ agreed to let Hunter handle it. He wasn't even sure what that meant, as he'd been told by his lawyer not to expect any movement from WWE's side unless our side filed a lawsuit.

But the next day, Vince texted TJ, eighteen months after he broke his neck. He said he was so sorry for what happened, and that he was going against the advice of his team by apologizing, but felt it was the right thing to do.

I saw TJ reading that text, and I could see the hurt moving a little—the weight of the world becoming just that fraction lighter.

After that text, he started to look forward a little again. And that meant I could too. As much as the promise of our dream together had changed, our life together had not. And I loved him more in that minute of healing than I ever had in any minute that came before.

TJ was rising up again.

I was too.

THE ASHES

I loved working with Charlotte, and we had a bunch of really fun, great matches together across a few PPVs and TV tapings. We even got to have Bret and Ric at ringside again, like in our *NXT* match—now on a much bigger stage. But it had an extra-special component to it because Bret had just beaten cancer, and had made it public for awareness. The audience gave him the greatest reception when we walked through the curtain.

It made me so happy that Bret and I got to work together again, and I was so happy for him that he got to see again just how much people loved and respected him, maybe more now than when he was actively wrestling.

Bret and I even got a chance to do the Sharpshooter, at the same time, to Ric and Charlotte, which made me feel on top of the world.

Between the end of 2016 and the beginning of 2017, everything really started to come together, and it felt fresh and exciting. I turned heel and played a bad guy on TV for the first time in years, and I got drafted from *Raw* to *SmackDown*, which meant a whole new show and division to work with. I even got to work one on one with Nikki Bella, which was a rarity for us both as we were usually across the ring from each other in a tag match. And boy, did we have a blast beating the hell out of each other in a Falls Count Anywhere match, where everything was legal and everything was a weapon.

I felt so alive, and so creatively free. I was having fun, which I appreciated more than I can say. I also felt included, which meant the world to me.

Nikki even encouraged me to tap into more personal stuff when I was bad-mouthing her on screen—to really go for her throat. She was in a relationship with John Cena at the time, and both had been public on *Total Divas* about how Nikki wanted to get married but John didn't. So Nikki encouraged me to use that to get heel heat from the crowd and fuel the fire of our WWE story.

I really let loose on the microphone for the first time in my career, and she did the same. We knew if we could build this story, it would make our matches so much more meaningful, so we did everything we could to amp up the tension.

John was great, too, giving us ideas and advice for the matches themselves. He sat at the monitor backstage and watched every match, and kept helping us make our stories more meaningful, so that the psychology in the ring made sense. When someone takes the time to watch your match, it's a huge compliment, and he always did that for us.

Fit was our producer, and together, he, Nikki, and I were coming up with all kinds of different ideas for our matches and what we could do to make them really exciting. It was the first time I used kendo sticks and weapons, and the first time I got to fight through the crowd and around the arena, and I loved it. Nikki was hard hitting, and I was hard hitting, and we both used that side of ourselves to make the audience sit up and take notice.

I hoped the company would notice too. I had been the Divas champion, but ever since the company went all in on the Women's Revolution, I'd wanted to prove that I also could be a champion in this new era. The talent pool was deeper than ever, the women's matches were better than ever, and the opportunities to show what we could do were greater than ever.

And while I knew I wouldn't be champion at most points in my career, I really wanted to be champion at *this* point, because I felt in my heart that it might be the last time my dad would see it.

In the eighteen months since he'd gotten out of rehab the second time, and since I started approaching him as someone who was struggling greatly with their memory versus someone who was just choosing to be "out of it" all the time, our relationship had gotten much better. I was there every step of the way with him and my mom as we tried to help my dad live as normal a life as possible without drugs and alcohol.

But his deteriorating condition made it as tough as ever.

And tougher as time went on.

If I was on the road, I'd call, and when I was home, I was at their house all the time. My dad and I would have conversations a lot, but they were all about very surface-level things: "It's a beautiful day out!" or "I love that shirt! Blue looks great on you, Daddy." I tried to engage with him more deeply, but it was hard. His answers got shorter and shorter, a few words instead of sentences, and I started to realize that his world was getting smaller and smaller. He hardly talked some days, and got uncomfortable leaving the house. He stopped interacting with anyone except his family.

But when all else failed, we had wrestling.

Even when he forgot the most basic things, like names, days, and people, he remembered wrestling. He remembered the people, and the feeling of getting into the ring. He remembered he was a champion. He remembered that I was going to be a champion too.

But he'd forgotten I already was.

I would have given anything for him to see me be a champion once again, before it was too late. I felt everything was moving in the right direction for me in WWE, and I wanted nothing more than to parlay that momentum into something that would bond me and my dad one last time. That would show him that I was holding up my end of our legacy.

But it wasn't just for me that things were moving in the right direction.

After Vince texted TJ, it was like a huge weight lifted off his shoulders, and he was able to get to a place emotionally where he could move on. He decided to go to therapy every week to sort through his thoughts and feelings, and I could slowly see him returning to himself again.

"How do I go back to WWE?" he asked me one night after I got off the road. "How do I move on from what happened and become a part of something I love again? I miss my friends. I miss you. And I miss wrestling."

I teared up because I hadn't heard TJ say he wanted to be a part of wrestling for such a long time. TJ was thinking about what he loved again. He wanted to get out of the house, get back to what had given him purpose.

"How can I feel like I matter again?" he asked.

It hurt to hear he felt that way, because he mattered so much to so many people. "You're more than what you do, TJ."

"Then how come I don't feel that way?"

The pain in his voice, I'll never forget it. But as hard as it was for him to say and me to hear, his talking like that was a huge step toward healing. It meant that he was no longer pushing down the pain of losing his old life—he was now trying to make sense of his new one.

Wrestling was the thing that had always set TJ's soul on fire—it was who he was—and it had been taken from him. He couldn't go under that grief, he couldn't go around it, and he couldn't go over it; he had to go through it. And he did. And he came out stronger on the other side.

"You should call Vince," I said, "because you have so much to offer outside the ring."

And to my surprise, the next day, TJ did.

Vince missed a *Monday Night Raw* taping and flew to meet TJ in person and talk. The conversation went well, and TJ felt Vince was very sincere in his regret about how everything was handled. I think they found a lot of common ground, and Vince came to learn and appreciate a lot more about TJ and his outlook on life—how TJ was someone with an extraordinary amount of drive, a survivor but never a victim. Vince said he'd help TJ do whatever he wanted to do in the company, as soon as TJ figured out what that was.

Did he want to do a reality show? Be a commentator? Be the subject of a documentary?

TJ went from fighting since he was fifteen years old to getting his dream job in WWE, and when you're a wrestler, you always want that spotlight. But I think that entertainer side of him died when he got hurt and he didn't want the attention that way anymore.

He still wanted to be *around* all those things. Just not be the center of them.

So TJ told Vince, "I would like to shadow Jamie Noble." Jamie was a producer in WWE that TJ really, really respected, and still does. "Maybe I can just follow him around and see what happens?"

TJ said that if he couldn't be in the ring delivering the match, he wanted to be in the wings devising them. So once he and WWE sorted through an agreement that addressed his injury, TJ began the second leg of his career, in June 2017, as a producer in WWE.

Once he got enough experience, seeing what the producers did and learning everything he could, he'd start to produce matches on his own. He'd be responsible for structuring the matches with the wrestlers, so that they could each tell their own individual story within the context of the overall show—and make sure they did so in the time allotted for the live broadcast. He'd be a mentor and sounding board to the newer talent who were trying to figure it all out, and he'd be a bridge between the wrestlers and the creative team to make sure the overarching presentation of the wrestlers made sense. This way, from the second the wrestlers' entrance music hit to the time they came back through the curtain, they'd make an impact.

He'd be perfect.

Even if he hadn't gotten hurt, I think TJ always would have ended up as a producer at some point, because he has a mind for seeing matches visually and laying them out to help talent see the story they were going to tell. TJ was a lifelong fan, too, so he would always try to put himself in the mind of the fans and what they wanted to see in a match. The job was a great fit.

On the first day he came back, I couldn't have been more thrilled to roll up to the building with TJ beside me again. It was the week of the first-ever women's ladder match, and I was in it. And while I knew now that I could take on anything, it was amazing having TJ close again.

Even after he'd been away almost two years, everybody welcomed him back with open arms. TJ had been an enthusiastic student his whole life, and he loved learning as much as he could from all the other producers: Jamie Noble, but also Fit Finlay, Michael Hayes, Arn Anderson, and the others he started with.

I saw him shift from student to mentor with ease, even on that first day. He had so much to offer everyone who needed and wanted his help, just like he'd helped me all the way along my journey. Watching him coming alive again around the business made me so happy, and when we both got home after our week on the road, being able to share that familiar tiredness again—the kind where you know you've put in the work, and it feels so satisfying—made me even happier.

That first night back after coming home together again, we sat in our darkened, quiet house with our bags at our feet and just smiled at each other from across the room.

TJ had found a new purpose that unlocked new goals.

And I'd found some momentum that brought me closer to mine.

CHAMPION

It was a writer who told me that I was going to be facing Naomi for the *SmackDown* **Women's Title at** *SummerSlam***, one of WWE's biggest PPVs of the year.**

I was taken aback because it was mentioned out of nowhere at the end of a conversation about where a few storylines in our division were going. *We're going to do this, and then this, then this, and that'll get us to you versus Naomi at SummerSlam.*

I just nodded in agreement, because I wanted to play it cool. I think I might have even uttered a "Cool" just to make seem like I was extra easy about it. But in my head I just kept replaying the *you versus Naomi* part and trying not to burst with excitement.

The writer continued, "She'll retain the title and move on from there."

"Of course," I said, trying to sound like I was okay with not winning.

As much as I wanted it, I didn't really expect to win. I never expect to win. Vince saw me one way when I first came into the company, and after a while I began to see myself that way too.

Over the years, I think that kind of typecasting might have slowed my growth as a top-tier wrestler. Everyone who became a great was put in the ring over and over again against the greats. They had to feel that big-match pressure and let it shrink them or make them. There is no shortcut to that next level; you have to get there through the fire of nightly experience. And while I'd had an amazing career up to that point, I wasn't booked in the top tier night after night, pushing myself, stretching my talent, and growing under pressure.

But I believed in my talent. I had worked my way from being the Frumpy Diva to the Divas Champion, from the Farting Diva to the Forgotten Diva to the Utility Diva—and now a *SmackDown* Women's World Title contender.

This match against Naomi at *SummerSlam* was a marquee match against a great champion, and it would be taking place in New York, my dad's favorite place in the world. I'd be a liar if I said I didn't crave that storybook ending of standing in that ring, in that city, on that massive PPV with gold around my waist—and my dad sitting front row.

But it wasn't going to happen.

Until it was.

One week before *SummerSlam*, in Boston, I was told the finish of the match had changed, and I'd be going over and becoming the new *SmackDown* Women's Champion in New York—the place it all started for the Harts seventy-two years before.

Holy fuck.

I immediately went to tell TJ. But as soon as I saw him waiting for me in the hallway, grinning from ear to ear, I knew that he knew. He'd heard a couple of hours before in a producer's meeting but didn't want to blur the lines between our professional and personal lives by telling me before the company did.

I was in shock, because I didn't know if I'd earned the right to be the face of the division. But TJ stopped my overthinking before it started.

"Nat," he said, "haven't you paid your dues? Haven't you done everything they asked of you? Haven't you been a professional at all times? Put everyone else over? Haven't you trained harder than everyone else? Haven't you fought tooth and nail to get to this point? If anyone deserves to be a champion, it's you."

TJ's words just made everything even *more* meaningful for me. He couldn't be a star anymore; he couldn't win that singles title he'd always wanted and never got. But he still passionately wanted me to fulfill the dreams he couldn't.

I exhaled strongly, my body now filled with adrenaline. "Will you help me?" I asked. "I want this to be perfect."

TJ smiled at me, and I could see the pride in his eyes. "Just tell me what you need."

This was a full-circle moment for us both. Even though I had the one and only Fit Finlay assigned to our match, I wanted TJ involved, too, because that's how we started out. Together. I came into this business relying on TJ's knowledge, though as the years went on, I needed it less and less. But after all we'd been through together, I wanted this match to be *our* win.

I felt like this night could be magic, if I could get all the stars to align. So that's what I set about doing.

Naomi and I met in Florida on our day off, got in an empty ring, and walked through what we wanted to do, with TJ there to help sculpt the story.

Naomi is one of my favorite people to be in the ring with because she's so creative. We might have been fighting for her title in a few days, but she was one of my closest friends in the industry. We have been through the ups and downs of WWE together, and she was so wonderful about me winning the championship from her; she wanted to give me everything she had in that match because she felt I deserved it.

And for the first time in my career, I felt like it wasn't a bad thing to have something for myself. A career is about moments. Moments that only flash thanks to hundreds and thousands of hours of consistent, reliable, understated, uncelebrated work—if you're lucky.

I knew this could be one of those moments for me, and my feelings of guilt or embarrassment for wanting to grab it with both hands disappeared. Unlike with my Divas title win, I felt that if the company wanted it for me, and TJ and Naomi did, too, then I had no reason not to enjoy the experience, and really take it in.

I knew I wasn't someone who was going to get these high-level moments too often, so for once in my life I just stopped overthinking and let myself feel.

And I can't remember ever feeling so grateful and happy rolling around the ring as I did when Naomi, TJ, and I began mapping out the story of our match.

Fit loved for us to bring him ideas, so when we got to the Barclays Center for the match that day, we were able to come to the table with a loaded gun and say, "Here's what we have." Fit listened to everything and, like always, put his own amazing spin on it to make it even better. The match became this beautiful collaboration, with my two favorite producers working together and not even really knowing it. I wanted everything for this match to be perfect, and so far that was exactly how it felt.

I sat in hair and makeup that day, knowing my family would be watching and TJ would be backstage waiting when it was all over. We'd come a long way from the Dungeon. The gear I had made for the match was by the same woman, Terry Anderson, who used to make Bret and my dad's gear back in the day. It made me think of all my family who came before me in WWE and how I was the last one left.

I didn't feel scared. I didn't feel sad. I felt overwhelmingly grateful for the way they'd allowed me to climb the ladder that their bodies and sacrifices, their tragedies and triumphs, had built.

I was notified that Naomi's and my match was next and told to make my way to Gorilla. The nerves, the excitement, the feeling of being ready flooded my body. I felt an unshakable confidence I'd never had before. I was warmed up and ready to go. I was ready to represent my family. I was ready to be champion.

My music hit first, and I strode onto the entrance ramp of the Barclays Center, drinking it all in, feeling that crowd energy in my bones. I was a bad guy to them, still playing the heel, but they were a joy to me—although I hid it behind my arrogant and cocky persona.

Naomi was out next, and her music got the building rocking. And as soon as our ring introductions were made, I slapped her across the face to start the match out strong. Ding, ding, we were live!

The physicality in the match and the rush of wrestling one of my favorite opponents in front of a sold-out arena made me feel alive. I fired off with aggression for the whole match, while Naomi countered with her spectacular babyface offense. Back and forth, trading brute force with superhero athleticism, until we moved to the finish. I had Naomi in the Sharpshooter, where it looked certain she was done—only for her to kick me backward at the last second, sending me crashing head first into the bottom turnbuckle.

Suddenly, *she* sensed victory.

She hurried to the top turnbuckle and somersaulted backward toward me with her split-legged moonsault, only for me to suddenly raise my knees and watch her crash ribs first down on my waiting trap.

As she lay on mat in agony, I dragged her prone body into the middle of the ring and put her in the Sharpshooter once more, forcing her to finally tap out and make me champion.

The ring announcer's voice echoed through the Barclays Center. "Here is your winner by submission, and new *SmackDown* Women's Champion . . . NATALYA!"

I snatched my new title belt from the hands of the referee, because the cameras were on and I was the arrogant, entitled villain. Inside I was flooded with a picture book of Hart memories as I climbed the turnbuckle to gloat at the audience with my new prize.

While Natalya Neidhart the heel scowled at the people, Nattie Neidhart the person—the sister, the cousin, the niece, and the daughter—hoped her family gathered back home cheered as loud as the arena booed.

It took everything I had not to smile when I thought of how far I'd come.

And it took everything I had again not to cry when I saw my dad's empty seat in the middle of the front row.

I'd reserved seats for him and my mom, just in case, and even though I'd have given anything for him to be there, I knew time had run out. The kind of stress he would have felt, having to be around that many people, at that point in his disease, would have been really hard on him.

He no longer had the ability to regulate his emotions or create new memories. He was operating only off the past and becoming less and less anchored in the present. I wished more than anything in the world that he could have been front row, but I don't regret now that he wasn't, because I now know he wouldn't have remembered it anyway. That was simply the reality of his condition.

I got down from the turnbuckle, and as Naomi cried in the ring, I gloated at her in my heel character and I kissed my new title to rub it in. But as I looked at that championship in my hands, it really hit me—I finally did it. Like, I really finally did it. I spent my whole career thinking about how to make others look good, how to help others be stars, and now there I was, gold above my head in front of my family, feeling like they must have all felt.

I felt a pressure leave me. I could go down in the history books as a Women's Champion, seven years after I won the Divas Championship—the first-ever woman to win both titles.

And it's not that I thought the Divas Championship wasn't a real championship, but it signified a period in the business that often wasn't kind to women wrestlers. This Women's Championship was the one that signified change and progress and recognized that strong female Superstars could main-event PPVs, put on great matches, and be involved in top storylines—everything I had always wanted for us.

I climbed through the ropes and walked backward up the ramp. Natalya made sure to keep the sneering and jeering right in the camera. Nattie made sure to take it all in: the size of the moment, the weight of the title.

I could finally stop beating myself up. I could finally feel like I belonged, both in WWE and my family's history in this business. For that moment I was the lead, not the support.

My dad told me that titles don't mean everything in wrestling, but in a business where very few are remembered, I wanted a shot at being one of them.

As I left the ramp, holding that title above my head like the little girl in Florida who held her father's the same way thirty years before, I knew at that moment that even if it all ended the following day, I could always say I was the women's champion.

And I earned it.

I was worthy.

EPILOGUE

My dad died a year and one day after I won the title.

He woke up at around six o'clock in the morning and told my mom that he was feeling cold, so he was going to turn the heat up on the thermostat. My mom followed him to the kitchen. He reached for the thermostat, twirled like he was doing a little spin in a dance, and then collapsed on the kitchen floor. He hit the top corner of his head when he fell. The cut was very deep and there was a lot of blood. He died right then and there.

My mom called 911, and then my sister Jenni, who was the only one around that morning—I was in South Carolina getting ready for *Raw*—but she knew already that Daddy was gone. She said that she heard him take his last breath, and I really wish that she hadn't had to hear that, especially since she was alone with him. But I also feel a lot of comfort that she was there by his side until the very end, as she had always been, unconditionally.

Jenni called me as they took my dad to the ambulance. It was early in the morning, but I was already awake, getting ready for the morning's media. She asked if I was in a spot where I could talk and the first thing I asked was, "Is everything okay with Daddy?"

"No."

I knew, but I was afraid to ask. "Did . . . he die?"

"Yes."

My heart broke open in South Carolina that day. I knew it was coming but I wasn't ready. There was part of me that believed he was invincible. My dad—the man who loved me, protected me, scared me, frustrated me, shaped me—was gone.

But I dried my tears and stowed away my grief. I needed to be strong.

My immediate next call was to Vince. He picked up in one ring and listened as I told him what happened, and said that I was really sorry, but I couldn't make it to *Raw* that night because I needed to get home to my mom, as I desperately wanted to be there and take care of anything that needed taking care of.

And I wanted to see my dad, and say goodbye.

Vince was so kind and understanding; he told me to send him every single picture that I had, and that he was going to put together a beautiful montage video package for my dad to open the intro of *Raw* and give him a fitting send-off.

And that's what Vince did.

Seeing my dad's younger face again on the clips WWE showed in his honor—larger than life, pulling his goatee beard and cackling—made me realize that I was the last of my family involved in WWE. It got me thinking a lot about legacy, and how it's a privilege even to be *able* to think about it.

The roots never get the luxury of thinking that way, only the branches do.

In the early days, my grandfather spent his whole life just trying to keep those roots alive, and because of that, years later, the branches of Bret, Davey, Owen, my dad, TJ, Harry, and so many, many more got to start their lives high above the muck my grandfather started in.

At that moment, watching my dad's tribute, I felt so connected to my legacy—and so afraid of it.

I still feel that way today.

I don't have a lot of the wrestling side of my family left here to ask if I'm doing a good-enough job. I don't even know if I want the answer. But it's the weight and anxiety of the question that makes me want to be great. I want to hold my own. I want to advance. I want to be one of the many in my family that makes our name and work live on.

Because the biggest thing I've learned about legacy is just how delicate time makes it.

And that's why, after eighteen years in WWE, I've never been surer that my dad was right all along. In a business where everybody's finish is predetermined by someone else, the only way to truly win in wrestling is to beat the fucking House. And that's what I aim to do. In a family that's done it all, I can't be the first Hart world champion, I can't be the first Hart Hall of Famer, but I can be the first to overcome the odds, and be the first of us to leave this business we've all loved without being broke or broken.

And I'm now ready to do that on my own, guided by everything I've learned, everything I was taught, and staring down with confidence everything that's still to come.

ACKNOWLEDGMENTS

I would like thank my mom. I know you didn't want to be the focus of this book, but you've taught me how to persevere in ways that have helped me survive my toughest battles. Thank you for always reminding me to not take shit from anyone.

I would like to thank my sisters for their unconditional love and for understanding me in ways that only you two can. We had so much fun growing up together and creating the best memories of my life. It's an honor to share part of your story too.

I would like to thank TJ for having my back since day one. Thank you for helping me soar in the ring, TJ. All of my most special matches had you written all over them. You are the most loyal person I know and the realest.

Thank you to every woman I've ever worked with in the ring. When you step through the ropes together, a relationship is formed that can never be broken. In a world where we're all fighting to succeed and leave our mark, the trust, respect, and those unbreakable bonds live forever.

Thank you, Paul, for helping me bring this book to life. Thank you for helping me find the words and the light at the end of the tunnel in so many moments. Thank you for reminding me that the best is yet to come. Because it truly is.

ABOUT THE AUTHOR

Nattie Neidhart is a third-generation WWE Superstar who has wrestled at the highest level for nearly eighteen years. Her family, the Harts, built a wrestling dynasty spanning nearly eight decades. She is the first woman in the family to carry on the tradition and holds six world records. She and her husband, TJ, along with their eight cats, reside in Tampa, Florida, where they both still work for WWE and where they train aspiring wrestlers in their private training facility, the Dungeon.